AF505904

BYRON AND THE EYE OF APPETITE

Also by Mark Storey

CLARE: The Critical Heritage (*editor*)
THE POETRY OF JOHN CLARE: A Critical Introduction
POETRY AND HUMOUR FROM COWPER TO CLOUGH
THE LETTERS OF JOHN CLARE (*editor*)

BYRON AND THE EYE OF APPETITE

Mark Storey

Senior Lecturer in English
University of Birmingham

St. Martin's Press   New York

© Mark Storey 1986

All rights reserved. For information, write:
Scholarly & Reference Division,
St. Martin's Press, Inc., 175 Fifth Avenue, New York, NY 10010

First published in the United States of America in 1986

Printed in Hong Kong

ISBN 0-312-11124-X

Library of Congress Cataloging-in-Publication Data
Storey, Mark.
Byron and the eye of appetite.
Bibliography: p.
Includes index.
1. Byron, George Gordon Byron, Baron, 1788-1824 – Criticism and
interpretation.   2. Emotions in literature.   3. Byron, George Gordon
Byron, Baron, 1788-1824.   Childe Harold's pilgrimage.   4. Byron, George
Gordon Byron, Baron, 1788-1824.   Don Juan.   5. Don Juan in literature.
I. Title.
PR4392.E5S7   1986   821'.7   86-1961
ISBN 0-312-11124-X

Contents

Preface

Whatever form it takes, criticism no doubt presumes too much. My excuse for this particular act of presumption must be that some quite basic things still need to be said about Byron. Although I am anxious that we should 'see him whole', and see the connections between different aspects of his work, I do not regard what follows as anything other than a very incomplete, introductory account.

Byron's attempts to define poetry frequently refer to the passions ('Are not the passions the food and fuel of poesy?. . . Poetry is the expression of an *excited passion* . . .'), and it is the passions that form the connecting link between my six chapters. Interestingly, much of the contemporary response to his work focused on the 'power' of his verse, what Scott in his review of *Childe Harold* summed up as that 'powerful genius . . . searching the springs of passion and of feeling in their innermost recesses': there is a clear relationship between power and passion. Like the other Romantic poets, from whom he is too often separated by a critical *cordon sanitaire*, Byron is deeply curious about the nature of feeling, and how different varieties of feeling can lead to forms of knowledge. This is as true of the early tales as it is of the later satires. What I have tried to do is to pursue some of the ramifications of this obsession without trying to be comprehensive. It might seem odd for a study of Byron not to make more than passing mention of *Manfred*, or the dramas, or *The Vision of Judgment*; I can only plead that particular texts seem to demand especial attention. I am particularly interested in showing how some poems work, in terms of Byron's exploration of the extremes of feeling, and what the connections are between those passions and their accommodation in verse.

Again, it would have been possible to adopt a much more 'developmental' approach, examining the processes whereby Byron moves away from what he came to see as a 'wrong revolutionary poetical system', towards the constraints of the *ottava rima*. But enough has been said about that elsewhere; it should be evident that my aims are rather different, and do not include a careful chronological working-out of Byron's growth as a poet. I should also say that this book grew out of the chapter on Byron in my *Poetry and Humour from Cowper to Clough* (1979), and there are several points in that earlier essay that I have not reiterated here. I have wanted especially to examine some of the early tales, and to continue the process of rehabilitation begun by critics such as Robert Gleckner and Jerome McGann: it seems extraordinary that so much of the non-satiric writings can be even now dismissed, both in introductory works and in more scholarly accounts. *Childe Harold* demands full discussion, because it remains such a complex poem, and to some extent my third chapter is an attempt to clear the ground for the fourth; the two chapters on *Don Juan* examine some of the ways in which Byron works out in his major satire what he calls in *Childe Harold* 'the fitting medium of desire'. For all his apparent recklessness, Byron is a writer acutely conscious of literary propriety, and that is what this book is about – the paradoxes and perplexities of discerning and expressing the appropriate passions. Byron describes himself in a letter to Teresa Guiccioli as an 'Observer of the Passions', but his observation, as the first chapter suggests, is itself of a curiously complex kind – hungry, all-consuming, fascinated, but aware that satiety can lead to disgust. Such keen observation leads to the romantic tales, but also to the satires. The book begins and ends with the paradoxes of seeing, with the 'eye of appetite' that can, in the rare case of Aurora Raby, see 'matters which are out of sight'.

I should add that this book is not concerned with Byron's personality. I have no doubt that he could, and frequently did, behave abominably. The important fact is that such a man was capable of such poetry: Byron's scrutiny of the passions is often puzzled, anxious and wary, but it is, in the last resort, profoundly moving. I have quoted extensively, for what matters in this book is Byron's own voice.

There are some books to which I owe debts that cannot be repaid in source notes. Anyone wanting to get closer to Byron will need to read William J. Calvert, *Byron: Romantic Paradox* (Chapel Hill, NC, 1935); George M. Ridenour, *The Style of 'Don Juan'* (New Haven, Conn., 1960); Andrew Rutherford, *Byron: A Critical Study* (Edinburgh and London, 1961); Robert F. Gleckner, *Byron and the Ruins of Paradise* (Baltimore, 1967); Jerome J. McGann, *Fiery Dust: Byron's Poetic Development* (Chicago and London, 1968) and *'Don Juan' in Context* (1976). Leslie Marchand's edition of the *Letters and Journals* (1973–82) has become indispensable, as has McGann's Oxford English Texts edition of the *Complete Poetical Works* (3 volumes so far published, Oxford 1980–1). For *Don Juan* I have been glad to use the Penguin edition, edited by T. G. and E. Steffan and W. W. Pratt (Harmondsworth, 1973, rev. 1977).

As for personal debts, these are too many and too various to be recorded publicly. But most books would not get far if it were not for particular people: in this case, I want to thank Andrew Brown, Martin Pumphrey and Ian Small for their advice and support. James Boulton, Seamus Heaney, David Lodge, Raman Selden and J. R. Watson helped things along, perhaps unwittingly, at various stages. Anne Buckley has, again, been the ideal typist. My parents, Christopher and Gertrude Storey, have as always given me every encouragement; Olivia Smith has found time from her own labours to offer her committed interest and faith in what she was hardly allowed to see; Tom, Jonathan, Hester and Hannah Storey, with their truly Byronic understanding of the claims of feeling and laughter, have kept me going.

1 The 'Eye of Appetite'

*You speak of Lord Byron and me — There is this great differ-
ence between us. He describes what he sees — I describe what I
imagine — Mine is the hardest task.*
(Keats, September 1819[1])

The difference between Byron and Keats was not as great as
either poet would have wished: but it was sufficiently marked
for both of them to chew at it in fascination. Even if we might
want to challenge the evaluative implications of Keats's verdict
here, he is, as usual, being more perceptive than he might
realise. In fastening on Byron's concern with what he sees, he
does, of course, hope to diminish him; and posterity might
well have been glad to accept such diminishment, as sanction
for its own refusal to allow to Byron the accolade of Romantic
imaginative vision. It is as though Keats were speaking for all
the other major Romantic poets: behind his bold assertion
('you see the great difference', he goes on, apparently un-
aware of his appeal to the organ he denigrates) we might hear
a whisper of Wordsworth's ire at Crabbe's mere poetry of
'fact'.[2] It has become hard to think of the Romantic poets
outside the pale of the imagination: Coleridge's esemplastic
power (like his opium) has indeed had its own binding effect,[3]
and, just as Byron is being excluded with great firmness by
Keats, so he has been excluded by a poetic and critical tradi-
tion that owes more to Keats than anyone has been prepared
fully to admit. And Byron, in his haughty way, offers up his
own hostages to fortune, inviting the exclusion he receives.
His letters are as revealing as Keats's in what they tell us of his
attitude to his craft, and his proud boast just five years before
Keats's dismissal of his efforts was precisely that 'I could de-
scribe what I had seen better than I could invent'.[4] It was to
what he called with some amusement 'that very material
organ'[5] that his early, so-called oriental tales owed not merely

1

their existence but their value: he had been to Greece and Turkey and Albania, and to have been was to have seen.[6] And to have seen was to begin to know. 'How I do delight in observing life as it really is', he declares, and we can begin to see the complexities implied in that casual observation.[7] To observe life as it really is could well involve the most strenuous bending of the imagination's sinews. There could be more to sight than seeing. In other words, Keats's opposition between seeing and imagining might serve the truth less well than it serves his own purposes. Desperate needs require desperate measures.

If, though, we can for a moment remove Keats from his own pronouncement, and focus on the Byronic half of the equation, then we can see the important truth in all its baldness. Byron is indeed obsessed with what he sees and with how he sees it. It is impossible to know of the particularities behind Keats's comment, which poems he had in mind. The extraordinary thing is how all-embracing a comment it becomes, perceptive in a way it doesn't actually want to be. The poet who in disgust throws down the first two cantos of *Don Juan* onto the deck of the boat taking him to Italy wants to hug to himself the weight and the scorn of that gesture. It is of the nature of Byron's particular and peculiar resilience to allow that gesture, that unmagnanimous contempt, and then to refuse it. There is an early instance of this in 1813. When John Murray had responded to *The Giaour* with an uncertain sense of poetic and commercial propriety, it was typical of Byron to respond in his publisher's terms, turning into compliments what could have been taken as something less flattering. 'I question', he wrote, 'whether ever author before received such a compliment from his *master* — I am glad you think the thing is tolerably *vamped* and will be *vendible*.'[8] Ironically, commercial and poetic scruples were in the end satisfied in equal degree. Byron worked at the poem with an assiduousness that spoke more about his artistic conscience than he or his publisher might have acknowledged, and the poem sold well. In a much more complicated way Byron's work as a whole takes Keats's comment on itself and throws it back. *The Giaour, The Corsair, The Prisoner of Chillon, Parisina, Childe Harold's Pilgrimage, Don Juan* — all seem to say, 'Yes, Johnny Keats, with your piss-a-bed poetry and your f—gg—g imagination, you are right, we describe what we see. We acknowledge our limitations. But once we acknowledge them, they cease to be the limitations you imagine them to be. We can all make virtues out of necessity'.[9] Byron's work transforms dismissal into praise. It is in fact glad to be dismissed for the right reasons, in the knowledge that those right reasons will eventually counter the need for dismissal. In one sentence Keats has effected, from Byron's point of view, a summation devoutly to be wished. He has made one of the central points about a poet who has so often seemed to lack any central point at all. That 'very material organ' is very material indeed.

Byron's challenge to Keats is thrown down most brazenly in canto V of *Don Juan*. The hero (though that is not how he presents himself) and his friend Johnson have been bought at a slave market by the eunuch Baba, and taken back to the seraglio he serves with such untroubled ease. The setting — exotic, mysterious, naughty — has a suggestiveness that Byron plays on knowingly: the sexual ambiguity allows him to fend off the erotic. And this is where the challenge to Keats lurks, the Keats in particular of 'The Eve of St Agnes'. The similarity of the contexts points up the essential differences, even whilst those differences are ironically denied by a Byron lazily working at full stretch. For, at the centre of his most fully imagined poem, Keats places two figures locked in the eyes' embrace. As Madeline sleeps and dreams, Porphyro, in his closet, looks and looks, and we watch his gaze. The gaze, like the poem, is one of tenderness and awe and quietness, requiring as its ultimate reward the reciprocal gaze of Madeline, awake as well as in sleep. That Keats should recognise the delicacy and fragility of relationship here might be typical of his surprising genius; just as typical, if even more surprising, is that he should load this spiritual and loving spectacle with such rich and lavish ore, that he should risk the monastic quiet with the plenitude of this:

> And still she slept an azure-lidded sleep,
> In blanched linen, smooth, and lavender'd,
> While he from forth the closet brought a heap

> Of candied apple, quince, and plum, and gourd;
> With jellies soother than the creamy curd,
> And lucent syrops, tinct with cinnamon;
> Manna and dates, in argosy transferr'd
> From Fez; and spiced dainties, every one,
> From silken Samarkand to cedar'd Lebanon.
>
> These delicates he heap'd with glowing hand
> On golden dishes and in baskets bright
> Of wreathed silver; sumptuous they stand
> In the retired quiet of the night,
> Filling the chilly room with perfume light.
>   ('The Eve of St Agnes', xxix–xxx)

It is a brilliant passage, provided we can say that without concurring with the implications of Keats's self-denigrating comment about being 'cheated into some fine passages'.[10] The brilliance resides not in any 'fine writing', but rather in Keats's extraordinary, wondrous ability to re-create with such physical fullness the sense of spiritual mutuality and repletion felt by the wondering Porphyro. This feast he brings is an offering, a token of humility and love. This sumptuousness is at one with the way, in the next stanza, 'Thus whispering, his warm, unnerved arm / Sank in her pillow', at one with his response when 'Her blue affrayed eyes wide open shone: / Upon his knees he sank, pale as smooth-sculptured stone', at one with the 'voluptuous accents' of the climactic stanza, where it is enough for Keats to glance at their 'solution sweet' before shifting with exquisite tact the angle of his vision, whilst the lovers with equal tact shift theirs.

Byron will have all of this, and yet will have none of it. Whereas Keats hangs poised 'like a throbbing star / Seen 'mid the sapphire heaven's deep repose', Byron hangs back, watching from the safer haven of the satirist. 'Distance is no object with me', he says in a letter, in that man-of-the-world tone that reveals unwittingly its more than worldly anxieties:[11] another instance of necessity claiming virtue for itself. We have here the same properties, but very different observations of proprieties. Whereas for Keats the intentness of the lovers' gaze works its own magic, which allows him to appeal without absurdity, but not without risk, to an exotic feast that could have come straight from the wand of Prospero (and in Keats's rich imaginings probably did), for Byron there is no magic, and gaze and feast remain linked but separate. As so often in Byron's major poetry, we have been prepared for the two parts of the equation. How the two men looked in the slave market was crucial to their 'prospects', and how in turn they should be looked at, or 'eyed over':

> No lady e'er is ogled by a lover,
> Horse by a blackleg, broadcloth by a tailor,
> Fee by a counsel, felon by a jailor,
>
> As is a slave by his intended bidder.
>> (*Don Juan*, V.xxvi–xxvii)

It is a small jump from the sale to the thought of food, a kind of minor Popean hiccough:

> And then the merchant giving change and signing
> Receipts in full, began to think of dining.
>> (V.xxix)

The jump once made, Byron begins one of his famous 'digressions'. When he declares in a letter that 'Everything in this life depends upon the weather and the state of one's digestion', it might well seem a carelessly delivered *bon mot*;[12] but, as he acknowledges in *Don Juan*, he cherishes his own commonplaces, and insists that we cherish them too.

In that nonchalant manner that characterises the poem, Byron slips into a digression which has become, by the time he declares it as such ten stanzas later, no such thing: a crucial theme has been heralded, the connection between eating and mortality. To isolate this particular instance is to do the poem a disservice, but then that is true generally of Byron: we are always having to put the cart before the horse. It is worth noting at this point that 'those hungry Jacobins, the worms' of the next canto earn their keep by the reference both to *Hamlet* and to the rest of the poem. Such concentration would not, at this juncture, serve Byron's purpose, although within the compass of a handful of stanzas (which is how they seem, thrown off and at us, if we care to catch them) concentration is very much of the essence. It is one of the small wonders of Byron's verse that he can effect such transformations, such alterations of pace.

> I wonder if his appetite was good
>   Or if it were, if also his digestion.
>   (V.xxx)

This allows him to ponder the phenomenon of post-prandial (and hint at post-coital) gloom, in a stanza with its own personal poignancy when set against Byron's epistolary references to Alexander, his sense that in some way he is in the same line – he will, he says, 'be content to die the death of Alexander' when he has achieved his conquests.[13]

> I think with Alexander that the act
>   Of eating, with another act or two,
> Makes us feel our mortality in fact
>   Redoubled. When a roast and a ragout
> And fish and soup, by some side dishes backed,
>   Can give us either pain or pleasure, who
> Would pique himself on intellects, whose use
> Depends so much upon the gastric juice?
>   (V.xxxii)

Byron summons up the idea of gross indulgence, without re-creating it. Those dishes all have their covers on. He has, in fact, in the previous stanza, used the word 'repletion', the word I applied to a partial effect of 'The Eve of St Agnes'; but for Byron repletion is an abstract concept, important because it is precisely that, cool and withdrawn. There is, though, no false fastidiousness about his attitude. The abstractions serve his purpose admirably in a passage which turns upon the very value, or otherwise, of abstraction ('who', he says, after all, 'Would pique himself on intellects'?). To startle us into the realisation that the question at the end of that stanza is not rhetorical, Byron recounts a tale of a soldier being idly killed in the street, outside his window: thoughts of mortality, in other words, become more than thoughts when we are confronted with a corpse, after supper.[14] Byron resorts to the verb he cannot avoid:

I gazed upon him, for I knew him well;
  And though I have seen many corpses, never
Saw one, whom such an accident befell,
  So calm. Though pierced through stomach, heart, and
    liver,
He seemed to sleep, for you could scarcely tell
  (As he bled inwardly, no hideous river
Of gore divulged the cause) that he was dead;
So as I gazed on him, I thought or said,

'Can this be death? Then what is life or death?
  Speak!' but he spoke not. 'Wake!' but still he slept.
                        (V.xxxv–xxxvi)

There is a terrible fascination about the scene, the com-
mingling of pain and pleasure that refuses to be unperplexed.
The gaze is prolonged, and it is a gaze that has to be indulged.
Much of Byron's poetry explores the ramifications of that
stare.

Just how un-Keatsian it is emerges after the 'digression',
when the newly bought slaves are themselves obsessed with
hunger. The questions they ask of each other have all the
urgency of people caught in a jam. Philosophising is not to the
point, unless it be of the proverbial kind ("Tis therefore',
significantly, 'better looking before leaping'). The important
thing is to survive, to keep your wits about you. But for Byron
that would be too easy: he needs to return to the ambiguities
of digestion, and to keep before us the connection between
that and mortality and seeing. As they approach the palace
('which opened on their view', again significantly), Byron's
sleight of hand is such that we could well slide over the three
words that condense that nexus of ideas – and to some extent
he wants us to slide over them. Their effect is subliminal, and
will surface three stanzas later.

And nearer as they came, a genial savour
  Of certain stews and roast meats and pilaus,
Things which in *hungry mortals' eyes* find favour,
  Made Juan in his harsh intentions pause
And put himself upon his good behaviour.
  His friend too, adding a new saving clause,

> Said, 'In heaven's name let's get some supper now,
> And then I'm with you, if you're for a row.'
>
> (V.xlvii; emphasis added)

Again, Byron's appeal is to the idea of sights and smells, rather than to sights and smells as such. 'Genial savour' is indicative of the verse's tenor, rhyming literally and in terms of ethos with the 'good behaviour' it encourages. But the idea is by now filled out to the extent that it is not merely an idea; it has its own range of reference, an elegant precision that owes all to the movement of the verse and thought since that casual 'I wonder if his appetite was good' of stanza xxx. It has taken twenty stanzas to reach its climax, and it is typical of Byron that, should we pause to notice the climactic moment, we are left behind, because it is rare for him to acknowledge what he has achieved. At the risk of being left behind, we have no choice but to pause.

> [They] smelt roast meat, beheld a huge fire shine,
>   And cooks in motion with their clean arms bared,
> And gazed around them to the left and right
> With the prophetic eye of appetite.
>
> (V.l)

If we wanted to pinpoint a precise moment at which Byron's challenge to Keats was at its height, this would be it. To do so would be misleading, in that the episode continues, as the seraglio is entered, and described in that paradoxical fashion cultivated by Byron to throw us off our guard ('I won't describe', he declares, even though 'description is my forte'), leading up to the encounter with the mistress, and Don Juan's precarious, epicene defence against her warm advances, fuelled, as we might expect, by her dark eyes. There is much more to be said about this canto and the way in which its potentially Keatsian lushness is hinted at but always kept in control. But by this stage we have the necessary elements of the contrast. The feast and the gaze have been set before us.

It is that very careful placing which announces the Byronic distinctiveness. I said that the gaze and the feast were linked but separate, that Byron had no concern for the magical. The paradox of this couplet that invites us to pass our eyes back over the first part of the canto, and forwards, prospectively ('prophetic') to the rest, is that it turns the tables on us, that it momentarily fuses the very things that it is apparently keeping apart, in that cool relationship that is for Byron not so much sanctuary from feeling as precaution against excess. Byron's path to the palace of wisdom is not Blake's. But at this point the startling fusion requires us to redefine our notions of Byronic detachment. The eye of appetite, hungry mortals' eyes, have become the hungry eyes of mortals, the eye wanting to consume what it gazes upon. The challenge to Keats is all the cheekier in that, at this point, we think of the melancholy lover 'feeding deep deep upon his mistress' eyes'. For a brief moment, Byron and Keats seem to be on the point of convergence, before going their separate ways. The possibility, though, is there, and we are, simultaneously, made to think of Wordsworth, and the terms he uses to discuss what he calls, in *The Prelude*, the 'tyranny of the eye'.

The Wordsworthian reference is worth pursuing, because Wordsworth so conciously outgrows 'the most despotic of our senses' even whilst admitting the sweet delights it held for him. He, too, finds himself talking in terms of greed and appetite. It is essential for him to refer to this time of his childhood, before he launches, in book XI, into the 'spots of time' passage where he is able to celebrate the imagination. It is as though he can only engage in that celebration at the expense of his early years:

> Here only let me add that my delights
> (Such as they were) were sought insatiably,
> Though 'twas a transport of the outward sense,
> Not of the mind, vivid but not profound:
> Yet was I often greedy in the chase,
> And roamed from hill to hill, from rock to rock,
> Still craving combinations of new forms,
> New pleasure, wider empire for the sight,
> Proud of its own endowments, and rejoiced
> To lay the inner faculties asleep.
>
> (*The Prelude* [1805], XI.186–95)

The terminology is that of 'Tintern Abbey', but the emotions less complex and contradictory:

> The sounding cataract
> Haunted me like a passion: the tall rock,
> The mountain, and the deep and gloomy wood,
> Their colours and their forms, were then to me
> An appetite: a feeling and a love,
> That had no need of a remoter charm,
> By thought supplied, nor any interest
> Unborrowed from the eye.
> ('Tintern Abbey', ll.76–83)

The shift from sight to sound is a sufficiently famous crux not to require amplification here, the way in which the eye is 'made quiet by the power / Of harmony and the deep power of joy' whereby 'We see into the life of things'. But, as in all his great poems, things are never quite what they seem, or what he might wish, and Dorothy's presence is a disturbing reminder of his own disturbance, however much of joy it might bring. She represents the very thing he has lost, and which he refuses here to mourn, as he is to refuse, less flexibly, in the 'Immortality' Ode. One of the most moving parts of the poem focuses on his gaze upon her, and he, perforce, resorts to the despotic claims of the eye. As he 'catches' the 'language of his former heart', he is himself caught, rather like the wedding-guest, pinned by the eye of the mariner:

> [I] read
> My former pleasures in the shooting lights
> Of thy wild eyes. Oh! yet a little while
> May I behold in thee what I was once,
> My dear, dear Sister!
> ('Tintern Abbey', ll.117–21)

It is a moment of intense poignancy in a poem that concentrates on this isthmus between past and future. Wordsworth lingers at the very point where the poem's logic least demands it. He has talked about a blind man's eye, he has talked about the body being laid asleep, he has begun to look ahead with what he thinks of as his inner, and superior, eye. Dorothy has been nowhere in sight: she has, so far as the poem is concerned, not existed. With his perverse form of truth and honesty, Wordsworth concentrates, suddenly, all of his energies upon her, and, in drawing his eyes towards her, her own eyes remind him of what his once were like. It is as though the 'tyranny of the eye', when we meet it in *The Prelude*, is being asked to do too much, to carry too great a burden, to fudge a complex issue for the sake of philosophical clarity. The move from outer to inner vision is not as straightforward as Wordsworth would sometimes like to think, or like us to think; even the disjunction of 'see' and 'feel' (Coleridge, in his 'Dejection' Ode, has 'I see, not feel, how beautiful they are'), which he implies in the 'Immortality' Ode, is not a necessary distinction, though it would make life easier, in some ways, if it were. Perhaps this is why the 'burden of the mystery' of 'Tintern Abbey' has particular appeal, not simply to our sense of honesty but just as much to our sense of poetic, even philosophical, integrity.

This brings us back to the perceptiveness of Keats, who understood well enough what the 'burden of the mystery' might imply, perhaps more wittingly than he understood the implications of his seeing how Byron saw.[15] What is interesting is that 'Tintern Abbey' provides the link between the two perceptions. Wordsworth stands at the centre of his poem, in the middle of the landscape, at the turning-point of his life, and, in looking at Dorothy, looks, as it were, at himself in the mirror, and watches his own eye; Byron's obsessive gaze is on a par with this, as it is on a par with the appetitive glances of Keats's major verse. But Wordsworth wants to press on to supposedly higher things, Keats wants to climb the steps to gaze upon Moneta's brow. Byron insists on lingering as Wordsworth lingers in 'Tintern Abbey', harking back to the hungry eye of youth, to the wide-eyed gaze that, precisely because it is so tyrannical, demands respect.

The narrative poems for which Byron was famous in his own day have become, subsequently, sticks with which to beat him. Byron's own equivocal attitude towards them has been used as an excuse to be less than equivocal ourselves; but, if we took his own protestations seriously and consistently, we should very soon have nothing left to read.[16] It may well be that, whatever absolute standards we choose to apply to the tales will, in the end, find them wanting in some respect or another. But there is still a considerable amount on which to remark. The particular aspect I want to pursue here is Byron's seizing on the optical theme in poems which focus on ideas of power. It is not enough to dismiss these poems as varieties of Gothic horror, however much they might owe to that tradition in its various manifestations. What Byron does is to take these tales of exotic splendour and mystery, and examine them from different perspectives. The Giaour, Lara, Conrad might all represent a particular aspect of Byron's character, his desire for action and adventure, and we could clearly explain them on that psychological level. Even to begin to do so, though, would be to realise the contradictory impulses within his character, and within these poems. It is one of the central advantages of his imagery of the eye that it allows for such contradictions, without necessarily collapsing into confusion.

In some respects *The Giaour* is the most interesting of the tales, if only because of the confessedly fragmentary nature of the piece. Byron had as precedent Samuel Rogers, but *The Voyage of Columbus* soon pales beside Byron's 'Fragment of a Turkish Tale'. *The Giaour* is not so much a fragment as fragments, and Byron made it the more so the more he worked at it. He was conscious of the inherent contradiction of his accretive processes: 'The general horror of *fragments* makes me tremulous for the Giaour', he wrote,[17] but it had not stopped him adding to it, additions which, as he said, 'render it a little less unfinished (but more unintelligible) than before'.[18] We might say that, as with many of the tales, the element of unintelligibility is an important part of the narrative and of our response to it. The poems are to do with secrets and mysteries, some of which they insist on keeping to themselves – *Lara* is the most extreme example of this. The highly wrought fragmentary nature of *The Giaour* allows for a kaleidoscopic narrative that mocks our normal expectations of time and perspective. It is a short step from Byron's obsessive concern with events as observed, to concern with the major characters who make their impact on and through the eye.

One of the central narrators is the fisherman, who is sometimes placed in the context of another narrative, sometimes allowed to tell his own tale. It is to his eye that the action first presents itself (after a complex introductory passage which I discuss at some length in the next chapter, but which, it is worth noting here, contains towards its conclusion, with reference to the lost freedom of Greece, the notion of the 'stranger's eye' – 'There points thy Muse to stranger's eye / The graves of those that cannot die!': the implication is partly that we, the readers, are strangers, and this is to be a recurrent theme throughout Byron's work). At this stage in Byron's career, it is typical that syntactically there is uncertainty as to the weight to be given to the 'glancing' of the first line of this quotation – a further reminder that Byron is to become adept at breathing life into defunct usages, at giving back to clichés the force they had before they became clichés:

> Far, dark, along the blue sea glancing,
> The shadows of the rocks advancing,
> Start on the fisher's eye like boat
> Of island-pirate or Mainote . . . .
> (*The Giaour*, ll.168–71)

The narrative voice changes abruptly, the fisherman speaks with the urgency of the present tense, as he watches the black horse thunder across the sands, bearing the apparently loathsome Giaour with his 'evil eye'. The change into the preterite is as sudden, before another, briefer, sortie back into the present. With these lurches of tense go the lurches of perspective, as we watch the fisherman transfixed by the figure that he sees but cannot comprehend:

> On – on he hastened – and he drew
> My gaze of wonder as he flew:
> Though like a demon of the night
> He passed and vanished from my sight;
> His aspect and his air impressed
> A troubled memory on my breast;
> And long upon my startled ear
> Rung his dark courser's hoofs of fear.
> He spurs his steed – he nears the steep,
> That jutting shadows o'er the deep –
> He winds around – he hurries by –
> The rock relieves him from mine eye –

> For well I ween unwelcome he
> Whose glance is fixed on those that flee . . . .
>
> (ll. 200–13)

What Byron is doing here is to draw our attention not so much to the action as to his, and our, contemplation of it. Barely has the Giaour been seen before he disappears, and the manner and effect of that disappearance matter as much as what has been seen. There is a fine ambiguity about the fisherman's response. His 'gaze of wonder' is drawn from him almost against his better judgement. What meets his gaze to some extent conquers it. But the relief felt at the moment of disappearance is double-edged: if the fisherman is relieved to see him go (and the paradox is apt, in that to see someone go is to observe their absence), so the Giaour is relieved of his glare. Each is in the other's power. It is this reciprocal nature of the optic contract that is one of the poem's chief concerns.

In terms of the narrative, the mysterious death of Leila, loved legitimately by Hassan, less so but more magnetically by the Giaour, is at the core of events. But, as in the jumbled sequence of a dream, the precise relation it bears to other segments of the narrative is not at all clear: the poem exploits that disturbing element of dreams, the sharp-edged clarity that goes hand in hand with its very opposite. It rarely makes sense to recount a dream, because we cannot capture that elusive combination within the normal confines of sequential narrative. Byron's achievement in *The Giaour* lies partly in having the best of both worlds. The fragment describing Leila's death, the unceremonious dumping of her body, tied up in a sack, in the sea, is an instance of this. We must assume that, once again, the fisherman is the narrator, but he is far from being an omniscient one. He is indeed like the spectator of his own nightmare. The only way he can describe what happens is to describe how he sees it. But his sight is mocked and what he gazes upon withdraws, relieving itself from his sight like the Giaour going behind the rock:

> Sullen it plunged, and slowly sank,
> The calm wave rippled to the bank;
> I watch'd it as it sank, methought
> Some motion from the current caught

> Bestirr'd it more, – 'twas but the beam
> That chequer'd o'er the living stream –
> I gaz'd, till vanishing from view,
> Like lessening pebble it withdrew;
> Still less and less, a speck of white
> That gemm'd the tide, then mock'd the sight;
> And all its hidden secrets sleep,
> Known but to Genii of the deep,
> Which, trembling in their coral caves,
> They dare not whisper to the waves.
>
> (ll.374–87)

Far from dwelling on the scene, Byron condenses it to a moment, and then soars on the wings of rhetoric in a passage of some magnificence. But he has told us enough, all we need to know. We are left to make the connections between the two events, the sudden disappearance from sight of the two main protagonists, almost before we have seen them. It is as though they define themselves by their absence, hugging their secrets to themselves. Dead, and covered in a sack, Leila is a mere thing, a mere pebble inflicting momentary disturbance on the placid surface of the sea, something that teases the eye of the beholder. She has ceased to be a person; she has, like the Giaour, no name; she, like him, has become a function of the narrative, serving to pull our eyes from their sockets as we gaze at the point in time and space when there was a hint, but no more, of her existence.

The forward thrust of the narrative, as is common enough in tales of mystery and intrigue, is retrospective. However jealously they might guard their secrets, the protagonists are sooner or later obliged to yield up at least something. So economically has Byron established his frame of reference that it is no surprise – rather, it seems inevitable – that he should begin to describe Leila through her eyes. He is to do such things better in later narratives (an instructive comparison would be with *Parisina*, ll.173–82). But the important point is that he knows what he wants to do, even if he does not do it very well. He knows that the eye can serve purposes other than those of power and might, or, rather, that power and might can take gentler forms than that represented by the Giaour on his steed. This is all a bit too cloying, even coy: only the prim would dismiss it accordingly.

> Her eye's dark charm 'twere vain to tell,
> But gaze on that of the Gazelle,
> It will assist thy fancy well,
> As large, as languishingly dark,
> But Soul beam'd forth in every spark
> That darted from beneath the lid,
> Bright as the jewel of Giamschid.
> Yea, *Soul,* and should our prophet say
> That form was nought but breathing clay,
> By Alla! I would answer nay;
> Though on Al-Sirat's arch I stood,
> Which totters o'er the fiery flood,
> With Paradise within my view,
> And all his Houris beckoning through.
> Oh! who young Leila's glance could read
> And keep that portion of his creed
> Which saith, that woman is but dust,
> A soulless toy for tyrant's lust?
> On her might Muftis gaze, and own
> That through her eye the Immortal shone. . . .
> *(The Giaour,* ll.473–92)

As so often in these tales, Byron's appeal to the trappings of the Orient might strike us as meretricious. We might not accept, so readily as Madame de Staël, his approbation of the East: 'Stick to the East', she told him, 'that is the only poetical policy',[19] and he duly defended *The Giaour* and *The Corsair* on those grounds – 'It is my Story and my East that I want to make palpable.'[20] But beneath the bright frippery is this girl's gentle eye, which others read and learn from; and we, as readers, are brought into that cycle of looking and learning. As, however, this lengthy passage continues, and Leila turns into a swan, so we are checked at that very point at which we begin to stare too eagerly. We should keep our distance. Byron brings us up sharp against the stern abstractions that lie behind this paragraph, pulling us back, away from the very contemporary exoticism that he wishes to parade, back to the sober injunctions that we associate with a previous age. The character of the couplet changes, and in the reminder of Leila's 'high and graceful' gait we are ourselves brought to heel, if there was any danger of our succumbing to the lushness of the setting.

Those subtler abstractions of *Don Juan*, referred to earlier, are at least hinted at in this most surprising of places, and we retire, somewhat abashed.

> Thus armed with beauty would she check
> Intrusion's glance, till Folly's gaze
> Shrunk from the charms it meant to praise.
> (*The Giaour*, ll.512–14)

The implied comment is at the expense of us all. In her living beauty, as well as her dead nothingness, Leila mocks the spectator who would look too closely, even too well. The narrator and the reader are left to ponder their inadequacy.

In a passage parallel to this, Byron portrays the Giaour, later in the poem, as he finds sanctuary in a monastery, after the murder of Hassan. The Giaour might not be the epitome of moral virtue, but he has established his supremacy, he has justified that initial gaze of wonder that implicates anyone who indulges it:

> Dark and unearthly is the scowl
> That glares beneath his dusky cowl –
> The flash of that dilating eye
> Reveals too much of times gone by –
> Though varying – indistinct its hue,
> Oft will his glance the gazer rue –
> For in it lurks that nameless spell
> Which speaks – itself unspeakable –
> A spirit yet unquelled and high
> That claims and keeps ascendancy,
> And like the bird whose pinions quake –
> But cannot fly the gazing snake –
> Will others quail beneath his look,
> Nor 'scape the glance they scarce can brook.
> (ll.832–45)

It is a measure of the poem's cumulative force that the 'glance' of that last line can support the work it is asked to do, that we are taken back to the ambiguity of its first appearance ('along the blue sea glancing') and led to understand the deeper ambiguity that underlies the very notion of the glance. The ambiguity is the more daunting in that it fends us off. But within the self-contained, even self-defeating world of the Giaour and Leila (and therein lies the sad irony of the poem, that the recognised truths lead only to tragedy) – within that world, ambiguity can at least momentarily give way to reciprocity. The Giaour's justification is possible because, as he 'meditates and gazes' on his own life, he forsakes the sole tyranny of his eye, and acknowledges the alteration to his vision effected by the person he loved. Their love has led to her death, his incarceration, his despair – by the end of the poem he has left as little 'trace' as Leila's bundled body on the flood. And yet

> She was a form of life and light –
> That seen – became a part of sight,
> And rose – where'er I turned mine eye –
> The Morning-Star of Memory!
>
> (ll.1127–30)

The Corsair allows itself more room in which to explore a similar kind of psychology. It might not have the technical narrative interest of *The Giaour*, but it compensates for this lack with its more 'commanding art' (to use one of the attributes of its hero). Initially the piratical Conrad might seem no more than a replica of the Giaour, equally hypnotic, equally powerful and vengeful. His power is such that his qualities seem to have transferred themselves, in his absence, to his followers.

> They game – carouse – converse – or whet the brand;
> Select the arms – to each his blade assign,
> And careless eye the blood that dims its shine:
> Repair the boat, replace the helm or oar,
> While others straggling muse along the shore;
> For the wild bird the busy springes set,
> Or spread beneath the sun the dripping net;
> Gaze where some distant sail a speck supplies,
> With all the thirsting eye of Enterprize . . . .
>
> (*The Corsair*, I.48–55)

Typically, Conrad is a man of few words, known by his eye and hand, so awesome that the poem dares to open with his absence, as the others await his return from a voyage of plunder. He is the archetypal man of action, alone and aloof. He appears almost to be represented by the watch-tower that stands guard over the bay. But the complexities of the poem are forced upon us in Byron's account of this tower, as the pirates go to wait and look for their leader: the tower seems almost inappropriate in a setting of such natural beauty and fecundity.[21] It is one of those reminders of the natural world that we do not always expect in Byron's verse, and which therefore still have the power of surprise. In this instance, it is as if two kinds of power were being postulated, that represented by the eye-like tower, and that represented by the elements. People are seen to be rather slow and cumbersome in a landscape of such vitality, and the thirst that is ministered to is of a different order from the 'thirsting eye of Enterprize'. The syntactic contortions of this sentence mirror the way in which, when he is eventually seen, Conrad is set apart from all the properties and people, and set apart, furthermore, in the act of looking. The great man of action is a mere straggler.

> Ascending slowly by the rock-hewn way,
> To where his watch-tower beetles o'er the bay,
> By bushy brake, and wild flowers blossoming,
> And freshness breathing from each silver spring,
> Whose scattered streams from granite basins burst,
> Leap into life, and sparkling woo your thirst;
> From crag to cliff they mount – Near yonder cave,
> What lonely straggler looks along the wave?
> In pensive posture leaning on the brand,
> Not oft a resting-staff to that red hand?
>
> (I.123–32)

The possible direction of the poem is hinted at, this early on. Small wonder that the pirates 'watch his glance with many a stealing look'. He is a man of loneliness and mystery, and one of his mysteries is the nature of his power. Conrad dominates the poem, certainly, in the way that the watch-tower dominates the landscape. But in both cases it is an uncertain kind of domination, tinged with as much doubt as the pirates' eyes. The validity of the watch-tower is questioned by brake, flowers and spring: its beetling brows are admonished as pungently as the 'eye of Enterprize' which is Conrad's stamp. The poem contains within itself the interrogation of its premisses — and, by extension, even more so those of *The Giaour*. As in *The Giaour*, we have a hero who is darkly Promethean ('In Conrad's form seems little to admire / Though his dark eyebrow shades a glance of fire'), a source of bafflement to those who look at him. But Byron probes more deeply the nature of this bafflement, its reflection of a bafflement within the hero himself.

> Though smooth his voice, and calm his general mien,
> Still seems there something he would not have seen . . . .
> (*The Corsair*, 1.207–8)

The antithesis is telling, illuminating with its echo of the similar plight of Childe Harold: the cool exterior is definitely that, a means of concealment. As with Harold, Byron is here determined to keep his own distance, to imply even that he is as much in the dark as the rest of us. But the Corsair is a more interesting customer than the Childe Harold of the first two cantos. We are getting closer to the core of the mystery than we did in *The Giaour*, where it is really the fisherman who is vouchsafed a sight, in the hero, of something he would rather not have seen. Here Conrad is the one who has seen, but we do not know what. His eye is the source of his sad perplexity (and hence of ours), but it is also, paradoxically, his defence. With his eye he can stave us off. We are inevitably reminded of that glance of Leila's in *The Giaour* which so decorously held us at arm's length. This is all rather more grandiloquent and bombastic, as Byron succumbs to the easy temptations of a rhetoric that will (he hopes) keep us within due bounds. Byron's concern for his hero is such that he appears both to offer a criticism of him and to rebut it, to 'roll back' on us the 'scrutiny' we are briefly tempted to bring to bear: it is, after all, the gaze of the observer, rather than of Conrad, that is 'cunning'. Conrad's eye is 'searching'. Hope and mercy do not put up much of a fight.

His features' deepening lines and varying hue
At times attracted, yet perplexed the view,
As if within that murkiness of mind
Worked feelings fearful, and yet undefined;
Such might it be – that none could truly tell –
Too close enquiry his stern glance would quell.
There breathe but few whose aspect might defy
The full encounter of his searching eye;
He had the skill, when Cunning's gaze would seek
To probe his heart and watch his changing cheek,
At once the observer's purpose to espy,
And on himself roll back his scrutiny,
Lest he to Conrad rather should betray
Some secret thought, than drag that chief's to day.
There was a laughing Devil in his sneer,
That raised emotions both of rage and fear;
And where his frown of hatred darkly fell,
Hope withering fled – and Mercy sighed farewell!
(The Corsair, I.209–26)

Conrad's evil – and it is described as such – is, in part, attractive to Byron because it is tempered with love. Just as the Giaour had found, in Leila, a source of inspiration that led to her death and Hassan's, and spiritually to his own, so Conrad is in some sense redeemed by the underbelly of his passionate hatred of mankind in general – that other passion that 'asks the name of love'. Redemption is, indeed, the concept that Conrad treasures when he thinks of his beloved Medora, even whilst he recognises the contradiction that she represents. She herself puts well that contradiction, when he goes to her, prior to his departure on another campaign:

How strange that heart, to me so tender still,
Should war with nature and its better will!
(I.396–7)

Medora is saying what the emblems of watch-tower and verdant landscape had hinted at, that Conrad is in conflict with the elements. The conflict is for Medora a bitter paradox, because it means he is in conflict with her.

That contradiction on which the poem is based is subtly

touched upon in the lines preliminary to the song Medora sings, in self-consolation for his absence. We are reminded of hill and tower, and the relation of each to the other; and in the ambiguity of the third line we get a brilliant merging, not just of the conflicting qualities represented by Conrad and Medora (he wild, she soft), and by Conrad within himself, but also of the two figures, in that in hearing her song he seems to appropriate her to himself. All this is done by the dislocation of syntax that allows 'wild and soft' to hang over into the next line, inviting us to relate the phrase directly to him, but inviting also the possibility that it relates to her, or to both. She is a creature of nature, a 'bird of beauty'; none the less 'his', a possession that is also in some way removed from him. Her accents come to him from a distance:

> Thus with himself communion held he, till
> He reached the summit of his tower-crowned hill:
> There at the portal paused – for wild and soft
> He heard those accents never heard too oft;
> Through the high lattice far yet sweet they rung,
> And these the notes his bird of beauty sung . . . .
>
>   (I.341–6)

It is characteristic of the Byronic impulse of these narrative poems that the hope offered by love should be so quickly dashed. Conrad acknowledges what Medora refuses to accept, the necessity of parting: 'Since all must end in that wild word – farewell!' (I.455). Such necessity is cruel, and Byron plays with it obsessively in much of his poetry. He knows only too well the pain of separation. In a light moment he might say, 'it is very odd the fuss people make about partings',[22] but only a few days later he can be more honest: 'how do I abhor these partings! – I know them to be of no use – and yet as painful at the time as the first plunge into purgatory'.[23] Both *The Corsair* and *The Bride of Abydos* have as their pivotal points of action partings that reveal the truth. It is another way in which the distance between people is no simple measure of their closeness.

In 'The Eve of St Agnes' Keats has the beautiful line 'But dares not look behind, or all the charm is fled' to refer to the suspended plight of Madeline, caught between dream and waking. Byron dwells on a comparable moment, and is compelled to dramatise it at length, exploring the implications for both lovers. Medora will not say farewell, will not accept its inherent despair, will not even accept that Conrad has gone. Byron captures in these lines, as he had not in the *The Giaour,* the pathos of love that is doomed. He does not sidestep the melodrama, the stylised gesture. But the bitter pain of looking at who and what is leaving you is reflected in verse that anticipates the 'swimming looks' of *Don Juan* and the sickening sight of *The Siege of Corinth*. Medora, too, has seen what she would not have seen:

> O'er every feature of that still, pale face,
> Had sorrow fixed what time can ne'er erase:
> The tender blue of that large loving eye
> Grew frozen with its gaze on vacancy,
> Till – Oh, how far! – it caught a glimpse of him,
> And then it flowed – and phrenzied seemed to swim
> Through those long, dark, and glistening lashes dewed
> With drops of sadness oft to be renewed.
> 'He's gone!' – against her heart that hand is driven,
> Convulsed and quick – then gently raised to heaven;
> She looked and saw the heaving of the main;
> The white sail set – she dared not look again;
> But turned with sickening soul within the gate –
> 'It is no dream – and I am desolate!'
>
> *(The Corsair,* I.491–504)

Conrad is well aware that he cannot afford the backward glance. The verb Byron employs tells its own tale – Conrad 'mans' himself and turns away, when he catches sight of his tower and thinks of Medora watching him as he leaves. When he finds himself, in disguise, in the enemy camp in the next canto, he is once again 'with self-possession mann'd'. He is the man of action with a job to do. There is in his world no place for Medora, even though she is his sole means of redemption. So Conrad, as we can now perhaps more fully understand, has seen what he would not have seen.

The narrative follows its relentless course. Conrad is caught in action by the Pacha, Seyd, and imprisoned. But his imprisonment is due to his lack of ruthlessness. He spends precious time removing to safety the women of the harem, in particular Gulnare, the jealously guarded favourite of Seyd. Resolutely undefeated by his feelings for Medora, he is caught off his guard at one blow by 'the weaker prey'. In reminding his men that 'man is our foe' he reminds them too that '*we* have wives', and reintroduces into his philosophy a contradiction that is soon acted out in the drama. By keeping the action amongst the men he has explicitly to acknowledge the women, and in that acknowledgement makes himself and the men open to the dangers of unmanning. If he saves Gulnare only to be defeated himself, she has it in her power to save him, which of course, from Conrad's point of view, is a further kind of defeat. It is no comfort to him that she 'mans' herself to kill Seyd, and thus effects Conrad's escape. The distinction he wants, and needs, to keep between the sexes is undermined, and he is perplexed. He allows himself the luxury of rescue, and muses on the contradiction that he confronts. They sail back home, to be greeted by the pirates' comrades. In the moment of greeting we are ourselves confronted with the irony that the pirates gaze, now, at Gulnare, and in that hint of amusement that Byron indulges in is the suggestion that Conrad's scruples are not to be scorned, that it is essential to his integrity that he can feel 'he yet can conquer and command'.

> They sailed prepared for vengeance – had they known
> A woman's hand secured that deed her own,
> She were their queen – less scrupulous are they
> Than haughty Conrad how they win their way.
> With many an asking smile, and wondering stare,
> They whisper round, and gaze upon Gulnare;
> And her, at once above – beneath her sex,
> Whom blood appalled not, their regards perplex.
>
> (III.508–15)

This mutual perplexity is a comment on the poem's larger sense of inverted values. Perhaps that is the distinguishing feature of *The Corsair*, when set alongside *The Giaour*, in that here Byron has moved into a complex debate on values that are mutually dependent and mutually contradictory. *The Giaour* had deliberately skirted moral issues, more interested in the perplexities of narrative, more interested in the elemental power of those dark glances than in their implications. But *The Corsair* sets up oppositions that are not to be easily reconciled. The extremes of *The Giaour* are challenged, and Conrad is consequently a much more vulnerable figure.

It is this vulnerability that is emphasised in *The Corsair's* grim conclusion. In sight of home, Conrad cannot forbear to embrace his rescuer. That embrace makes it a false home-coming.

> Oh! what can sanctify the joys of home,
> Like Hope's gay glance from Ocean's troubled foam?
> (III.565–6)

The 'troubled foam' suggests that there is something too blithe about that glance, something ominous in the abstract noun that seems to belong to an already questioned convention. Hope has so far proved a frail vessel. And so it turns out. Medora's vain look before that bitter parting finds its echo here in Conrad's, as he gazes impatiently both on Medora's dark tower and on the 'lingering oar' that delays his hoped-for reunion with her. As he bursts into her room, he casts the look he had previously withheld, and sees the result to be what he had hoped to deny by not looking when he left. But he has known what he will find, and as he enters her room and settles her body he enacts with eloquent silence his own guilt and his recognition that it was from this room that Medora had gazed out to sea, gazed as she had so often gazed before, waiting for his return. In their final conversation, she had half joked about how she would imagine he was not coming back, and how he would then reappear:

> Thus Conrad, too, will quit me for the main;
> And he deceived me – for – he came again!
> (I.448–9)

His return has, this time, been marked by real deception, a deception she has mutely witnessed. The fixity of her gaze at their parting had been prophetic, and is answered now by Conrad.

He turned not – spoke not – sunk not – fixed his look,
And set the anxious frame that lately shook:
He gazed – how long we gaze despite of pain,
And know, but dare not own, we gaze in vain!
In life itself she was so still and fair,
That death with gentler aspect withered there;
And the cold flowers her colder hand contained,
In that last grasp as tenderly were strained
As if she scarcely felt, but feigned a sleep,
And made it almost mockery yet to weep:
The long dark lashes fringed her lids of snow,
And veiled – thought shrinks from all that lurked below –
Oh! o'er the eye death most exerts his might,
And hurls the spirit from her throne of light!
Sinks those blue orbs in that long last eclipse. . . .
                                        (III.599–613)

The mockery of tears is Conrad's final unmanning: his wild eyes absorb his 'mother's softness' after all, and he weeps like a child, before steeling himself to the world. The vain gaze that links the two main dramatic moments in the poem achieves its ironic apotheosis. If there was ever an appropriate time to dare to look, it is now past:

There is no darkness like the cloud of mind,
On Grief's vain eye – the blindest of the blind!
Which may not – dare not see – but turns aside
To blackest shade – nor will endure a guide!
                                        (III.658–61)

In *The Bride of Abydos* Byron presents the obverse of this coin: it is, if this be possible, even bleaker. The less-than-manly Selim has to prove himself, if he is to thwart the plans of his so-called father Gaffir and win the hand of Zuleika. The only way he can win is to adopt the tactics of the enemy, to arm himself and fight. But, again, it is his redeeming grace, his abiding love for Zuleika, that makes it impossible for him wholly to transform himself into the figure he would wish to be. Whereas Conrad, in parting, had kept his look steadfastly ahead, Selim fails this initial test, at the very point where he is about to win: he cannot refrain from the backward glance, and Byron poses the desperate question

> Ah! wherefore did he turn to look
>   For her his eye but sought in vain?
> That pause – that fatal gaze he took –
>   Hath doom'd his death – or fixed his chain. . . .
>   (*The Bride of Abydos*, II.563–6)

The worlds of action and of contemplation do not mix, and yet each seems to demand something of the other. It is tempting at this point to look ahead to an infinitely more complex and more touching moment in *Don Juan*, when Haidée leaves Juan asleep. The pause, the hesitation – however movingly gentle – carries with it ominous overtones:

> Young Juan slept all dreamless, but the maid,
>   Who smoothed his pillow as she left the den,
> Looked back upon him and a moment stayed
>   And turned, believing that he called again.
> He slumbered, yet she thought, at least she said
>   (The heart will slip even as the tongue and pen),
> He had pronounced her name, but she forgot
> That at this moment Juan knew it not.
>   (*Don Juan*, V.cxxxv)

The paradox at the centre of *The Bride of Abydos* is explored in two contrary tales, *The Siege of Corinth* and *Parisina*, which seem to represent the two poles of Byron's vision in the early years, and which look ahead to the more complex working-out of the paradox in *Don Juan*. Once again it is a matter of reviving outworn clichés. If we gaze greedily on what we would, or would not, see, we can end up sickened. Medora had discovered that when she realised that Conrad was gone, and her soul was sickened. That, in *The Corsair*, is a metaphysical point. But, just as in *Don Juan* the eye of appetite can have an appositely literal application, so Byron has occasion, in *The Siege of Corinth*, to demonstrate the literal way in which a sight can be sickening. The besieged hero, Alp, at the centre of the poem, paces the battlements during a lull in the fighting. His eyes fall on a gruesome feast:

> And he saw the lean dogs beneath the wall
> Hold o'er the dead their carnival,
> Gorging and growling o'er carcase and limb;

They were too busy to bark at him!
From a Tartar's skull they had stripped the flesh,
As ye peel the fig when its fruit is fresh;
And their white tusks crunched o'er the whiter skull,
As it slipped through their jaws, when their edge grew dull,
As they lazily mumbled the bones of the dead,
When they scarce could rise from the spot where they fed;
So well had they broken a lingering fast
With those who had fallen for that night's repast.
(The Siege of Corinth, ll.409–20)

Alp's response is as we should expect: he 'turned him from the sickening sight', and in that turn away he is doing more than acknowledge the loathsomeness of what he sees – he is responding to the implications of that sight. The dogs need to gorge just as Seyd, in *The Corsair*, needs to 'glut his eye'. Ironically, the Keatsian fullness of vision as depicted in 'The Eve of St Agnes' leads to a repletion that is uncloyed, that has nothing to do with satiety. Byron here hints at the revolting nature of what we look upon, at the way in which we might move from gazing in horror to not gazing at all. If this is what the eye has to offer, the eye were better closed. There is something desperate in Byron's journal entry, 'my heart begins to eat itself again . . . to prevent me from returning, like a dog, to the vomit of memory, I tear out the remaining leaves of this volume. . . . O fool I shall go mad.'[24]

But in *Parisina*, one of Byron's most compact narratives, the eye were not better closed. It is not that much hope is offered: the plot of incest and vengeance ends with bitter justice and even more bitter remorse. But, although Parisina's charms are seen as 'fatal', and are clearly so in that Hugo is seduced by them into loving his father's bride, she and he both maintain a dignity that asserts itself through the eye. Her wide stare removes the need for words:

Her eyes unmoved, but full and wide,
Not once had turned to either side –
Nor once did those sweet eyelids close,
Or shade the glance o'er which they rose,
But round their orbs of deepest blue
The circling white dilated grew –

> And there with glassy gaze she stood
> As ice were in her curdled blood;
> But every now and then a tear
> So large and slowly gathered slid
> From the long dark fringe of that fair lid,
> It was a thing to see, not hear!
> (Parisina, ll.328–39)

For his part, at the moment of execution, Hugo refuses to have a 'kerchief' bound across his eyes. That, for him, would be the 'last indignity': 'let me die / At least with an unshackled eye' (ll.450–1).

If each of them has the courage to look and stare death in the face, Azo's sad lot is to go on living. The irony and futility of revenge is contained in the bitter lack of contact between his children (by his new marriage) and himself: 'on his cold eye / Their growth but glanced unheeded by' (ll.534–5). They have become to him a look, a glance which he cannot return. He who lives is the one who has lost most. The others are dead, but they did at least take with them their wide eyes.

Some of the ambiguities of seeing are most startlingly and dramatically rendered in canto II of *Don Juan*. After the love affair between Juan and Julia, abruptly terminated by Don Alfonso's unexpected return, the move from love-sickness to sea-sickness to cannibalism is both apt and shocking.[25] The shipwreck is one of Byron's most famous set pieces, and justly so: his celebrated dependence on fact finds its apogee here, as also does his ability to combine the incongruous, the terrible and the tender, the awful and the outrageous. There is good cause for the laughter of despair.

I have already mentioned the long section in canto V which focuses on the need for food, and the paradoxes inherent in that need (the discussion could easily be extended to the later 'English' cantos, where vast stretches are given over to the details of eating, so that the poem becomes something of a versified menu). There is an alarming moment in canto II when Byron gives a hint of what is to come, and incidentally anticipates that other recurrent theme, the need for what he calls 'due precision':

But man is a carnivorous production
  And must have meals, at least one meal a day.
He cannot live like woodcocks upon suction,
  But like the shark and tiger must have prey.
Although his anatomical construction
  Bears vegetables in a grumbling way,
Your labouring people think beyond all question,
Beef, veal, and mutton better for digestion.

And thus it was with this our hapless crew,
  For on the third day there came on a calm,
And though at first their strength it might renew,
  And lying on their weariness like balm,
Lulled them like turtles sleeping on the blue
  Of ocean, when they woke they felt a qualm
And fell all ravenously on their provision
Instead of hoarding it with due precision.
                            (*Don Juan*, II.lxvii–lxviii)

In their desperation, the survivors eat Juan's dog, but this of
course cannot do more than postpone starvation. The hither-
to unspoken thought gets voiced: they will have to begin
eating each other. This is one of those crucial moments when
Byron acts out the terrible power of the eye, as it becomes a
consumer of the most awful and awesome kind:

                          Savagely
    They glared upon each other. All was done,
      Water and wine and food, and you might see
    The longings of the cannibal arise
    (Although they spoke not) in their wolfish eyes.
                            (II.lxxii)

There is an echo there of the 'eye of Enterprize' in *The Corsair*,
of the glutted eye of Seyd in *The Bride of Abydos*. But what in the
tales might (even if wrongly) have been shrugged off as a
figure of speech is here transformed into the most terrible
inevitability. If they are to survive, they have to resort to
cannibalism. The consequences cannot yet be foreseen, and in
their despair they set about the preparations:

The lots were made and marked and mixed and handed
  In silent horror, and their distribution
Lulled even the savage hunger which demanded,
  Like the Promethean vulture, this pollution.
None in particular had sought or planned it;
  'Twas nature gnawed them to this resolution,
By which none were permitted to be neuter,
And the lot fell on Juan's luckless tutor.

(Don Juan, II.lxxv)

Byron has already, in canto I, mentioned Prometheus, in an important passage which I shall discuss in a later chapter (see p. 165); it is significant that the reference back should be made at this point, that in describing the 'longings of the cannibal' Byron should allude to this particularly potent myth of creativity. As his earlier comment makes plain, Prometheus was 'unforgiven' for his theft of fire from heaven; the poet, like Adam, like Prometheus, is similarly cursed with this lack of forgiveness, condemned to the daily torture of the pecking vulture. But the compressed phrase 'Promethean vulture' underscores the irony: the poet, like the men in the boat, is both Prometheus and vulture, the embodiment of John Clare's later description of himself as the 'self-consumer of my woes'.[26] These people are both eaters and eaten. The creative act is, by extension, one of necessity and revulsion. Quite brilliantly, the verb Byron uses – 'gnawed' – makes his dreadful point for him. The imagery of cannibalism pervades the natural and the moral universe. But, as Byron goes on to demonstrate, such extremes in such extremities (again the appeal by implication to 'due precision') have extreme consequences – 'For they who were most ravenous in the act / Went raging mad.' So, what was necessary and awfully natural leads to madness and death. The awfulness is the stronger because of Byron's measured tones, the balance he keeps within his verse, the decorum which lends nobility to the quiet death of Juan's tutor Pedrillo.

Literary sanction is sought for these horrors, and in appealing to Dante Byron manages to claim some kind of wry respectability for his verse. Having shown us the full grotesqueness – so much worse than the sickening sight that confronts Alp in *The Siege of Corinth* – he then turns round, typically, and says it's not really so bad after all. Friendship, politeness and fairness become the paradoxical norms:

> And if Pedrillo's fate should shocking be,
>   Remember Ugolino condescends
> To eat the head of his archenemy,
>   The moment after he politely ends
> His tale. If foes be food in hell, at sea
>   'Tis surely fair to dine upon our friends
> When shipwreck's short allowance grows too scanty,
> Without being much more horrible than Dante.
>   (*Don Juan*, II.lxxxiii)

Byron, not for the first time, will have it both ways. And when Juan, the sole survivor, opens his 'swimming eyes' to confront the beautiful Haidée, Byron emphasises that, however idyllic the setting, however strong the passions, food is necessary. After this extraordinary scene in the boat (and see later, pp.195–8), we are likely to think of any food with a certain degree of distaste; there is an appositeness in the caution displayed by the handmaid Zoe in the face of Juan's 'most prodigious appetite' (II.cliii). We get an echo of the Promethean vulture:

> And feeling still the famished vulture gnaw,
> He fell upon whate'er was offered, like
> A priest, a shark, an alderman, or pike.
>
> He ate, and he was well supplied, and she,
>   Who watched him like a mother, would have fed
> Him past all bounds, because she smiled to see
>   Such appetite in one she had deemed dead.
> But Zoe, being older than Haidée,
>   Knew (by tradition, for she ne'er had read)
> That famished people must be slowly nurst
> And fed by spoonfuls, else they always burst.
>   (II.clvii–clviii)

Zoe treats him like a child, to save him from the 'self-slaughter' of his companions:

She snatched it and refused another morsel,
  Saying, he had gorged enough to make a horse ill.
(II.clix)

The wide eyes of appetite, hungry mortals' eyes, are necessary
and yet necessarily dangerous. The long, rapturous account
of Haidée's and Juan's love for each other is spelled out in
terms of their mutual gaze; but such mutuality is darkened by
the remembrance of those wolfish eyes in canto II. A gaze is
not far removed from a glare. When the two of them gaze
upon the sunset at the beginning of canto IV, it is as though the
very act of gazing spells its own end. Haidée's eye is ominously
prophetic:

That large black prophet eye seemed to dilate
  And follow far the disappearing sun,
As if their last day of a happy date
  With his broad, bright, and dropping orb were gone.
Juan gazed on her as to ask his fate;
  He felt a grief, but knowing cause for none,
His glance inquired of hers for some excuse
For feelings causeless, or at least abstruse.
(IV.xxii)

Haidée's instincts are sadly right: she, like the Giaour, the
Corsair, Medora, has seen what she would rather not have
seen.

Byron addresses himself to the implications of these drama-
tic conflicts on a number of occasions: *Don Juan* provides some
of the readiest instances. For all the pain of seeing it is none
the less necessary to go on doing so. He is scornful of those, his
critics, 'who have imputed such designs as show / Not what
they saw, but what they wished to see' (IV.vii). To see can even
be to admire and to wonder (some, he says, call it 'incon-
stancy'):

'Tis the perception of the beautiful,
  A fine extension of the faculties,
Platonic, universal, wonderful,
  Drawn from the stars and filtered through the skies,
Without which life would be extremely dull.

> In short it is the use of our own eyes,
> With one or two small senses added, just
> To hint that flesh is formed of fiery dust.
> (II.ccxii)

There is an interesting digression on this extension of seeing to admiration in canto V, at the point where Juan and Johnson meet Gulbeyaz in the harem. The interest arises partly from the contradiction, within two stanzas, of what Byron says more than once in his letters. In 1811 he writes, 'Well did Horace write *nil admirari* . . .' and in 1819, to Teresa Guiccioli, '*Never to feel admiration* – and to enjoy myself without giving too much importance to the enjoyment in itself – to feel indifference to human affairs – contempt for many but hatred for none – this is the basis of my philosophy.'[27]

But this is not what he says in *Don Juan*:

> They bowed obeisance and withdrew, retiring,
> 　　But not by the same door through which came in
> Baba and Juan, which last stood admiring
> 　　At some small distance all he saw within
> This strange saloon, much fitted for inspiring
> 　　Marvel and praise, for both or none things win.
> And I must say, I ne'er could see the very
> Great happiness of the *nil admirari*.
>
> 'Not to admire is all the art I know'
> 　　(Plain truth, dear Murray, needs few flowers of speech)
> 'To make men happy, or to keep them so',
> 　　(So take it in the very words of Creech).
> Thus Horace wrote we all know long ago,
> 　　And thus Pope quotes the precept to re-teach
> From his translation, but had none admired,
> Would Pope have sung, or Horace been inspired?
> (V.c–ci)

The indifference espoused by the letter-writer is that of the man for ever trying to escape from himself; it is an indifference that certainly fuels much of the satirical writing, once we acknowledge that it is, in fact, feigned. Hazlitt's phrase 'the eloquence of indifference' is an astute (if accidental) summing-up of one aspect of Byron's work.[28] The satirist cannot afford to admire too much: his eye has to be un-clouded. At the same time, the particular quality of Byron's satire derives from something that is the very opposite of indifference (which can so easily become a form of apathy). The essential movement towards feeling (charted in various ways throughout this book) owes much to the admiration admired here. The poet depends on inspiration which is de-pendent on a sense of wonder – 'Man's a strange animal . . . . Man's a phenomenon, one knows not what, / And wonderful beyond all wondrous measure' (I.cxxviii, cxxxiii). Not to won-der is not to feel. The celebration of particular kinds of love, in *Childe Harold's Pilgrimage* and *Don Juan*, is made possible by virtue of what he calls, in *The Giaour*, the 'gaze of wonder'. Just as his heroes indulge in such a gaze, so he as poet looks with intentness on the world around him. In canto XI of *Don Juan* he gives what might appear to be a catalogue of world weari-ness:

> Talk not of seventy years as age. In seven
>   I have seen more changes, down from monarchs to
> The humblest individual under heaven,
>   Than might suffice a moderate century through.
>
> (XI.lxxxii)

But it turns into something less cynical: the repeated affirma-tions ('I have seen . . . . I have seen . . . . I have seen . . . .') become a justification for the poem. He has obeyed his own injunctions to keep his eyes open. It is important, however, to emphasise the hard-won nature of that clarity, and its limita-tions.

At the beginning of canto XIV Byron contemplates the problems of philosophical certainty: he is reverting to the 'sea of speculation' he had talked of in canto IX.xviii in rather less solemn tones (in spite of the quotations from *Hamlet*). He had put the dangers neatly:

> 'Tis true we speculate both far and wide
>   And deem because we see, we are all-seeing.
>
> (IX.xvi)

That is a corrective to any grand, self-congratulatory designs the open-eyed poet might have. But in the later canto we seem to get the quintessence of Byron's views on the problems of seeing. Without any incongruity, he sends us back to the image, not just of eating and digestion, but of cannibalism.

> If from great Nature's or our own abyss
>   Of thought we could but snatch a certainty,
> Perhaps mankind might find the path they miss,
>   But then 'twould spoil much good philosophy.
> One system eats another up, and this
>   Much as old Saturn ate his progeny,
> For when his pious consort gave him stones
> In lieu of sons, of these he made no bones.
>
> But System doth reverse the Titan's breakfast
>   And eats her parents, albeit the digestion
> Is difficult. Pray tell me, can you make fast
>   After due search your faith to any question?
> Look back o'er ages ere unto the stake fast
>   You bind yourself and call some mode the best one.
> Nothing more true than not to trust your senses,
> And yet what are your other evidences?
>
> (XIV.i–ii)

To set forth on the 'sea of speculation' is to be back in the boat with Juan and Pedrillo. Such compulsions, though, have few compunctions. However steep the precipice, we find ourselves in a position comparable to Julia's, except that we have at least a modicum of self-awareness.

> When the mountains rear
> Their peaks beneath your human foot, and there
>   You look down o'er the precipice, and drear
> The gulf of rock yawns, you can't gaze a minute
> Without an awful wish to plunge within it.
>
> 'Tis true, you don't, but pale and struck with terror,
>   Retire. But look into your past impression
> And you will find, though shuddering at the mirror
>   Of your own thoughts in all their self-confession,
> The lurking bias, be it truth or error,

> To the unknown, a secret prepossession
> To plunge with all your fears – but where? You know not
> And that's the reason why you do – or do not.
>
> (XIV.v—vi)

That is both teasing and absolutely true to the central dichotomy of Byron's vision. The abyss is there, we want to peer into it, to find the truth, even if it means hurling ourselves into it like Empedocles: the impossibility of knowledge and certainty explains either course of action. It is not surprising that such keen glances cause indigestion, which perplexes

> Our soarings with another sort of question.
>   And that which after all my spirit vexes
> Is that I find no spot where man can rest eye on
>   Without confusion of the sorts and sexes,
> Of being, stars, and this unriddled wonder,
> The world, which at the worst's a glorious blunder,
>
> If it be chance, or if it be according
>   To the old Text, still better . . . .
>
> (XI.iii—iv)

Soon after this, Juan in London is attacked by footpads: ironically their cry of imprecation is 'Damn your eyes!' (XI.x). It is a cry that Byron echoes in his more pessimistic moments. He finds himself, along with many of his hereos, thinking that some things are best not seen.

The contradictions and the inconsistencies of sight manage to avoid nihilistic confusion. Alp might be sickened at Corinth; Hugo on the other hand might insist on keeping his eyes open at the moment of death. In doing so though, his staring orbs, whilst retaining their dignity, have the hopeless, helpless quality of a blind man's eye. There is a moment when Byron confronts this paradox head on:

> I will not swear that black is white,
> But I suspect in fact that white is black,
> And the whole matter rests upon eyesight.
>   Ask a blind man, the best judge . . . .
>
> (XII.lxxi)

At this *volte-face* we are half-invited to laugh: it is not an invitation we can readily refuse. But the Dedication to *Don Juan* puts the matter in a rather different light. For there the prime appeal, in an age of carnage, 'Transferred to gorge upon a sister shore', is to the 'blind old man' with his 'helpless eyes', the poet of epic sublimity, John Milton. And it is, perhaps, Milton, better than anyone, who would understand what Byron meant by 'the prophetic eye of appetite'.

2 The 'Fever at the Core': The Poetry of Passion

There may be some truth in the contention that Byron, in poems such as *The Giaour* and *The Corsair*, was producing a kind of poetry that his audience wanted.[1] But much more than mere opportunism lies behind this long string of narrative poems, stretching from *The Giaour* through later efforts such as *The Prisoner of Chillon* and *Parisina* to *Mazeppa* and *The Island* (this last interrupted the composition of *Don Juan*). Clearly, Byron was fascinated by the possibilities of narrative verse, even if *Childe Harold's Pilgrimage* and *Don Juan* both, in their very different ways, seem to announce his apparent indifference to anything we might understand by the term: he returns to the narrative form repeatedly, experimenting with perspectives, narrators, settings, in his attempts to elevate the verse tale, as popularised by Scott, into something more sublime. Whatever the formal peculiarities, though, I would want to argue that these reflect Byron's thematic obsessions, obsessions that he addresses in different ways in his major satires and which are there throughout his writing life. In spite of his own teasingly nonchalant remarks, there is every reason for taking these poems seriously. His determined immersion in so many narrative tales answers a specific aesthetic need which can be stated quite baldly: these poems are, to an obsessive degree, about varieties of passion, about heightened states of feeling, to which a loftily moralistic line cannot be applied. Byron is exploring not just the compulsions and imperatives of passion but also the dangers and inadequacies: the complexities of what it means to feel, particularly to feel on the borders or at the extremes of experience, constitute a thematic point of major importance, mirrored in the tortured, often fragmented, nature of the writing. In his satires he finds other means of tackling these complexities, but the obsessions remain.

His 'snake of a poem',[2] *The Giaour*, is, as I have suggested, perhaps the most highly structured of all his narratives: this is partly due to its piecemeal composition, the numerous changes it went through in manuscript, and from one edition to another.[3] The fragmentary nature of the structure is the necessary concomitant of the events and emotions under scrutiny. A brief summary of the plot would contain the following points: Hassan, a Moslem chieftain, loves his consort Leila; but she is loved also by the Christian Giaour, and Hassan, learning of her infidelity, has her killed in the traditional fashion (drowned, like a kitten, in a sack); the Giaour kills Hassan in combat, and then retreats into a monastery, where he tells his tale and dies. Put like that, it could well sound absurd, as could the substance of many a heightened and extravagant narrative. But Byron puts it not at all like that, and the poem requires several readings for that sequence of events to emerge as the narrative framework: the uncertainty and the mystery, the temporal transposition of events, the sentences left hanging in mid-air – these are all part of the narrative suspense, but, just as importantly, part of the emotional pattern of the poem. We are not allowed to stand still in any one fixed relation to events: different narrators, jumbled tenses, further a disorientation which prevents any easy identification or judgement. For Byron, this is extremely important, that we cannot remain settled in our attitudes or our reactions: he is working on us, in a way that could remind us of some of Wordsworth's devices in *Lyrical Ballads*, but which is in fact, I think, much more adventurous. For a start, Byron would never have dreamt of saying that each of his poems had a 'worthy purpose';[4] but that does not mean, as many critics have suggested, that his purposes are totally unworthy, that he is cavalierly exploiting Gothic horrors for his own wicked delight, revelling in a world where evil triumphs, where pirates and bandits and outlaws are regarded as appealing rogues. The hallmark of many of these poems, is, in fact, suffering, and we might bear in mind Coleridge's astute description of Lear as the perfect example of the *persona patiens*:[5] just as there is a philological connection between patience and suffering, so suffering and passion are inseparably linked. *The Giaour* and *The Prisoner of Chillon* are both, then, about aspects of passion, and the monastery to which the Giaour retreats finds its echo in the confines of Bonnivard's narrow cell. Both confront a 'vile repose' which is the apparent antithesis of their passionate thirst for life, but which is also, in some respects, the inevitable result of a passion that is too wild. The extremes of feeling can lead to the extremes of suffering. This is the terrible, potentially tragic, paradox that fascinates Byron.

In his confession at the end of the poem, the Giaour addresses the Friar, explaining the nature of his love for Leila. This sums up the distance Byron puts between this love and that of ordinary mortals, and the volcanic image has its special significance when we recall that that is how Byron thought of the imaginative act:[6]

> The cold in clime are cold in blood,
>   Their love can scarce deserve the name;
> But mine was like the lava flood
>   That boils in Aetna's breast of flame.
> I cannot prate in puling strain
> Of ladye-love, and beauty's chain;
> If changing cheek, and scorching vein –
> Lips taught to writhe, but not complain –
> If bursting heart, and madd'ning brain –
> And daring deed, and vengeful steel –
> And all that I have felt – and feel –
> Betoken love – that love was mine,
> And shewn by many a bitter sign.
> 'Tis true, I could not whine nor sigh,
> I knew but to obtain or die.
> I die – but first I have possest,
> And come what may, I *have been* blest;
> Shall I the doom I sought upbraid?
> No – reft of all – yet undismay'd
> But for the thought of Leila slain,
> Give me the pleasure with the pain,
> So would I live and love again.
>
> (*The Giaour*, ll. 1099–120)

It is characteristic of these Byronic heroes that they find it hard fully to explain their feelings. We should not be surprised at some of the short-hand at work here: it is, after all, the Giaour's boast that he cannot resort to flowery literary terms. He knows he has felt, and the indications are there in all their starkness – those extremes that require the simple, yet extreme, images of the volcano. And that this is no easy trope is suggested, locally, by that slight tremor in the fourth line, whereby he talks not of his own 'breast of flame' but, directly, of Aetna's, so that simile becomes metaphor, and hero and volcano merge in that personification. This declaration of his passionate love for Leila is at the core of the Giaour's experience. It is important to acknowledge, however, that the blessing of which he speaks is, apart from anything else, a spiritual blessing. It is one of the poem's many nice ironies that the Friar finds something abhorrent in the Giaour's single-minded pursuit of a love with such religious connotations.

The Giaour continues,

> Yes, Love indeed is light from heaven –
>   A spark of that immortal fire
> With angels shar'd – by Alla given,
>   To lift from earth our low desire.
> Devotion wafts the mind above,
> But Heaven itself descends in love –
> A feeling from the Godhead caught,
> To wean from self each sordid thought –
> A Ray of him who form'd the whole –
> A Glory circling round the soul!
>
> (ll.1131–40)

Again, we might challenge the poetic success of these lines. But we need to emphasise the insistence on love as heavenly light: when the Giaour spoke earlier of the 'pleasure' and the 'pain' it was no simple fleshly desire he was celebrating. And, even if, as he admits, his own love might have been imperfect, Leila's was not in any way so, which leads to the remorseless logic that lies behind these lines, and by extension, behind the events of the poem:

> She was my life's unerring light –
> That quench'd – what beam shall break my night?
> Oh! would it shone to lead me still,
> Although to death or deadliest ill!
>
> (ll.1145–8)

To lose such love is to lose everything: the volcano erupts again, in 'phrensy' and in 'madness', so that the cycle of passion is complete. The Giaour tells the Friar to report to an unnamed friend what he, the Giaour, has become, 'what thou dost behold!':

> The wither'd frame, the ruined mind,
> The wrack by passion left behind –
> A shrivelled scroll, a scatter'd leaf,
> Sear'd by the autumn blast of grief!
>
> (ll. 1253–6)

This inherent conflict of volcanic passion – between physical intensity and spiritual elation – lies at the base of the poem, tentatively in the early versions, but increasingly as Byron works on it and revises it. The conflict runs deep, colouring structure and imagery. It is Selim, in *The Bride of Abydos*, who warns his beloved Zuleika that 'I am not . . . what I appear!'; there is not much in Byron's world of passion that is what it seems to be. This much is apparent from the opening lines of *The Giaour*.

Byron initially offered six lines which, by themselves, would have told a reader very little:

> No breath of air to break the wave
> That rolls below the Athenian's grave,
> That tomb which, gleaming o'er the cliff,
> First greets the homeward-veering skiff,
> High o'er the land he saved in vain –
> When shall such hero live again?
>
> (ll. 1–6)

This mere hint at Themistocles, the champion of Greek freedom, is not self-explanatory, and Byron eventually added more than a hundred lines that have become crucial to the emotional tone of the poem. But even in that opening fragment we get some idea of the poem's sobriety. What presents itself as 'A Fragment of a Turkish Tale' seems to offer no suggestion of action – the final question implies that there will be no such hero in the future – and in any case Themistocles might as well have saved his energies, since freedom has gone. It is, in fact, very hard to determine, syntactically, the focal point of this sentence; consequently, it is difficult to know what the significance is of that lack of wind. As our eyes and mind move between sea and cliff and back again (the rhymes underscore the restless lurching from line to line) we wonder about the tomb on the headland – in what sense is it a greeting, in what sense an admonishment? Death seems to be very much part of this landscape (and this seascape). The contradictions are left: something essential to a complete understanding is missing.

Byron is seldom interested in allowing for complete understanding; but his lengthy amplification of this enigmatic opening indicates just how anxious he is to tease out the contradictions. By a sudden alteration of perspective, the scene is apparently transformed into a paradise:

>   Fair clime! where every season smiles
> Benignant o'er those blessed isles,
> Which seen from far Colonna's height,
> Make glad the heart that hails the sight,
> And lend to loneliness delight.
> There mildly dimpling – Ocean's cheek
> Reflects the tints of many a peak
> Caught by the laughing tides that lave
> These Edens of the eastern wave;
> And if at times a transient breeze
> Break the blue chrystal of the seas,
> Or sweep one blossom from the trees,
> How welcome is each gentle air,
> That wakes and wafts the odours there!
>
>   (ll.7–20)

The Edenic reference is, for Byron, extremely potent: in *Cain* he is to focus all his dramatic energies on the implications of the expulsion from the Garden, and of course the central implication is not comforting. Eden is a temporary, transitory state, seldom to be trusted. So it proves in *The Giaour*. After a passage in which nature is depicted in harmony with itself, and with heaven, we get the first hint of nature's ways perverted: the grotto becomes a refuge for the pirate, a means of stealthy attack; the sailor's song, echoing that of the nightingale, is transmogrified into the groans of one assaulted. At this point Byron speaks out against mankind's folly, his destruction of the natural Eden, his destruction of freedom (whereupon the Themistoclean reference takes on its true significance).

> Strange – that where Nature lov'd to trace,
> As if for Gods, a dwelling-place,
> And every charm and grace hath mixed
> Within the paradise she fixed –
> There man, enamour'd of distress,
> Should mar it into wilderness,
> And trample, brute-like, o'er each flower
> That tasks not one laborious hour;
> Nor claims the culture of his hand,
> To bloom along the fairy land,
> But springs as to preclude his care,
> And sweetly woos him – but to spare!
> Strange – that where all is peace beside
> There passion riots in her pride,
> And lust and rapine wildly reign,
> To darken o'er the fair domain.
> It is as though the fiends prevail'd
> Against the seraphs they assail'd,
> And fixed, on heavenly thrones, should dwell
> The freed inheritors of hell –
> So soft the scene, so form'd for joy,
> So curst the tyrants that destroy!
>
> (ll.46–67)

If this is an attack on tyranny, on inverted values (and this inversion helps retrospectively to explain the bewildering changes of focus in the opening lines), it is put, primarily, in terms of passion, a passion sadly at odds with the gentler wooings of the natural world. We can see that the terms of the poem's emotional debate – to be acted out in the narrative proper – are being carefully defined in what amounts to a prologue. The passion that is to be the hallmark of the hero is equated here with the essential characteristic of the human race – pirates, brute-like, tyrants all.

It would, though, be a mistake to assume that the Giaour is simply a personification of such tyranny. The point about

Greece as it now presents itself to the poet is that it requires further heroics, a challenge to the 'tyrant's power', a challenge which will of necessity involve the ferocity of fighting. The history of Greece urges its offspring to 'Snatch from the ashes of your sires / The embers of their former fires'. The volcanic emotion which the Giaour is to speak of later clearly has its anticipation here, which should make us wary of assuming that all passion is the same, and is to be unequivocally condemned. Much depends upon the qualifications, on who is doing the condemning. The fisherman narrator, when he first sees the Giaour, thundering on horseback across the sands, exclaims,

> I know thee not, I loathe thy race,
> But in thy lineaments I trace
> What time shall strengthen, not efface;
> Though young and pale, that sallow front
> Is scath'd by fiery passions brunt,
> Though bent on earth thine evil eye
> As meteor-like thou glidest by,
> Right well I view, and deem thee one
> Whom Othman's sons should slay or shun.
>
> (ll.191−9)

This particular narrator has his own reasons for the view he takes, even as he acknowledges his lack of knowledge. 'Fiery passion' receives its fullest *apologia*, as we have seen, from the Giaour himself, in his final confession. But the poet is anxious to explain that the Giaour is, if a wreck, a mighty one ('It was no vulgar tenement . . .'−l.872): 'The close observer can espy / A noble soul, and lineage high' (ll.868−9). That is unequivocal, and necessarily so, when the Giaour has no one else to speak for him, when he has to nurse his own sorrow in isolation. The poem, in essence, is an attempt to make of the reader a 'close observer', in so far as that is possible when the result can be so uncomfortable ('Oft will his glance the gazer rue' − l.837). To this end, Byron inserts a long, ruminative passage in the middle of the Giaour's confession, whereby he hopes to define the unbending, brittle nature of a particular kind of passion − which in turn helps to explain the grudging admiration of that 'But . . . ' clause in the passage quoted above (even an enemy finds the man fascinating, if only because he has, in one sense, time on his side).

> To love the softest hearts are prone,
> But such can ne'er be all his own;
> Too timid in his woes to share,
> Too meek to meet, or brave despair;
> And sterner hearts alone may feel
> The wound that time can never heal.
> The rugged metal of the mine
> Must burn before its surface shine,
> But plung'd within the furnace-flame,
> It bends and melts – though still the same;
> Then tempered to thy want, or will,
> 'Twill serve thee to defend or kill;
> A breast-plate for thine hour of need,
> Or blade to bid thy foeman bleed;
> But if a dagger's form it bear,
> Let those who shape its edge, beware!
> Thus passion's fire, and woman's art,
> Can turn and tame the sterner heart;
> From these its form and tone are ta'en,
> And what they make it, must remain,
> But break – before it bend again.
>
> (ll.916–36)

Byron's fatalism cannot be avoided: much of his earlier work is permeated with the varieties of Calvanism he had taken in with his mother's milk. But what is interesting here is that the Giaour emerges, because of this fiery passion over which he seems to have had no choice, as a figure of tragic dimensions. There is a marvellous – and marvelling – description of him caught for a split second in stillness before he disappears from view. It is described as a moment of restraint, of hesitation, of bewilderment, as though he is in a 'waking dream'. Such moments in this poem are surprisingly frequent, moments of repose of various kinds, set off against the surrounding turbulence: these alterations of pace reinforce the shifts in perspective, and in particular the paradoxes of mood and emotion.

There are two aspects of this account of the Giaour, caught in this frozen moment; first of all, his appearance to the observer-narrator, an appearance reminiscent, above all, of death:

> He stood – some dread was on his face –
> Soon Hatred settled in its place –
> It rose not with the reddening flush
> Of transient Anger's hasty blush,
> But pale as marble o'er the tomb,
> Whose ghastly whiteness aids its gloom.
> His brow was bent – his eye was glazed –
> He raised his arm, and fiercely raised;
> And sternly shook his hand on high,
> As doubting to return or fly . . . .
>
> (ll.234–43)

Secondly, there are the metaphysical reflections that accompany this observation, once the Giaour has disappeared. This passage is highly charged, gathering up into itself much of the concentrated energy of the early part of the poem, and anticipating, in its complex sense of time and eternity, later tales such as *The Prisoner of Chillon*, or the magnificent reflections of the last two cantos of *Childe Harold's Pilgrimage*. There are times when we want to accuse Byron of overblown rhetoric, but this is not one of them:

> 'Twas but a moment that he stood,
> Then sped as if by death pursued;
> But in that instant, o'er his soul
> Winters of Memory seemed to roll,
> And gather in that drop of time
> A life of pain, an age of crime.
> O'er him who loves, or hates, or fears,
> Such moment pours the grief of years –
> What felt *he* then – at once opprest
> By all that most distracts the breast?
> That pause – which pondered o'er his fate,
> Oh, who its dreary length shall date!
> Though in Time's record nearly nought,
> It was Eternity to Thought!
> For infinite as boundless space

> The thought that Conscience must embrace,
> Which in itself can comprehend
> Woe without name – or hope – or end.
>   (*The Giaour*, ll.259–76)

Against that recurrent sense we get in Byron's narrative poems of his heroes fleeing from something 'they know not of', seeking, like Childe Harold, an escape in restlessness, we should set such moments as this, when the 'vacant bosom's wilderness' (l.939) is revealed, when there is another kind of feeling, as intense as any that comes with constant motion. That is why it needs to be said that there are two passages in particular in *The Giaour* which epitomise the currents within the poem, where we can see very clearly the oppositions between which Byron moves. (He was the first to acknowledge that his mind was basically antithetical.)

To take the second passage first: in preparing for the confrontation between the Giaour and Hassan, Byron resorts to a kind of epic simile which is both obvious and central to his vision of antithetical forces. To say that it is obvious is to point, not to its triteness, but to its inevitability: a poem that has begun so complexly and compellingly with the sea has earned the right to place it at the poem's emotional and eventful core.

> As rolls the river into ocean,
> In sable torrent wildly streaming;
>   As the sea-tide's opposing motion,
> In azure column proudly gleaming,
> Beats back the current many a rood,
> In curling foam and mingling flood;
> While eddying whirl, and breaking wave,
> Roused by the blast of winter rave;
> Through sparkling spray in thundering clash,
> The lightnings of the waters flash
> In awful whiteness o'er the shore,
> That shines and shakes beneath the roar;
> Thus – as the stream and ocean greet,
> With waves that madden as they meet –
> Thus join the bands whom mutual wrong,
> And fate and fury drive along.
>   . . .

> Ah! fondly youthful hearts can press,
> To seize and share the dear caress;
> But Love itself could never pant
> For all that Beauty sighs to grant,
> With half the fervour Hate bestows
> Upon the last embrace of foes,
> When grappling in the fight they fold
> Those arms that ne'er shall lose their hold;
> Friends meet to part – Love laughs at faith; –
> True foes, once met, are joined till death!
>
> (ll.620–54)

The sense of frenzy as river and ocean meet is an image not just of the opposing armies: it is a potent emblem of the passion that the poem is exploring. We are perhaps at this point invited to attempt some distinction between the passions of the respective protagonists. But the declared mutuality of their wrong, their fate, and their fury, makes such distinction apparently impossible; similarly (echoing the greeting offered by cliff to skiff in the opening lines of the poem) stream and ocean greet each other, and the telescoped syntax drives home the essential ambiguity of this maddened and maddening greeting. It then makes perfect sense for Byron, at the end of this paragraph, to talk of love and hate: he is fascinated by their relationship, by the ways in which the possessive grasp of the one mirrors that of the other (possession, after all, is an aspect of his love for Leila that the Giaour exults in, even as he mourns possession's inevitable loss). The ultimate irony, the bitterness of experience, is contained in that final couplet – which stands out in all its epigrammatic force because of the way Byron has worked across the line breaks in the earlier part of this final sentence, so that we gain momentary relief from the rush of breathless couplets, only to be brought up sharply by the final turn. A meeting of friends has within its very nature a potential parting, which paradoxically for a moment seems more than a merely cynical acknowledgement of the way life works – before, of course, the second half of that line disabuses us; enemies are in a perverse way true, and by implication truer, because they avoid such a parting, in that their embrace lasts 'till death'. The paragraph as a whole lends to this couplet a weight of feeling that we soon realise is true to the pathos of the poem as a whole. The natural forces of opposition guarantee the authenticity of that fatal embrace. The frenzy of passion, whatever its dreadful consequences, has its own validity. If we are in any doubt about this, Byron's account of the fall of Hassan should confirm the point in all its fullness:

> Fall'n Hassan lies – his unclos'd eye
> Yet lowering on his enemy,
> As if the hour that seal'd his fate,
> Surviving left his quenchless hate;
> And o'er him bends that foe with brow
> As dark as his that bled below.
>
> (ll.669–74)

This image of the Giaour bending over his implacable foe recalls, quite vividly, the other passage I want to discuss, the passage towards the end of the prologue which was almost universally acclaimed by Byron's contemporaries. The echo demands a hearing.

After Byron has unleashed his venom against destructive tyrants who have trampled on nature's Eden, he has a quite extraordinary paragraph, in which the syntax seems to turn inside out, as the sentence is lost and then refound. The gaze of the living is replaced by that of the dead, in a reversal typical of the poem's movement: it is, in fact, only after twenty-odd lines that we realise we have been launched upon a simile. What is of particular interest here is the lavish attention paid to the image of death and decay: what the Giaour is to loathe as 'the languor of repose' is here, at least for a moment, translated into 'rapture'.

> He who hath bent him o'er the dead,
> Ere the first day of death is fled;
> The first dark day of nothingness,
> The last of danger and distress;
> (Before Decay's effacing fingers
> Have swept the lines where beauty lingers)
> And mark'd the mild angelic air –
> The rapture of repose that's there –
> The fixed yet tender traits that streak

> The languor of the placid cheek,
> And – but for that sad shrouded eye,
>   That fires not – wins not – weeps not – now –
>   And but for that chill changeless brow,
> Where cold Obstruction's apathy
> Appals the gazing mourner's heart,
> As if to him it could impart
> The doom he dreads, yet dwells upon –
> Yes – but for these and these alone,
> Some moments – aye – one treacherous hour,
> He still might doubt the tyrant's power,
> So fair – so calm – so softly seal'd
> The first – last look – by death reveal'd!
> Such is the aspect of this shore –
> 'Tis Greece – but living Greece no more!
> So coldly sweet, so deadly fair,
> We start – for soul is wanting there.
> Hers is the loveliness in death,
> That parts not quite with parting breath;
> But beauty with that fearful bloom,
> That hue which haunts it to the tomb –
> Expression's last receding ray,
> A gilded halo hovering round decay,
> The farewell beam of Feeling past away!
> Spark of that flame – perchance of heavenly birth –
> Which gleams – but warms no more its cherish'd earth!
>
> (ll.68–102)

It is extremely difficult to do justice to this passage, so bursting is it with the concerns of the poem as a whole, even whilst apparently offering itself as a detachable piece of 'fine writing'. We should not be misled by this appearance – it is a consequence of the fragmentary nature of *The Giaour*, in which there are many passages which are, in a superficial sense, self-contained. Part of the shock of this passage derives from the sudden change of pace and tone after the attack on tyranny and the riot of passion. We move from an image of a country bordering on the mythical, and from a teeming rhetoric of anger, to one of Byron's 'emblems of emotion', to a particularity and a quiet eloquence whose primary quality is exploratory. Ethel C. Mayne's comment of 1924 holds good:

she describes the 'trailing anacoluthon' as 'that strange slipshod loveliness, where He never fulfils his destiny as the subject of the opening phrase. Bent o'er the dead he remains immoveable to the end of time.'[7] That is a perfect matching of response to Byron's verse. As I have suggested, the image of the mourner bent over the dead anticipates that of the Giaour bent over Hassan on the battlefield. In both instances there is the implication of eternity. The sense of repose belongs both to the dead and to those who mourn, to Hassan and to the Giaour, to the trampled, butchered scene and its observer — how extraordinary is Byron's ability, in his desire to make of us the ideal close observers of his drama and its emotions, to glide from that suspended 'He' to 'We', more than twenty lines later: not only is the anacoluthon left trailing, it absorbs us into itself in one of those recurrent moments in this poem in which the gazer is transfixed by what he gazes upon. On this occasion Byron manages, by implication, to perform, to act out, the process he is later, in *Don Juan*, to describe more coolly, whereby we become what we see. His triumph here is to lure the reader into the poem. Once we are in there, we are caught: in view of what I have just been saying, we are the Giaour, we are Hassan, we look at our own expulsion from Eden, our own death.

As with so much in this poem, there is an ambivalence around this central concept of death: just as the Athenian tomb gleams, so the body here has its own special beauty. Byron is later to explore various ramifications of the related notion of marble sculptures, frozen and yet apparently alive. In this poem the Giaour is described as 'pale as marble o'er the tomb', in that crucially frozen moment of inaction before he rounds the corner and disappears from view: the connection is clearly not fortuitous. We are on that same isthmus between events, that same moment of repose which is, in its essence, helpless. The punning qualification is a sharp reminder that Byron was exploring modes of hesitant precision long before the virtuosity of *Don Juan*:

> Hers is the loveliness in death,
> That parts not quite with parting breath . . . .

In the last few lines of this paragraph, Leila's love for the

Giaour is foreshadowed: his account of the heavenly light, a 'Glory circling round the soul', finds its counterpart here in the 'gilded halo hovering round decay, / The farewell beam of Feeling past away!' In terms of the imagery, then, Leila is subsumed into this paragraph as much as the male protagonists. And this is important in a poem where separate identities are hardly the point: the multiple narrative perspectives, whatever their many functional purposes, are indicative, by virtue of their oddly blurring effect, of the blurred relationship between events and between people. In *Childe Harold's Pilgrimage*, this can be a problem, both for Byron and for the reader; it is one he eventually acknowledges. But in *The Giaour* the transferences, the complex interweavings of relationships, are central to the poem's emotional tone. As these lines imply, what is at issue is the nature of feeling, and it can be no accident that feeling as it fades is so closely placed to 'Expression's last receding ray'. Byron's obsession is with the nature of feeling, with its necessity; just as throughout *Don Juan* he refers obliquely to *Macbeth*, so here he resorts to an echo in voicing his greatest dread:

> Where cold Obstruction's apathy
> Appals the gazing mourner's heart . . . .

Byron's Greek was good enough to know that apathy means lack of feeling; he knew, too, that how and what we feel is intimately tied to how and what we speak.

By comparison with *The Giaour*, *Lara* tends to get rather short critical shrift, even from such champions of the narrative poems as Robert Gleckner. Many have been content to see it as an adjunct, a rather feeble continuation of the more fully developed *Corsair* (and that is how Byron seems to have viewed it). But, as Gleckner persuasively suggests, it has similarities with *The Giaour*, and I should like to pursue some of these without accepting his rather grudging critical view of the poem. Although *Lara* is centred on mystery, on things untold and unrevealed, its relative simplicity of plot and structure allows it to serve as a comment on some aspects of the far richer *Giaour*.

As a character, Lara approaches the state of the Giaour in the monastery: even at the start of the poem he is, to some degree, a wreck.

> Short was the course his restlessness had run,
> But long enough to leave him half undone.
> (Lara, I.23–4)

The narrator is scarcely interested in what has brought him to this point ('It skills not, boots not step by step to trace / His youth through all the mazes of his race' – I.21–2); what matters is the stark contrast between the merriment of those who are at home to receive him, and his emptiness. His absence had become such a part of things that his return makes him seem unreal, a ghostly figure in an unreal present:

> They see, they recognise, yet almost deem
> The present dubious, or the past a dream.
> (I.53–4)

Byron's fascination with this conflict recurs throughout his work, and is a dominant *motif* in this poem. The very first stanza, for all its emphasis on mirth and gladness, has its fair share of qualifications, indications of reluctance in those bright, fixed smiles.

> The Serfs are glad through Lara's wide domain,
> And Slavery half forgets her feudal chain . . . .
> (I.1–2)

But the contrast is none the less there, and Lara's initial appearance is presented with a characteristic Byronic twist: 'He comes at last in sudden loneliness' (I.43). Strictly speaking, it is his arrival that is 'sudden'; but the loneliness gets its surprisingly right, and rightly bleak, epithet. *The Giaour* had explored loneliness; many of its most vivid images had been of isolation. Lara's loneliness is highlighted, and related very specifically to the 'flagging wing' of 'weary Time'. He is a shell of what he once was, an epitome of what the Giaour terms 'The wrack by passion left behind'. In Lara's case

> That brow in furrow'd lines had fix'd at last,
> And spake of passions, but of passion past;
> The pride, but not the fire, of early days,
> Coldness of mien, and carelessness of praise;
> A high demeanour, and a glance that took
> Their thoughts from others by a single look . . . .
>
>   (I.67–72)

There seems little that he has in common with other people, little sense of aim or purpose. What feeling he does have is too deep for knowledge:

> And some deep feeling it were vain to trace
> At moments lighten'd o'er his livid face.
>
>   (I.83–4)

Lara is rather like the Ancient Mariner, in that he has been across the world and undergone experiences the rest of us know nothing of; but he is totally unlike the Mariner (and unlike the Giaour in this respect) in his silence, his refusal to tell others of his experience. Curiosity is left frustrated. There is, however, an important stanza in which the puzzle he presents is stated rather more fully. Although we should have to admit the lameness of the verse here, what we are being told is of considerable significance.

> 'Twas strange – in youth all action and all life,
> Burning for pleasure, not averse from strife:
> Woman – the field – the ocean – all that gave
> Promise of gladness, peril of a grave,
> In turn he tried – he ransack'd all below,
> And found his recompence in joy or woe,
> No tame, trite medium; for his feelings sought
> In that intenseness an escape from thought:
> The tempest of his heart in scorn had gazed
> On that the feebler elements hath rais'd:
> The rapture of his heart had look'd on high,
> And ask'd if greater dwelt beyond the sky:
> Chain'd to excess, the slave of each extreme,
> How woke he from the wildness of that dream?

> Alas! he told not – but he did awake
> To curse the wither'd heart that would not break.
>   (I.115–30)

The received notion of the 'Byronic hero' gets an airing here: certainly in tone this stanza seems closer to some of the tiredness of the early cantos of *Childe Harold's Pilgrimage* than to the detailed explorations of *The Giaour*. Just as Byron the narrator is anxious to distance himself, initially, from the wilder excesses of Harold, so he is ready here to restrain his enthusiasm for Lara's early intensity. What we have here is some pale echo of a Marlovian overreacher, caught in a nightmare world where he is no better, no more free, than his serfs; his passions might have served an immediate purpose, as escape from thought, but they in turn have to be escaped from. The tempest of this stanza is far removed from that fierce, contentious stanza at the centre of *The Giaour*.

After some further passages of scene-setting, a dramatic event leaves everyone puzzled. There is a terrible cry in the middle of the night, and Lara is found lying in a faint on the floor, his sword half-drawn, his face twisted in rage, his 'gladiator's look' 'fix'd in horrible repose'. The only person he can speak to, when he recovers, is the mysterious pageboy, about whom we have been told very little, but on whom he clearly depends. Now, this shriek might well seem to have come out of the pages of a Gothic novel; but Byron uses the episode in three important directions, which owe little to the Gothic tradition. First, he underlines the nightmare quality of the experience, so that we as readers are left in the position of the serfs, deeming 'The present dubious, and the past a dream'; secondly, he begins to fill in the bonds between Lara and his pageboy, and these are to constitute a major aspect of the narrative; and, thirdly, he tries to give at least some account of his hero, in terms of the bewildered, contradictory reactions of everyone else at court. The more we are told, the more Lara comes alive as a psychological creation. Once again, character is inextricably bound up with the manifestations of passion:

> With more capacity for love than earth
> Bestows on most of mortal mould and birth,

> His early dreams of good outstripp'd the truth,
> And troubled manhood followed baffled youth;
> With thought of years in phantom chace misspent,
> And wasted powers for better purpose lent;
> And fiery passions that had poured their wrath
> In hurried desolation o'er his path,
> And left the better feelings all at strife
> In wild reflection o'er his stormy life . . . .
>
> (I.321–30)

The studied coldness that follows on this wilful passion (wherein he puts onto the shoulders of fate the responsibility for his own actions), has a curious effect: it simultaneously isolates him and makes him a figure of power over others. Lara impresses himself on everyone who sees him, however much they might resist him:

> Vain was the struggle in that mental net,
> His spirit seemed to dare you to forget!
> (I.381–2)

It is this characteristic which helps to further the action. At a celebration in Otho's hall, Otho's friend Sir Ezzelin recognises Lara from the distant past, a recognition Lara publicly denies but privately knows to be well justified. At the first moment of meeting, their eyes reveal their secrets:

> At length encountering meets the mutual gaze
> Of keen enquiry, and of mute amaze . . . .
> (I.409–10)

The shift from 'mutual' to 'mute', and back again, under-scores well enough the secrets shared between these men, and underlines, too, the peculiar nature of this poem, in which silence plays such a part. The relationship (the mutuality) between Lara and his page is one in which few words are spoken: Kaled's love for Lara is shown 'in reverence and in deeds alone; / In mute attention; and his care, which guessed / Each wish, fulfilled it ere the tongue expressed' (I.556–7). If Kaled understands his master as does no one else in Otho's hall, it is because he shares some of his characteristics; in

particular, he has 'A latent fierceness that far more became /
His fiery climate than his tender frame' (I.580–1). And, if
Lara and Kaled share a mutual and a mute regard, the same
can be said of Lara and Ezzelin. In confronting Ezzelin, Lara is
having to confront that part of himself he has striven to
conceal.

The appointment between the two men is, mysteriously, not
kept by Ezzelin; in an argument Otho leaps to the defence of
Ezzelin's honour; in their brief duel Otho is wounded, and
Lara leaves the court, 'Nor cast on Otho's towers a single look'
(II.96). In his description of the duel, Byron touches on the
conflict between passion and control:

> And fiercer shook his angry falchion now
> Than when his foe's was levell'd at his brow;
> Then all was stern collectedness and art,
> Now rose the unleavened hatred of his heart;
> So little sparing to the foe he fell'd,
> That when the approaching crowd his arm withheld,
> He almost turned the thirsty point on those
> Who thus for mercy dared to interpose;
> But to a moment's thought that purpose bent,
> Yet look'd he on him still with eye intent,
> As if he loathed the ineffectual strife
> That left a foe, howe'er o'erthrown, with life;
> As if to search how far the wound he gave
> Had sent its victim onward to his grave.
>
> (II.75–88)

It becomes clear that the poem is an exploration of the puz-
zling combination represented by Lara. His passion, his
hatred, is balanced by a cold collectedness that is not entirely
at his bidding; but alongside his absolute rage is this curiously
metaphysical intensity of concern as to how close his opponent
is to death. He is himself, at this moment, an image of per-
plexity. What could be seen on one level as an angry brawl
becomes, on another, a look at the relationship between life
and death, in particular that border country Byron has
already hinted at in his words on the world of dreams at the
end of canto I: it is to become something of an obsession in *Don
Juan* (see p. 205). This moment of puzzled poise 'between two

worlds' (as he is to put it in *Don Juan*) seems to be related to the narrow dividing line between 'unleavened hatred' and 'stern collectedness and art'.

The poem takes something of a sociological turn, as discontented peasants rally to Lara's side against the 'tyranny' of Otho. Clearly Byron is in at least two minds as to Lara's motivation; although at times his hero seems a mere opportunist, a considerable claim is made for him:

> Stern, unambitious, silent, he had been
> Henceforth a calm spectator of life's scene;
> But dragg'd again upon the arena, stood
> A leader not unequal to the feud;
> In voice – mien – gesture – savage nature spoke,
> And from his eye the gladiator broke.
>
> (II.258–62)

This balances the desolation that sweeps over the land once 'distempered passions lent their force' (II.270). The poem becomes one of carnage which leads to the inevitable death of Lara.

In the course of this second part of the poem, more weight is given to the relationship between Kaled and Lara. As Lara lies dying, Otho and his troops arrive to witness the strange, alien converse of these two.

> They seem'd even then – that twain – unto the last
> To half forget the present in the past;
> To share between themselves some separate fate,
> Whose darkness none beside should penetrate.
>
> (II.450–3)

One particular secret is finally revealed: Kaled is, after all, a woman. If we think of the poem as a sequel to *The Corsair*, then she is Gulnare to Lara's Corsair. But such speculation is deliberately eschewed. Their love goes unquestioned:

> Is human love the growth of human will?
> To her he might be gentleness; the stern
> Have deeper thoughts than your dull eyes discern,

> And when they love, your smilers guess not how
> Beats the strong heart, though less the lips avow.
>
> (II.531–5)

What happened to Ezzelin is briefly hinted at: the implication
is that Lara killed him. But by this stage the poem has really
outgrown its plot; it has become a poem about the past, a past
that has no memorial. As later, with Haidée and her father on
the island, it is the poem that provides the memory, and, in
doing so, retains and perpetuates the mystery. And, like
Haidée, Kaled dies because of her love for the dead Lara. At
the end, we might catch a pre-echo of Keats's 'Isabella', with-
out its idiosyncratic grotesqueness. We should certainly not
pass lightly by this emblem of helpless sorrow:

> And she would sit beneath the very tree
> Where lay his drooping head upon her knee;
> And in that posture where she saw him fall,
> His words, his looks, his dying grasp recall;
> And she had shorn, but sav'd her raven hair,
> And oft would snatch it from her bosom there,
> And fold, and press it gently to the ground,
> As if she staunch'd anew some phantom's wound.
> Herself would question, and for him reply;
> Then rising, start, and beckon him to fly
> From some imagin'd spectre in pursuit;
> Then seat her down upon some linden's root,
> And hide her visage with her meagre hand,
> Or trace strange characters along the sand –
> This could not last – she lies by him she lov'd;
> Her tale untold – her truth too dearly prov'd.
>
> (II.612–27)

As narrative, then, *Lara* can be seen to be rather thin. What
the poem does is to emphasise this central area of experience
which makes little sense to others, but which is self-validating.
As in *The Giaour*, much of the passion is taken for granted; but
we do not get the kind of explanation that takes up the last
part of the earlier poem – it is as though Byron is anxious to
confront a different, but related, kind of challenge. He wants
to do away with explanations that will satisfy the rationalists

amongst us: that address to our 'dull eyes' puts us as readers
fairly firmly in our place, and in doing so anticipates the sort
of assault he is to make on us in *Don Juan*, where we become,
amongst other things, 'atrocious'. *Lara* is part of that larger
process whereby we are taught to see properly; but at the same
time one of the lessons is that, just 'because we see, we're not
all-seeing' (see p. 35). This poem represents part of the yawn-
ing abyss into which we would peer and plunge at our peril.
Byron gives sufficient indication of the vitality of the passions
involved here, of their devastating consequences, but also of
their 'gentleness'. In his account of the chains that bind the
two lovers together, he seems to anticipate some of the para-
doxes of freedom and constraint that are to get fuller treat-
ment in later narratives:

> They were not common links that form'd the chain
> That bound to Lara Kaled's heart and brain;
> But that wild tale she brook'd not to unfold,
> And seal'd is now each lip that could have told.
>
> (II.535–8)

The central opposition inherent in the sway of passion finds
its most startling outlet in two complementary poems, *The
Prisoner of Chillon* and *Mazeppa*. These tales may be taken as
the most compressed and perhaps most polished statements
of those conflicting impulses which fascinated Byron all his
life, and which preoccupied him in all his narrative poems.
The one immediately noticeable difference between these two
tales and those I have so far discussed is the approach, here,
towards the dramatic monologue. In *The Prisoner of Chillon*,
the speaker throughout is the historical figure Bonnivard, the
sixteenth-century Frenchman held captive in the castle which
Byron visited in 1816; in *Mazeppa*, the framed, central narra-
tive is spoken by the eponymous seventy-year-old 'hetman' of
King Charles of Sweden. Such a radically different focus of
attention has major implications for Byron's development.
His relationship as poet with his material is often complex –
Childe Harold's Pilgrimage is the prime example, but *Don Juan*,
too, plays heavily on the ambiguities that arise from not know-
ing precisely where the poet stands in relation to his narrator

or to his hero. We have seen something of how, in *The Giaour*, Byron experimented, very daringly, with a form of fragmented, multiple narrative in which the constantly fluctuating perspectives refuse, on our part, any too ready identification with particular points of view; the effect of such a strategy is to leave us perplexed, suspended in an oddly open-ended kind of way. Many of the other narratives are less experimental in this respect, but we could say that their main feature is related to *The Giaour's* narrative technique – what makes *Lara*, *The Bride of Abydos*, *The Corsair* so compelling, for all their acknowledged carelessness, is that central element of mystery, the hidden core of the heroic figures who do their utmost to preserve their secrets. In adopting a first-person narrative technique Byron is deliberately dispensing with that element of mystery: having shown us various instances of what such characters look like from the outside, and how they strike the uncomprehending and the hostile, he now explores the psychology from within. In doing so, he performs a rather remarkable feat. For he manages to present us with plausible characters placed in fully realised settings, particularised and detailed, whilst at the same time implying that such characters are not outside the pale of our knowledge: there is in fact a very strong sense in which they become fully representative of their condition. In other words *The Prisoner of Chillon* is not just about Bonnivard, it is about the nature of imprisonment; *Mazeppa* is not just about a rather humorous old Swede with a good story to tell, it is about the nature of passion and freedom. There are good reasons for considering the two poems together, and for regarding them in many ways as the fitting culmination of Byron's narrative strategies.

The Prisoner of Chillon picks up, in its opening stanza, two themes reminiscent of *The Giaour*. The Giaour had declared to the Friar that he 'loathed the languor of repose', whilst admitting a certain ambiguity in his attitude ('Yet lurks a wish within my breast / For rest – but not to feel 'tis rest'); he had also described himself as 'The wrack by passion left behind'. Bonnivard talks of himself as a 'wreck' and refers to his limbs, 'rusted with a vile repose'. The difference is that the Giaour's wish for a rest that he cannot actually feel as such is fulfilled, and he dies, finding in death the release he had never had when alive; the savage irony of this poem is that Bonnivard's entire monologue is uttered, as we soon realise, after he has been freed: but he can never be free again. All his natural ties have been destroyed:

> And mine has been the fate of those
> To whom the goodly earth and air
> Are bann'd, and barr'd – forbidden fare . . . .
> (*The Prisoner of Chillon*, ll.8–10)

He has languished in prison for his beliefs, and those of his father: a complete family has been broken. Byron is not particularly interested in the reasons for the imprisonment and the persecution: what concerns him is the effect of a perversion of nature, for not only is Bonnivard barred from nature; whatever aspects of nature can reach him are themselves imprisoned. The second stanza, with its relentless, repetitive cataloguing of the terms and conditions of imprisonment, is a brutal summary of what Byron had put forward, more tentatively and more rhetorically, at the beginning of *The Giaour* – the destruction of nature by humankind:

> There are seven pillars of Gothic mould,
> In Chillon's dungeons deep and old,
> There are seven columns, massy and grey,
> Dim with a dull imprison'd ray,
> A sunbeam which hath lost its way,
> And through the crevice and the cleft
> Of the thick wall is fallen and left;
> Creeping o'er the floor so damp,
> Like a marsh's meteor lamp:
> And in each pillar there is a ring,
>   And in each ring there is a chain;
> That iron is a cankering thing,
>   For in these limbs its teeth remain,
> With marks that will not wear away,
> Till I have done with this new day,
> Which now is painful to these eyes,
> Which have not seen the sun so rise
> For years – I cannot count them o'er,
> I lost their long and heavy score,
> When my last brother droop'd and died,
> And I lay living by his side.
> (*The Prisoner of Chillon*, ll.27–47)

The sun, in these circumstances, serves no purpose; and that image permeates the stanza, in that even when free the prisoner finds only pain in the sight of the rising sun, the very thing he had longed for for more years than he can remember. John Clare, in his despairing poem of removal, 'The Flitting', echoes, with dreadful pertinence, Byron's depiction of an alienated nature:

> The sun een seems to lose its way
> Nor knows the quarter it is in . . . .[8]

Just as with Clare, so with Bonnivard: the lost, imprisoned sun is an emblem of himself, of his futility. And, as an index of the poem's metaphoric strength, we relate the marks of the iron teeth in his limbs with the rust of the first stanza: the startling metaphor has behind it a startling literalness.

The three brothers are locked away together, but unable to see each other in their immobility, except by 'that pale and livid light / That made us strangers in our sight' (*The Prisoner of Chillon*, ll.52–3). Nature conspires in their alienation, in that terrible separateness that Byron so often dwells on, in his poems of parting: here, even though together, they are 'yet apart', and their very voices, as they talk and sing in their attempts to remain sane, become restricted and impersonal, ghostly reminders that they are losing their own identities, almost merging with their bleak surroundings. This denial of their own nature, and of the natural world at large, is the more tellingly stressed in those stanzas which describe his brothers precisely in terms of nature. His youngest brother

> was beautiful as day —
> (When day was beautiful to me
> As to young eagles, being free) —
> A polar day, which will not see
> A sunset till its summer's gone,
> Its sleepless summer of long light,
> The snow-clad offspring of the sun:
> And thus he was as pure and bright,
> And in his natural spirit gay,
> With tears for nought but others' ills,
> And then they flow'd like mountain rills,

> Unless he could assuage the woe
> Which he abhorr'd to view below.
>   (ll.80–91)

A person so described is destroyed when the sun itself is a dim imprisoned ray.

A further irony of their imprisonment is that the very place mocks them: Lake Leman conspires with the castle wall to make a 'double dungeon', so that there is an added poignancy to the characterisation of their 'dark vault' as a 'living grave'. They are made aware of nature's freedom, but it is a freedom that is of no use to them. The movement of the verse captures both the activity of the elements above them, and their own terrible indifference, their numbed acceptance that death would be preferable:

> We heard it ripple night and day;
>   Sounding o'er our heads it knock'd;
> And I have felt the winter's spray
> Wash through the bars when winds were high
> And wanton in the happy sky;
>   And then the very rock hath rock'd,
>   And I have felt it shake, unshock'd,
> Because I could have smiled to see
> The death that would have set me free.
>   (ll.117–25)

The brazen assonance fills out the apathy that Byron alluded to in the Shakespearean echo in *The Giaour*.

One brother dies, then the other, 'the favourite and the flower': once again, the simple imagery of sunlight serves its purpose, as the slow death gets its tender Byronic attention.

> He faded, and so calm and meek,
> So softly worn, so sweetly weak,
> So tearless, yet so tender, kind,
> And grieved for those he left behind;
> With all the while a cheek whose bloom
> Was as a mockery of the tomb,
> Whose tints as gently sunk away
> As a departing rainbow's ray;

> An eye of most transparent light,
> That almost made the dungeon bright . . . .
>> (ll.186–95)

At the moment of death, this young brother comes close to recapturing his role as the day's sunlight; but Byron will have no sentimentality here, and that 'almost' in the last line of that quotation emphasises the impossibility of our deriving any lasting hope from such an illusion. This in turn helps to account for what is in many ways the most extraordinary, most powerful, stanza in the whole poem. Byron talks frequently of the abyss, of the complete loss of understanding and sensation; but there are few passages where he does so more starkly.

> What next befell me then and there
>   I know not well – I never knew –
> First came the loss of light, and air,
>   And then of darkness too:
> I had no thought, no feeling – none –
> Among the stones I stood a stone,
> And was, scarce conscious what I wist,
> As shrubless crags within the mist;
> For all was blank, and bleak, and grey;
> It was not night, it was not day;
> It was not even the dungeon-light,
> So hateful to my heavy sight,
> But vacancy absorbing space,
> And fixedness without a place;
> There were no stars, no earth, no time,
> No check, no change, no good, no crime,
> But silence, and a stirless breath
> Which neither was of life nor death;
> A sea of stagnant idleness,
> Blind, boundless, mute, and motionless!
>> (ll.231–50)

The echoes of 'The Ancient Mariner' need no comment: what is remarkable about them here (as opposed, say, to the more obvious allusions at the beginning of *Childe Harold's Pilgrimage*), is how much Byron has absorbed the Coleridgean experience into his own poetic consciousness, so that we can talk of echoes without in any way implying any leaning on influence. Bonnivard gives voice here to what the Giaour calls 'the vacant bosom's wilderness', the terrible sense of nothingness for which 'futility' would be quite the inappropriate word. Byron has managed, in his precise way, to present the horror in its fullness, the paradox of 'fixedness without a place', of being 'bound' and yet on the 'boundless' sea. This is not life-in-death, nor death-in-life; it is 'neither . . . of life nor death', the furthest extreme to which the human spirit can be taken. On this 'sea of stagnant idleness' there will be no dance of the watersnakes.

Not that hope is not, cruelly, offered, in the next stanza, where Byron teases Bonnivard, and us, with what might seem like Coleridgean, even Wordsworthian, expectations. A bird sings outside, but the comfort is precarious:

> A light broke in upon my brain, –
>   It was the carol of a bird;
> It ceased, and then it came again,
>   The sweetest song ear ever heard,
> And mine was thankful till my eyes
> Ran over with the glad surprise,
> And they that moment could not see
> I was the mate of misery;
> But then by dull degrees came back
> My senses to their wonted track;
> I saw the dungeon walls and floor
> Close slowly round me as before,
> I saw the glimmer of the sun
> Creeping as it before had done,
> But through the crevice where it came
> That bird was perch'd, as fond and tame,
>   And tamer than upon the tree;
> A lovely bird, with azure wings,
> And song that said a thousand things,
>   And seem'd to say them all for me!
>   (ll.251–70)

In spite of his awakening sense of reality, Bonnivard allows himself to think the bird is a sign of hope, a 'visitant' possibly 'from Paradise', even his brother's soul; he makes an attempt to identify himself with the bird, who 'seem'd like me to want a mate'. But, just as he begins to imagine the bird is a spiritual surrogate for his dear, dead brother, it flies away, leaving him as isolated and forlorn as the Keats of the 'Ode to a Nightingale'. The gap between reality and aspiration is wider then ever, and he sees himself as a blot on the natural scene, a frowning cloud ruining a bright sunny sky. In his state of despair he has become as destructive a force as the prison bars. When his guards release him from his chains, to let him pace his cell, his 'liberty' consists in the repeated measuring of his narrow bounds; he is working out the image of the next stanza, where he declares that there would be no point in escape: 'the whole earth would henceforth be / A wider prison unto me' (ll.322–3). However, although such an exchange would be without point, he is tempted to climb up to the window of his cell, 'and to bend / Once more, upon the mountains high, / The quiet of a loving eye' (ll.329–31).

Once more, the Wordsworthian spirit is invoked only to deceive, for what he sees through the bars he would prefer not to have seen.[9] If we recognise a hint of Wordsworth here, it is the saddened, stoic Wordsworth of the Matthew poems, where any appeal to nature recoils on the appellant. Nature, in all its freedom and joy, is a mockery to him, an oppression to his eye, a kind of parody of his own plight: the island that he sees reminds him of his dungeon, not just because of its size, but because of the three trees that are so clearly the mirror image of the three withered brothers.

> A small green isle, it seem'd no more,
> Scarce broader than my dungeon floor,
> But in it there were three tall trees,
> And o'er it blew the mountain breeze,
> And by it there were waters flowing,
> And on it there were young flowers growing,
>   Of gentle breath and hue.
>
> (ll.344–50)

His younger brother had been a 'flower'; the eagle he sees riding the blast recalls the free eagles in flight that formed part of the image cluster surrounding his first description of his brother. Small wonder that, when he climbs down from his foothold, the dungeon has become his own grave. Like the Giaour, he would welcome the rest that was the final rest; unlike the Giaour, he is not granted that rest, but is, instead, finally freed, by which time freedom means nothing to him. He has become, in so far as it is possible, reconciled to his imprisonment, at one with the mice and the spiders. But reconciliation is the wrong word.

> It was at length the same to me,
> Fetter'd or fetterless to be,
> I learn'd to love despair.
> (ll.372—4)

What this amounts to is the triumph of despair over hope. It is hard to see in this poem other than the extension to its logical conclusion of the pessimism that overtakes so many of the narrative poems. In *The Prisoner of Chillon* we are vouchsafed the most intense understanding Byron will give us, in his narratives, of the terrible vacancy at the core of his 'Gothic' heroes. Of course, Byron is not the kind of schematic writer who would allow us to fit all this into a neat pattern: Bonnivard is much more than just another version of the Giaour or Lara. But what we have here is an extended portrayal of that stagnation which those figures most fear, 'cold Obstruction's apathy', where even the normal, healthy love of man for nature, brother for brother, is shown to be useless. Anything, we are led to conclude, would be better than this. This is the passion of suffering. After such unrelieved Stygian gloom, the brighter world of *Mazeppa* is especially inviting. It lies at the opposite pole from *The Prisoner of Chillon*, and it offers hope where the other can only offer despair.[10]

An initial contrast is made between King Charles of Sweden, fleeing wounded from battle, and his Cossack prince, Mazeppa. Charles is not the mighty warrior he would wish to seem, any more than Napoleon would prove in his assault on Moscow — Byron is quick to point to that parallel in his opening stanza, and his ambivalence towards Napoleon eventually colours our subsequent reactions to a warrior of less heroic stature. Charles's escape is not merely at the expense of others: 'thousands fell that flight to aid' (*Mazeppa*, l.19). There is an unexpected humour in this poem, foreshadowing the wit of the *ottava rima* poems, and it emerges early on in Byron's description of the wounded King:

> A king must lay his limbs at length.
>   Are these the laurels and repose
> For which the nations strain their strength?
> They laid him by a savage tree,
> In outworn nature's agony . . . .
>
> (Mazeppa, ll.30–4)

The King can keep his pangs under control, but only as if they were his vassals. He is in fact surrounded by his enemies, nature itself offers a 'savage' form of repose (we might briefly wonder to whom that 'agony' belongs), and the nations no longer lie subdued around him. However, whereas the King is only, at this point, 'kinglike' in a determinedly self-conscious, rather ridiculous way, the Ukraine's hetman, Mazeppa, goes about his business, 'calm and bold', entirely unselfconscious. His first concern, significantly, is not for himself, but for his horse: the two seem to be similar, with their priorities right, clearly earning the narrator's approval.

> But he [the horse] was hardy as his lord,
> And little cared for bed and board;
> But spirited and docile too,
> Whate'er was to be done, would do.
> . . .
> That steed from sunset until dawn
> His chief would follow like a fawn.
>
> (ll.66–77)

Mazeppa and his horse seem to combine similar qualities of calmness and boldness: what is true of the one is true of the other. The poem's narrative helps explain this.

Mazeppa responds to the King's invitation to tell the assembled company how he learned to ride, how he and his horse have become a latter-day Alexander and Bucephalus. Mazeppa recalls the king for whom he acted as page when young: the recollection and the irony are bolstered by the almost jaunty verse:

> A learned monarch, faith! was he,
> And most unlike your majesty;
> He made no wars, and did not gain
> New realms to lose them back again;
> And (save debates in Warsaw's diet)
> He reign'd in most unseemly quiet;
> Not that he had no cares to vex;
> He loved the muses and the sex;
> And sometimes these so forward are,
> They made him wish himself at war;
> But soon his wrath being o'er, he took
> Another mistress, or new book . . . .
>   (ll.131–42)

In this relaxed atmosphere (*Sardanapalus* is the obvious comparison: to indulge in passionate pleasure is to be neither indolent nor epicene), Mazeppa, with his 'strength, youth, gaiety', falls in love with the young wife of an aged count. The description of his love requires quotation, since it both looks back to earlier attempts by Byron to capture the timid rapture of love, and looks ahead to the more fully drawn-out complexities of *Don Juan*. As so often, he starts with the eye, and, as so often again, expands the image in such a way that it becomes a part of nature: the vocabulary of melting and expiration furthers the reciprocity of the two lovers.

> She had the Asiatic eye,
>   Such as our Turkish neighbourhood
>   Hath mingled with our Polish blood,
> Dark as above us is the sky;
> But through it stole a tender light,
> Like the first moonrise of midnight;
> Large, dark, and swimming in the stream,
> Which seem'd to melt to its own beam;
> All love, half languor, and half fire,
> Like saints that at the stake expire,
> And lift their raptured looks on high,
> As though it were a joy to die.
> A brow like a midsummer lake,
>   Transparent with the sun therein,
> When waves no murmur dare to make,

> And heaven beholds her face within.
> A cheek and lip – but why proceed?
> I loved her then, I love her still:
> And such as I am, love indeed
>   In fierce extremes – in good and ill.
> But still we love even in our rage,
> And haunted to our very age
> With the vain shadow of the past,
> As is Mazeppa to the last.
>
> (ll.208–31)

Byron is anxious to emphasise the fierceness of this love, its tenacious hold, 'a strange intelligence, / Alike mysterious and intense, / Which link the burning chain that binds, / Without their will, young hearts and minds' (ll.238–41). It is in fact a form of imprisonment, a giving-up of one's own will and destiny, which should give us pause, as we remember *The Prisoner of Chillon*. But the contrast between Mazeppa and Charles is made again, and again it is the King who is seen to fall short, in his ignorance of 'those gentle frailties'. At the same time, such passions will brook no control, and therein lies their danger and potential cause for despair:

> In sooth, it is a happy doom,
>   But yet where happiest ends in pain.
>
> (ll.296–7)

The poem assumes, at this point, a rather different aspect: for all the literal details of the wild ride Mazeppa is forced to make, strapped to the back of an unbroken horse, this headlong dash is the most vivid symbolic depiction of uncontrolled passions; the cuckolded husband gets his most appropriate revenge. Some of Byron's most energetic couplets are to be found in this long central section, as the horse pounds on through the 'wild wood', evading the pursuing wolves, as Mazeppa longs only for death. He does actually think he is dying as he loses consciousness, and sees himself, like Childe Harold, as a piece of flotsam and jetsam on the ocean:

> I felt as on a plank at sea,
> When all the waves that dash o'er thee,

> At the same time upheave and whelm,
> And hurl thee towards a desert realm.
>
> (ll.553–6)

To an extent, Mazeppa's death takes place here: he confronts the worst, and wakes to learn that he has survived, that the horse is carrying him across a river; Mazeppa is born again, 'rebaptized'; for all his confusions he takes some pleasure in the horse's determined progress:

> My courser's broad breast proudly braves,
> And dashes off the ascending waves,
> And onward we advance!
>
> (ll.590–2)

But it is not to be an easy triumph: the element of nightmare persists. To reach the top of the riverbank is but to be confronted with further hurdles. Byron shows here the obverse of the terror in the castle at Chillon:

> a boundless plain
> Spreads through the shadow of the night,
> And onward, onward, onward, seems,
> Like precipices in our dreams,
> To stretch beyond the sight . . . .
>
> (ll.605–9)

None the less, some symbolic barrier is passed, and the sun rises to find them in some strange, alien world. This is all very beautifully done, with the sun's solitary grandeur set against that of the world.

> Methought that mist of dawning gray
> Would never dapple into day;
> How heavily it roll'd away —
> Before the eastern flame
> Rose crimson, and deposed the stars,
> And call'd the radiance from their cars,
> And fill'd the earth, from his deep throne,
> With lonely lusture, all his own.

> Up rose the sun: the mists were curl'd
> Back from the solitary world
> Which lay around, behind, before.
> (ll.645–55)

Nature is reasserting itself; the horse reaches its goal, its own home where a thousand horses come to meet them, free and riderless, thundering along like the waves of the sea. The horse falls and dies, the other horses sniff around the dazed Mazeppa, and then return to the forest. It is a most moving moment; for all the despair that Mazeppa feels, there is a clear sense of achievement, a sense that some kind of spiritual home has been found, that the dead horse is at this point as important as Mazeppa. The horse has brought his charge to the land where his fellow horses are free in their 'plunging pride'; they are, in their way, as magnificent as the sun. A modern reader will think of the end of Lawrence's *Rainbow*; a reader sympathetic to Byron's purposes will see the advantages of precision and concision over quasi-mystical rhetoric. No one needs to ask what happens here.

> What booted it to traverse o'er
> Plain, forest, river? Man nor brute,
> Nor dint of hoof, nor print of foot,
> Lay in the wild luxuriant soil;
> No sign of travel, none of toil;
> The very air was mute;
> And not an insect's shrill small horn,
> Nor matin bird's new voice was borne
> From herb nor thicket. Many a werst,
> Panting as if his heart would burst,
> The weary brute still stagger'd on;
> And still we were – or seem'd – alone.
> At length, while reeling on our way,
> Methought I heard a courser neigh,
> From out yon tuft of blackening firs.
> Is it the wind those branches stirs?
> No, no! from out the forest prance
>   A trampling troop; I see them come!
> In one vast squadron they advance!
>   I strove to cry – my lips were dumb.

The steeds rush on in plunging pride;
But where are they the reins to guide?
A thousand horse, and none to ride!
With flowing tail, and flying mane,
Wide nostrils never stretch'd by pain,
Mouths bloodless to the bit or rein,
And feet that iron never shod,
And flanks unscarr'd by spur or rod,
A thousand horse, the wild, the free,
Like waves that follow o'er the sea,
  Came thickly thundering on,
As if our faint approach to meet;
The sight re-nerved my courser's feet,
A moment staggering, feebly fleet,
A moment, with a faint low neigh,
  He answer'd, and then fell;
With gasps and glazing eyes he lay,
  And reeking limbs immoveable,
    His first and last career is done!
On came the troop – they saw him stoop,
  They saw me strangely bound along
  His back with many a bloody thong:
They stop, they start, they snuff the air,
Gallop a moment here and there,
Approach, retire, wheel round and round,
Then plunging back with sudden bound,
Headed by one black mighty steed,
Who seem'd the patriarch of his breed,
  Without a single speck or hair
Of white upon his shaggy hide;
They snort, they foam, neigh, swerve aside,
And backward to the forest fly,
By instinct, from a human eye.

(ll.656–708)

Mazeppa hovers in that twilight world of waking dream, of life and death, which we have seen in *Lara*, and will see repeatedly in *Don Juan*.

I know no more – my latest dream
  Is something of a lovely star

Which fix'd my dull eyes from afar,
And went and came with wandering beam,
And all the cold, dull, swimming, dense
Sensation of recurring sense,
And then subsiding back to death,
And then again a little breath,
A little thrill, a short suspense,
    An icy sickness curdling o'er
My heart, and sparks that cross'd my brain –
A gasp, a throb, a start of pain,
    A sigh, and nothing more.

(ll.783–95)

This is a most wonderful anticipation of the *Don Juan* mode without the benefit of the *ottava rima*: such a detailed and animated re-creation of this 'short suspense' that can seem stretched out to eternity is worthy of his major satire, and it is no surprise, with *Don Juan* in mind, to find Byron resorting to his image of the woman bending over the watching man. The beginnings of Mazeppa's pain are a recognition of his ability to feel more than apathy; he has overcome his 'need' of death, he has suffered for his earlier passions, but he is now able to cultivate a passion that is like the Cossack maid's black eyes, 'wild and free', which of course is what the horses were. His eventual release, unlike Bonnivard's, is to genuine freedom. Mazeppa represents the triumph of passion; he has escaped from the imprisonment of his first love; he has escaped from the terrifying, imprisoning ordeal of his punishment, strapped to the wild horse. Whereas the Giaour, Conrad, Lara, Bonnivard all succumb to literal or metaphoric deaths, Mazeppa expands, like Dudù and like Aurora Raby, into the warmth of life.

3 'A Whirling Gulf of Phantasy and Flame': *Childe Harold* (i)

If *Endymion* is Keats's albatross, then *Childe Harold's Pilgrimage* is Byron's. But the Ancient Mariner was to a large extent defined by his burden, and it would be absurd to think of him without it. Certainly Keats, for all his adolescent embarrassment about it, felt the exposure provided by *Endymion* was necessary, as though in finally wrenching himself free from it he was announcing his obligations and directions. Byron in his more breezy way threw his poem at the public, and was as pleased with it as his first audience seemed to be when they lapped up the first two cantos and asked for more, which he duly provided. It was only subsequently that it became something of a problem for readers of his poetry. The romantic tales, *Manfred*, *The Prisoner of Chillon*, the brilliant satires could all be categorised and accounted for (or so it seemed): but *Childe Harold* induced that kind of critical foot-shuffling that tells us not only about the critics' desire for neatness and order but also about what a work is actually doing. This again is where a comparison with Keats is instructive, in that both poets resolutely refuse to be drawn into the critical frameworks we all set up to cope with recalcitrant literary objects. Our desire to chart progress, development towards maturity, is constantly checked by the poet's sidestepping of his own declared intentions. Not every poet has the ability, or even the inclination, to see his work, either in anticipation or retrospectively, in grandiose Wordsworthian terms, with every piece of brick and mortar contributing towards the architectural whole, the Gothic cathedral of his imagination. Neither Keats nor Byron had that kind of vision, and we are wasting our time if we hope to find it. This of course involves us, and them, in certain paradoxes, in that they both clearly had some grand designs: Keats would not have spent the larger part of his creative life writing, and sometimes laboriously rewriting, long narrative poems if he did not believe it was in that kind of structure that he would work out his own aesthetic salvation; and Byron, as *Don Juan* testifies, set store by the very epic tradition he was both invoking and subverting. It might be easier for us, after Poe, and after Matthew Arnold's famously stated preference for Wordsworth's lyric genius, to rest our claims for the Romantics on their shorter poems, their odes and songs; but they would be justifiably miffed if they knew what we were up to. So far as Byron is concerned, *Don Juan* might be his exasperating masterpiece: but to say that is to have to acknowledge that in our exasperation it might also seem a mess. And, if that is true of *Don Juan*, how much more of a mess and perhaps less of a masterpiece *Childe Harold*. But that does not allow us to pass by on the other side, any more than it allows us to indulge in an act of condescending critical charity. If the Arnoldian injunction to see a thing as it really is makes, when applied to literature and how we see it, philosophical nonsense, at least the urging to see it whole has some point, especially if it undercuts his, and our, other tendencies to go for the juicy bits.

To attempt to see *Childe Harold* whole involves a recognition of its resistance to such viewing – particularly perverse, we might feel, in a work that is largely about just that: what we see and how we see it. But the perversity on reflection (and again the poem invites the metaphor) is justified when we realise that it is that very resistance of the object to the eye which ends up as the poem's major preoccupation. 'Ends up' is the appropriate phrase, reminding us of the frustrations involved in a considered reading of this work that sometimes does not want so to be considered; if there is something infuriatingly casual about that 'ending-up' then it is because Byron works in a casual way. It is at this juncture that 'wholeness' might seem to be the inappropriate, and yet the most desirable, commodity. We do like to make sense of things, especially when we can't.

To approach *Childe Harold* in this way is at least to treat it seriously and on its own terms. It will involve us in awkwardness and unpleasantness. We cannot simply refuse the moralistic delights of pointing out the bad bits and indulge in a

Coleridgean searching for the 'beauties' of the piece: Byron does not often deal in such 'beauties', and such a course would in any case merely bring us back to the Arnoldian gathering of pearls. So from the outset we have to acknowledge the oddness of this poem, its unevenness of structure and tone, the impurity, even, of its diction, its waywardness; we have to acknowledge that it was written over a number of years, in response to personal events, of very different kinds and degrees, in Byron's own life, that it was published piecemeal, with prefaces to individual cantos announcing changes in direction and intention. We might even have to admit that it is a mess. But it requires more than merely nerve and cheek to construct a poem of four cantos on an outlandish and extravagant theme, to tempt us into seeing it as a mess, and then by some curious process of retrospective osmosis force us into a reappraisal of our notion of mess. Whereas Pope in the *Dunciad* had seen into the maws of Chaos and trembled at what he saw, the Romantics were acutely conscious of, and fascinated by, a chaotic world. This is not to say, as we sometimes say all too easily of, for example, *The Waste Land*, that the fragmentary nature of the work mirrors the age that spawns it; rather, it is to say that with the Romantics the notion of chaos and mess has to be redefined; it is to say, further, that *Childe Harold* is a poem to do with definitions, definitions that are elusive and not always comforting. And, as definitions are about limits, horizons, boundaries and ends, that is another way of saying that the poem not only ends up in a way that takes itself by surprise; it is a poem about that very process, about ending-up.

> My task is done — my song hath ceased — my theme
> Has died into an echo; it is fit
> The spell should break of this protracted dream.
> The torch shall be extinguish'd which hath lit
> My midnight lamp — and what is writ, is writ, —
> Would it were worthier! but I am not now
> That which I have been — and my visions flit
> Less palpably before me — and the glow
> Which in my spirit dwelt, is fluttering, faint, and low.
>
>   (*Childe Harold* IV.clxxxv)

Childe Harold, then, is a provisional poem; in this it clearly looks ahead to *Don Juan*, without necessarily anticipating it. (Byron in fact went out of his way to remove some of the more specific anticipations, getting rid of overtly satirical passages that seemed, as he revised, to challenge even his loosely held notion of decorum.) It is provisional of necessity, in that it does not know, any more than its hero, where it is going. There is wryness in the notion of pilgrimage, because pilgrims are usually very firmly bent on a particular destination. Byron plays on this from the very beginning, when he manages to invoke the religious connotations we should expect and then to turn them upside down: monks and nuns get rather a bad press in this poem. So that 'pilgrimage' turns out to be a grand name for something that is anything but: the combination of the Grand Tour and sackcloth and ashes is sufficiently odd and unsettling for us to wonder quite what is going on. If the poem, and the poem's hero, and the poem's author (and, as we shall see, there is some confusion there, too) stagger with some uncertainty from pillar to post, then we too, as readers caught up in this escapade, get involved in the provisional nature of the exercise. We, too, cannot see round the next corner. It is only with the benefit of hindsight that we are able to chart the route we've travelled, the corners we've negotiated: and this is another of the poem's central paradoxes, that we can, in the last resort, see, if not where we are going, then where we have been. But it is as though even that granting of hindsight is itself provisional. As Wordsworth says disarmingly,

> the hiding-places of my power
> Seem open; I approach, and then they close;
> I see by glimpses now; when age comes on,
> May scarcely see at all . . . .
> (*The Prelude*, [1805] XI.336–9)

There are some rather remarkable similarities between Wordsworth and Byron: one of the most interesting is the problem of the relation between past and present, public and private, the problem of perspective, of seeing things that have an unnerving habit of disappearing. A simple clue in *Childe Harold* to the relativity of Byron's vision is provided by the 'ifs' and 'buts': he is too fond of such words for us to regard them as stylistic mannerisms. He knows that, just as he thinks he has got something into perspective, something else comes along to knock it awry. It doesn't require a detailed examination of the concordance to make the point, simply an alertness to the texture of the verse – 'ifs' and 'buts' and 'yets' vie, in their shyly obtrusive way, for our attention. As with Greek particles, in Byron's poetry it is frequently the little words that count. As we survey the landscape of his text, we become increasingly conscious that the horizon is pitted with such words. That is the significance of the poem's provisional nature.[1]

To say that something is 'provisional' is in itself rather odd: the word implies both foresight (as in, to provide for the future) and also lack of it (not seeing beyond the moment). It is a peculiarly apt word for *Childe Harold*, especially as etymologically it reminds us of that concept of seeing which is central to the poem. But, as I argued in the first chapter, to describe what we see is no simple matter, and *Childe Harold* is the perfect demonstration of this. The poem charts a journey in which the protagonist has to learn what it is he is looking at, and then how to look at it, which in turn affects what he is looking at, and how he reacts to it, and how that affects the way he tells us about it. This is an extraordinarily complex process, and it might well be that the poem suffers from Byron's initial inability to see the complexities of seeing; but in the end it is the poem's triumph that he breaks through that barrier, and once he has done so there is no need to make the tour again. It is a necessary journey, precisely because it makes itself unnecessary, just as the poem writes itself out of existence.

The poem's initial problems might well seem to be formal. *Childe Harold* announces itself as a curiosity, reaching for some of that medieval quaintness that had already served Coleridge well enough, if misleadingly, in 'The Ancient Mariner', and which was to be a hallmark of Keats's 'La Belle Dame Sans Merci'. The subtitle, 'A Romaunt', takes us back, as does the Addition to the Preface, to the world of courtly romance, just as the appellation 'Childe' is a conscious reminder of the

Border minstrelsy. But that does not in fact tell us all that much: whatever the world of this poem, it is self-evidently not that of the ballads; and, if the occasional song, such as 'Goodnight' in the first canto, is an overt allusion to a particular ballad (in this case 'Lord Maxwell's Goodnight'), the structure of the poem as a whole is much more complex. Nineteenth-century readers steeped in Spenser would recognise the Spenserian stanza, but they might not recognise the uses to which it was being put. No reader could actually mistake this poem for Spenser. Byron was in no danger of being overwhelmed by his model, as was Keats with his Miltonic *Hyperion*. But, then, Byron was nodding at Spenser from a distance: his Preface declares his debt to James Beattie, to James Thomson, and to the Italian Ariosto. It is an odd trio to be celebrating, but Byron's eclecticism in his choice of influences establishes itself as a rather important fact. The point about Beattie and Thomson was that they had both employed the Spenserian stanza in ways that appealed to late-eighteenth- and early-nineteenth-century poets anxious to reconcile their interest in the past with an awareness of the present. Spenser had demonstrated in *The Faerie Queene* that the nine-line stanza allowed for a flexible combination of narrative and description. Keats was to exploit its potentialities in 'The Eve of St Agnes' (1820), as was Shelley in *The Revolt of Islam* (1818) and, more spectacularly, in his homage to Keats, *Adonais* (1821). Keats was to spend many an hour poring over Thomson's Spenserian *Castle of Indolence*, in his eyes almost as good as the real thing. Wordsworth's *Prelude*, but more particularly his early, descriptive verse, owed at least something to Beattie's Spenserian poem of childhood and nature, *The Minstrel*. Beattie knew what he was doing, and Byron knew that he knew.

'Not long ago', Beattie had said conveniently enough for Byron to quote him, 'I began a poem in the style and stanza of Spenser, in which I propose to give full scope to my inclination, and be either droll or pathetic, descriptive or sentimental, tender or satirical, as the humour strikes me; for if I mistake not, the measure which I have adopted admits equally of all these kinds of composition.' Byron, looking, rather surprisingly we might think, for 'authority', latched onto this, and decided to use the Spenserian form for his own poem, so that he could embrace a similar kind of variety of mood. He is not one to remain content with consistency, and he sees in the Spenserian stanza, especially as employed by Beattie and his contemporaries, the chance to experiment (the Preface does actually say that 'these [first] two cantos are merely experimental'). Byron's mind darts and flickers, and in 1812 it is some comfort to have literary sanction for his idiosyncrasies. But, if we are in any danger of thinking that that settles it all, and that we can proceed to lump his poem with Beattie's and Thomson's, then the poem will soon disabuse us of that; and the sly reference to the Italian poets, especially Ariosto, is filled out in a typically elusive comment of Byron's, that the poem is written 'according to the plan of Ariosto, that is, no plan at all'.[2]

As it happens, the Spenserian stanza, unless it is used by Spenser, has not necessarily all the advantages attributed to it by Beattie: certainly a poem of four long cantos finds itself, rather, at some disadvantage. Byron discovers, perhaps too late, that there are limits to the kinds of variety possible. What might have been variety when it was still a twinkle in his eye can turn out to be unease, or at least a variety of attempts at something tantalisingly elusive. There are certainly shifts of tone, and we often get the impression, especially in the first two cantos, that they are rather awkward, sometimes clumsy, often self-conscious. It is rather as though Byron required some formal sanction, and yet landed himself with something not altogether congenial to his temperament. The 'no plan at all' side of it was fine, of course; but the stanza does impose its own rigorous requirements. It is no service to Byron to pretend he solves this problem with any degree of consistency.

And yet this very uncertainty as to the form's possibilities, and to his place in a tradition he is invoking, becomes, at first, part of the poem's necessary drift and, eventually, a virtue. The plight of the restless poet, thrashing around to accommodate himself to a self-imposed straitjacket, mirrors that of his hero, restlessly roaming the earth in self-imposed exile. The poem is about false starts, and these have to do with the poet as much as with Childe Harold, so much so that by the end of the poem Byron gives up the pretence that they are separate beings, however strenuously, to begin with, he had denied the connection. The poem is very much to do with what such a poem can do, and it is here that the Spenserian stanza becomes something of a virtue. It is, after all, a self-enclosed, obfuscating form, ending with a couplet that announces rather thumpingly the end, the closure of something that seems, sometimes, to have escaped us. This elusive quality of the experience of reading is matched by the elusiveness of both hero and poet. *Childe Harold* is a poem about escape: Harold escapes from domestic confines, but he ends up confronting other confines even more daunting; and, as he attempts to escape, so things escape from him.

These related points are made at the very start of the poem – even before it begins, in the lines 'To Ianthe'. The very first stanza of this introductory poem seems to be announcing a rather heady brew of negatives:

> Not in those climes where I have late been straying,
> Though Beauty long hath there been matchless
> deem'd;
> Not in those visions to the heart displaying
> Forms which it sighs but to have only dream'd,
> Hath aught like thee in truth or fancy seem'd:
> Nor, having seen thee, shall I vainly seek
> To paint those charms which varied as they beam'd –
> To such as see thee not my words were weak;
> To those who gaze on thee what language could they speak?

This is not distinguished verse; it has that air of fustian the Romantics seem to resort to with distressing alacrity. But through the fog we can glimpse idiosyncratic concerns, the contradictions of the assertive negatives, the putative relation between truth and fancy, the emphasis on seeing, the apparent pointlessness of writing poetry at all. If this seems like a passing mood, then the first stanza of the poem proper makes us rethink that, reinforces our sense of uncertainty if only because the poet himself is uncertain.

> Oh, thou! in Hellas deem'd of heav'nly birth,
> Muse! form'd or fabled at the minstrel's will!
> Since sham'd full oft by later lyres on earth,
> Mine dares not call thee from they sacred hill:
> Yet there I've wander'd by thy vaunted rill;

> Yes! sigh'd o'er Delphi's long-deserted shrine,
> Where, save that feeble fountain, all is still;
> Nor mote my shell awake the weary Nine
> To grace so plain a tale – this lowly lay of mine.
>
> (*Childe Harold*, I.i)

This, after all, is not a conventional invocation to the Muse: the Muse is both heralded and yet reviled, apparently of heavenly birth and yet at the whim of any old poet; 'the vaunted rill' turns out to be a 'feeble fountain'; the Delphic shrine is deserted and quiet; the Muses are weary; it hardly seems worth the effort to wake them up in support of something as 'lowly' as this.

Immediately we move from this rather doleful start to contemplation of the hero of the piece, and this seems to be equally unpromising:

> Whilome in Albion's isle there dwelt a youth,
> Who ne in virtue's ways did take delight . . . .
>
> (I.ii)

The archaisms announce the unease, whether or not we take this as self-conscious irony at Byron's own expense. Harold is an enigmatic figure, a riotous 'shameless wight' trampling on his heritage like a spoilt child, giving himself up to sin with desperate abandon, until he reaches a point of self-disgust that urges him away from his home, his native land. He is isolated and solitary, a proud man who has forfeited the love of all around him. Systematising critics anxious to account for Harold have seen in him various aspects of the Solitary who is a common adornment of the late-eighteenth- and early-nineteenth-century literary landscape: but such labels do not get us very far.[3] There are two things in particular that stand out in these opening stanzas about the hero: first, what Byron will not, or cannot, say, about him, and, secondly, the rather curious connection that is made between the Childe and the poetic process.

The third stanza begins:

> Childe Harold was he hight: – but whence his name
> And lineage long, it suits me not to say;

> Suffice it, that perchance they were of fame,
> And had been glorious in another day . . . .

Retrospectively this assumes considerable significance: the poet is asserting a different kind of authority, withholding information from us. It is as though the Childe has an independent existence to which we are not privy. Another example of this process occurs in stanza xii of this canto, where the hero is on the point of departure:

> And then, it may be, of his wish to roam
> Repented he, but in his bosom slept
> The silent thought . . . .

There is something rather teasing about all this, and other examples merely emphasise the point. It is complicated by the second factor I have just mentioned, the connection between the hero and the poetic process. Stanza iii has hinted at this, when referring to the Childe's irredeemable evil:

> Nor all that heralds rake from coffin'd clay,
> Nor florid prose, nor honied lies of rhyme
> Can blazon evil deeds, or consecrate a crime.

The implication here, that there is something too appalling about the truth for poetry to contemplate, is another index of the way the poem will move, towards a discussion of what truth actually is, and how poetry can or should cope with it. Byron is really suggesting here that he would like to get away from the 'honied lies of rhyme', because they are inadequate. It is as though he is dismissing both his medium (self-chosen) and his material (equally self-chosen). This hint of potential emptiness is expanded in stanza viii — one of those places where 'Yet' occupies the supreme position, as though Byron were trying to retrieve this situation even whilst acknowledging the impossibility ('Yet' is followed by 'But'):

> Yet oft-times in his maddest mirthful mood
> Strange pangs would flash along Childe Harold's brow,
> As if the memory of some deadly feud
> Or disappointed passion lurk'd below:

> But this none knew, nor haply car'd to know;
> For his was not that open, artless soul
> That feels relief by bidding sorrow flow,
> Nor sought he friend to counsel or condole,
> Whate'er his grief mote be, which he could not control.

It is as though people's not knowing of the existence of something makes the possibility of that something disappear: others' indifference diminishes us to nothingness, just as his own apparent coldness causes him to sing, a little later,

> My greatest grief is that I leave
> No thing that claims a tear.

The eighth stanza, though, provides us with another way into the problem of closure. Although Childe Harold has not an 'open, artless soul' of the kind that would give expression to his suffering, he cannot in fact control it either. This is bound to cause severe, if interesting, psychological problems for Byron's hero; but stylistically, too, there are going to be problems, as the poem's strangely clotted language confirms. The poem, like its hero, finds it hard to be open and artless; finds it hard, too, to control those pent-up emotions. And in many respects that is one of the most important conflicts within Byron's work as a whole – hence the particular importance of reading *Childe Harold* with some care and attention. The old cliché about the inseparability of form and content is given renewed life as we see Byron coping with problems that are in the first place dramatic and psychological – how to present his chosen hero, how to be detached and yet sympathetic; in the second place stylistic – how to forge an appropriate language, and in the process of course discover truly what appropriateness entails; and, thirdly, coming full circle, psychological in a more personal sense – how to present himself, where to draw the line that divides him from the hero who is, initially and disarmingly, his surrogate.

Byron has chosen the romance form (as we have seen, by calling the poem 'A Romaunt' he is deliberately invoking medieval concepts of courtly chivalry): but he soon shows a strong desire to challenge it. On his travels, Harold goes to Portugal – it is his first port of call, in fact, after that very extraordinary song he sings before leaving. Expectations are high; there is excitement in the air as they espy 'new shores', Cintra's mountain, the river Tagus, 'His fabled golden tribute bent to pay'. Already the signposts towards disenchantment are there: Cintra, seat of the infamous Convention at which, in 1808, English generals had of their own accord allowed the defeated French to have their soldiers and artillery back to fight elsewhere in the war most Englishmen, including Wordsworth, Southey and Byron, saw as a fight for Spanish and Portuguese independence; the possible barb in 'fabled'; and then, in the final couplet, one of those curiously disturbing 'yets':

> And soon on board the Lusian pilots leap,
> And steer 'twixt fertile shores where yet few rustics reap.
>
> (I.xiv)

It would be hard to paraphrase that: we have to ask about the force of that 'yet' – is it temporal (as in, roughly, 'as yet', or 'still'), or is it suggesting the possibility of a 'but'; are there going to be more rustics reaping there one day? Where are these rustics; why aren't they reaping? If they're not reaping, what are they up to? Simple questions, no easy answers. The next stanzas pick up on these notes of uneasiness, confirming our sense that all is not quite right. We are, in the very first line, brought up against a typical cry in this poem – we soon learn to distrust 'goodly sights':

> Oh, Christ! it is a goodly sight to see
> What heaven hath done for this delicious land!
> What fruits of fragrance blush on every tree!
> What goodly prospects o'er the hills expand!
> But man would mar them with an impious hand:
> And when the Almighty lifts his fiercest scourge
> 'Gainst those who most transgress his high command,
> With treble vengeance will his hot shafts urge
> Gaul's locust host, and earth from fellest foemen purge.
>
> (I.xv)

So we had been right about that 'yet'; the 'goodly prospect' of a heavenly nature is undermined by a human 'But' – and the pun on the familiar landscape term should not go unnoticed: we might imagine we see goodly prospects, but no one there, actually in the landscape, enjoys 'goodly prospects'. This is an early warning that the gentlemanly picturesque approach is open to challenge.

The next stanza elaborates on the contrast, making even clearer the implication of poets in the false image we have, and give, of things:

> What beauties doth Lisboa first unfold!
> Her image floating on that noble tide,
> Which poets vainly pave with sands of gold,
> But now whereon a thousand keels did ride
> Of mighty strength, since Albion was allied,
> And to the Lusians did her aid afford:
> A nation swoln with ignorance and pride,
> Who lick yet loath the hand that waves the sword
> To save them from the wrath of Gaul's unsparing lord.
>
> (I.xvi)

The poets are firmly put in their place – 'vainly' and 'but' are the important words. And yet Byron is of course a poet, and we have just had our hero, Harold, unburdening himself in song. The only way he had been able to unlock his frozen heart was through poetry – and, as it happened, poetry of a particular kind, a ballad with its echoes both of 'Lord Maxwell's Goodnight' and, more importantly, of Coleridge's 'Ancient Mariner' ('And now I'm in the world alone, / Upon the wide, wide sea' is the most obvious allusion). John Galt had actually remarked of Byron as he set off on his voyages that he looked like the Ancient Mariner, and if we extend that connection beyond the personal and anecdotal into the fabric of the poem – as Harold's song invites us to – then the Mariner's role as exile and wanderer and poet, with a frightening imaginative vision to communicate, can be seen to parallel Harold's. We then begin to ask a rather daunting question: can we trust a poet who distrusts poetry? Those exclamatory gestures that opened stanzas xv and xvi begin to seem double-edged, whether we attribute them to Harold or the poet.

The next stanza takes us into the deserted town: it is an unwitting anticipation of Keats's 'Grecian Urn', except that Byron has no illusions at this stage about art's ability to cope with the disparities between seeming and being. What he does have difficulty with, interestingly enough, is the diction he should use to embrace disappointment, as though the poets' failure has ensured that no individual poet can find, yet, the right language with which to confront the truth.

> But whoso entereth within this town,
> That, sheening far, celestial seems to be,
> Disconsolate will wander up and down,
> 'Mid many things unsightly to strange ee;
> For hut and palace show like filthily:
> The dingy denizens are rear'd in dirt;
> Ne personage of high or mean degree
> Doth care for cleanness of surtout or shirt,
> Though shent with Egypt's plague, unkempt,
> unwash'd, unhurt.
>
> (I.xvii)

Byron's doubts as to poetry's role in all this are clearly expressed in what follows, though here again we realise retrospectively, in view of his scorn for the Convention of Cintra, the ambiguities of the paradisal references:

> Poor, paltry slaves! yet born 'midst noblest scenes –
> Why Nature, waste thy wonders on such men?
> Lo! Cintra's glorious Eden intervenes
> In variegated maze of mount and glen.
> Ah, me! what hand can pencil guide, or pen,
> To follow half on which the eye dilates
> Through views more dazzling unto mortal ken
> Than those whereof such things the bard relates,
> Who to the awe-struck world unlock'd Elysium's gates?
>
> (I.xviii)

This is more than the traditional cry of the poet who feels inadequate to his task: it turns out to be a much more despairing recognition of the failure of poetry to see things properly. The mention of the Garden of Eden reminds us of the cruel

fact that paradise has indeed been lost. Such acknowledge-
ment spells the doom of poetry, and there are sufficient re-
minders of this througout *Childe Harold*. It is no comfort, he
says later, for heroes to be remembered in song – the memo-
rial is a useless one:

> Teems not each ditty with the glorious tale?
> Ah! such, alas! the hero's amplest fate!
> When granite moulders and when records fail,
> A peasant's plaint prolongs his dubious date.
>
>   (I.xxxvi)

Or again,

> Thy name shall circle round the gaping throng,
> And shine in worthless lays, the theme of transient
> song!
>
>   (I.xliii)

A visit to Parnassus revives his faith, momentarily, in poetry.
But it is a faith undercut by the desolation of the place
('Though from thy heights no more one Muse will wave her
wing' – I.lx), and by his own self-doubts ('And now I view thee,
'tis, alas! with shame / That I in feeblest accents must adore' –
I.lxi). Passing by Lesbos, Harold is reminded of Sappho's
death: his observation has its triteness, certainly, but it fits into
an overall pattern of despair at poetry's apparent uselessness –

> Dark Sappho! could not verse immortal save
> That breast imbued with such immortal fire?
> Could she not live who life eternal gave?
> If life eternal may await the lyre,
> That only Heaven to which Earth's children may
> aspire.
>
>   (II.xxxix)

 This is a theme Byron returns to directly and powerfully in
the final cantos of the poem and obliquely it is a recurrent
concern. But I should now like to revert to that connection I
was anxious to make between the hero and poetry, to the point

about poetry's emptiness and failure being a reflection of Childe Harold's own sense of uncertainty. The connection is made that much more poignant by virtue of the obvious fact that Byron is a poet; but also because he sits in uneasy relation to his hero. I have already mentioned the combination of sin and revulsion which sends Harold into exile; he behaves according to dictates he does not really understand, and which make him an object of incomprehension to those around him ('If friends he had, he bade adieu to none . . .'). He is driven on by impulses that sometimes go contrary to his better interests: I.xxvii sums up the basic contradiction, whilst simultaneously pointing to the painful paradox that the truth he sees is something he would rather avoid. He is a Mephistophelian figure (rather like Lara), carrying his hell around with him, for ever trying to escape, unaware – or perhaps all too aware – that there is no escape, that the ceaseless, hectic activity is self-deception, a means of avoiding the issue:

> So deem'd the Childe, as o'er the mountains he
> Did take his way in solitary guise:
> Sweet was the scene, yet soon he thought to flee,
> More restless than the swallow in the skies:
> Though here awhile he learn'd to moralize,
> For Meditation fix'd at times on him;
> And conscious Reason whisper'd to despise
> His early youth, mispent in maddest whim;
> But as he gaz'd on truth his aching eyes grew dim.
>
> (I.xxvii)

If, as the next stanza suggests, the goal is not yet 'fix'd', the implication is that it will, eventually, be so; but, also, the onward flight is necessary, however blind and headlong it might seem. One concomitant of this is that Harold has to maintain the aloofness he has cultivated and which ends up defining him: he cannot afford to let the mask slip, to confront the truth about himself or about his relation with others.

Byron is certainly fond of dwelling on his hero's coldness. There is an interesting passage in canto II, where Byron is talking about Greece. It is important because of his own easily aroused emotions about a country that had lost its freedom, and for which he was eventually to die; it is also important structurally, in that we can see here very clearly how Byron sees his own relation to the hero who keeps slipping out of the poem. In one stanza he sets up a putative, impassive observer of Greece's suffering:

> Cold is the heart, fair Greece! that looks on thee,
> Nor feels as lovers o'er the dust they lov'd;
> Dull is the eye that will not weep to see
> Thy walls defac'd, thy mouldering shrines remov'd
> By British hands, which it had best behov'd
> To guard those relics ne'er to be restor'd.
> Curst be the hour when from their isle they rov'd,
> And once again thy hapless bosom gor'd,
> And snatch'd thy shrinking Gods to northern climes abhorr'd!
>
> (II.xv)

The following stanza presents us with a reminder of Harold's absence, paradoxically at the point where his presence is obliquely implied. In other words, mention of a cold heart brings Byron back to what is supposedly the main business, to what he should actually be doing. But at this stage in the poem the indication of his responsibilities as author has to be registered. If there is a hint of the carelessness that characterises itself as a virtue in *Don Juan*, there is also a reminder of that odd moment in canto I where he again 'forgets' himself, and then proceeds with the narrative, or at least says that is what he is doing:

> Now to my theme – but from thy holy haunt
> Let me some remnant, some memorial bear . . . .
> (*Childe Harold*, I.lxiii)

It is really a bit of a nuisance to have a 'theme'; how much pleasanter to dally. Similarly Harold, like a wayward child who insists on getting lost at every twist and turn, is a bit of a pest. Byron has to stop and look for him; and in asking the questions he does he forces us into asking questions about the nature of what he is doing. If he can lose his charge so easily, how do we gauge his sense of responsibility? If this poem is really about Childe Harold, how can he slip between the cracks?

> But where is Harold? shall I then forget
> To urge the gloomy wanderer o'er the wave?
> Little reck'd he of all that men regret;
> No lov'd-one now in feign'd lament could rave;
> No friend the parting hand extended gave,
> Ere the cold stranger pass'd to other climes:
> Hard is his heart whom charms may not enslave;
> But Harold felt not as in other times,
> And left without a sigh the land of war and crimes.
>
> (II.xvi)

If Harold is empty at the core, then so too is the poem, and by extension the poet; everyone is implicated in that forgetfulness.

By the end of canto II Byron has more or less given up the pretence of being interested in his hero. He has spoken of Harold's passing love; but much more central is his own for the choirboy Edleston, recently and suddenly dead, and such a loss, Byron implies, has to be incorporated into his poem even if in the process it makes the poem and the poet that much more redundant. He mentions first his own anticipated disappearance; just as he had called out in some alarm 'Where is Harold?', so later generations will wonder who or where Byron had been. It is as though he has come full circle – in his isolation and uselessness, he is in the position Harold occupied before he set out on his travels.

> For thee, who thus in too protracted song
> Hast sooth'd thine idlesse with inglorious lays,
> Soon shall thy voice be lost amid the throng
> Of louder minstrels in these later days:
> To such resign the strife for fading bays –
> Ill may such contest now the spirit move
> Which heeds nor keen reproach nor partial praise,
> Since cold each kinder heart that might approve,
> And none are left to please when none are left to love.
>
> (II.xciv)

Again, we might initially feel, a typical plaint, a typical posture: even Milton in 'Lycidas' was anxious about his claims on an impervious posterity. But it is obviously more than that: there is a world-weariness and desolation that forces us into thinking in far more personal terms than those of the conventional trope. The sudden shift in the next stanza underscores this personal element, reminding us of a different kind of loss and departure, and, in so doing, reminding us that the poem is about parting, from that very opening scene in canto I onwards; and parting, as it is put there, has all the Byronic paradox we should by now expect.

> Ye, who have known what 'tis to dote upon
> A few dear objects, will in sadness feel
> Such partings break the heart they fondly hope to heal.
>
> (I.x)

The role of 'buts' and 'yets' becomes even clearer in this context – they are words that help to keep things apart, to remind us of the distances resulting from departure. We might say in anticipation that the poem reaches its apotheosis when in IV.clxxv Byron declares,

> But I forget. – My pilgrim's shrine is won,
> And he and I must part, – so let it be, –
> His task and mine alike are nearly done . . . .

But at the end of canto II, it is Edleston Byron addresses:

> Thou too art gone, thou lov'd and lovely one!
> Whom youth and youth's affection bound to me;
> Who did for me what none beside have done,
> Nor shrank from one albeit unworthy thee.
> What is my being? thou hast ceas'd to be!
> Nor staid to welcome here thy wanderer home,
> Who mourns o'er hours which we no more shall see –
> Would they had never been, or were to come!
> Would he had ne'er return'd to find fresh cause to roam!
>
> (II.xcv)

Untutored by notes or extraneous information, we well might wonder what was happening here, and the confusion of pronouns seems to reinforce the point, as though that attempt to get back outside himself in the last line, back to Harold in the third person, were really half-hearted. The wanderer has ceased to be Harold, he is now the poet, and within two stanzas Byron is openly using the first person singular. Whereas previously it had been Harold who had been urging himself on, and then been urged on by the poet, it is now the poet, reluctantly coming back before the next round, helplessly crying out against the only form of existence he knows, desperately trying to find an identity now that one of its crucial components, Edleston, has gone ('What is my being? thou hast ceas'd to be'). So in the long run the poem is about identity. Harold was lost; now the poet too is lost, forced to 'plunge again into the crowd', where, as he knows only too well, solitude is felt more keenly. It is at this point that the second canto, and the first part of the poem, ends, with the sad realisation that the worst thing in life is

> To view each lov'd one blotted from life's page,
> And be alone on earth, as I am now.
>
> (II.xcviii)

He is back, as Keats later, with his sole self. It is a forlorn prospect.

The third canto brings all these tensions and complexities to the surface. There are biographical reasons for this rather remarkable shift, and I have referred to these elsewhere.[4] A gap of four years separates the publication of this part of the poem from the preceding cantos, and in that time Byron had gone through all the domestic inferno of scandal, separation and exile to Italy. There had been the affair with his married half-sister, Augusta Leigh; his marriage to Annabella Milbanke had turned out to be the disaster he prophesied. When the two women united in opposition to him, and when London society found Byron too much of an embarrassment to accommodate him quietly, he had, in April 1816, left England for good. This means, amongst other things, that parting can no longer be the sweet literary sorrow it might occasionally have appeared earlier; it means, too, that, in order to understand the change both in the poem's status and in its command, we need to have read those domestic pieces written in the intervening years. A study of the 'Epistle to Augusta' explains much, especially Byron's awareness of at least some of the ways in which he had gone wrong, his puzzlement and bafflement that he has ended up where he has, famous, fulfilled, reviled, lonely. Life has followed literature uncomfortably closely. A different kind of control is needed now, if he is to make sense of his life and of his work. It might seem to us, now, curious that after such an interval Byron should contemplate a continuation of the same poem. Our surprise should be tempered by two considerations: first, Byron knew well enough that his poem had followed the Ariosto 'no plan at all' formula sufficiently for him to be able to get away with a continuation in a different key; secondly, the changes in circumstance, themselves matters of deep philosophical as well as personal concern to him, gave him an opportunity to elaborate on, and expand, the hints of the first two cantos.

There is an astonishing increase in confidence that is immediately striking at the start of canto III. We were left, at the end of canto II, with his grief over the loss of Edleston, his foreboding that he was about to be pitched, Gulliver-like, into further turbulence that he could not avoid, which was in fact essential if he was to define himself further. Here we are thrown in at the deep end, with an address to his daughter. What is extraordinary about this first stanza is the sudden transition halfway through the fifth line, as though he were jolting himself out of a dream, or even lurching from one dream to another – the dislocation extends even to the syntax:

> Is thy face like thy mother's, my fair child!
> Ada! sole daughter of my house and heart?
> When last I saw thy young blue eyes they smiled,
> And then we parted, – not as now we part,
> But with a hope. –
>   Awaking with a start,
> The waters heave around me; and on high
> The winds lift up their voices: I depart,
> Whither I know not; but the hour's gone by,
>   When Albion's lessening shores could grieve or glad mine
>   eye.
>
>   (III.i)

He proceeds to embrace the voyage out with some enthusiasm: he is both a weed, 'flung from the rock', and therefore presumably out of control, and like a rider familiar with his steed.

Although the contradictory impulses are still there, the priorities have altered: the central figure in this oddly heaving seascape is now the poet, and, once he has launched himself onto the ocean with a recklessness reminiscent of what we had thought of as his hero, he then reminds us (and himself) of what the poem had originally been about. He can now be more open about his connection with Harold, and he deliberately makes the point that he is seizing the original theme with the same desperate verve with which he sets sail:

> Again I seize the theme then but begun,
> And bear it with me, as the rushing wind
> Bears the cloud onwards . . . .
>
> (III.iii)

The time in between then and now has of course altered perspectives; but that has been its main advantage. Byron is no longer caught in that uncertain area where he has to pretend he is not Childe Harold, whilst anxious to make some capital out of the confusion. It is true that it is not until the final canto that he spells out in his Preface that he no longer wants to 'draw a line which everyone seemed determined not to perceive', and that the distinction between hero and author has vanished. At this stage in the poem, he does, after the initial seven stanzas of canto III, draw himself up and offer an apology for this breach of decorum:

> Something too much of this:– but now 'tis past,
> And the spell closes with its silent seal.
>
> (III.viii)

But there is something rather half-hearted about that; the autobiographical intrusion cannot be taken away, and Byron does not want it to be. The assertion of self, and then the apologetic withdrawal, is all part of the poem's overall design.

These four stanzas explain why Byron expends so much energy on *Childe Harold*, and they deserve close examination: his doubts and uncertainties about poetry are fully stated, as are his doubts about himself; but, equally important, there emerges an embryonic poetic creed which is indissolubly linked to his sense of himself; and the ambiguity of self-awareness and self-forgetfulness, canvassed earlier in the poem, now receives the force it needs to make full sense. Byron is directing attention to the centre of the poem, to that sense of loss, lostness and nothingness which has been there all along, but only allowed to surface spasmodically. And there at the centre is himself, a creature without existence ('What am I? Nothing'), apparently, and yet with a potential existence, through poetry, that is its own justification. What had been 'phantasy and flame' might indeed become something of form and substance, the dream of selfishness might be avoided, the shifting world of meaningless shapes might be fixed, those airy images in some way held. The poem has dwelt repeatedly on the way in which images blur and alter, the frighteningly uncertain connections between the observer and what is observed, so that truth becomes a concept best approached obliquely. Now, Byron is saying, the poet can at least begin to make sense out of all that muddle.

> Since my young days of passion – joy, or pain,
> Perchance my heart and harp have lost a string,
> And both may jar: it may be, that in vain
> I would essay as I have sung to sing.
> Yet, though a dreary strain, to this I cling;
> So that it wean me from the weary dream
> Of selfish grief or gladness – so it fling
> Forgetfulness around me – it shall seem
> To me, though to none else, a not ungrateful theme.
>
> He, who grown aged in this world of woe,
> In deeds, not years, piercing the depths of life,
> So that no wonder waits him; nor below
> Can love, or sorrow, fame, ambition, strife,
> Cut to his heart again with the keen knife
> Of silent, sharp endurance; he can tell
> Why thought seeks refuge in lone caves, yet rife
> With airy images, and shapes which dwell
> Still unimpair'd, though old, in the soul's haunted cell.
>
> 'Tis to create, and in creating live
> A being more intense, that we endow

With form our fancy, gaining as we give
The life we image, even as I do now.
What am I? Nothing: but not so art thou,
Soul of my thought! with whom I traverse earth,
Invisible but gazing, as I glow
Mix'd with thy spirit, blended with thy birth,
And feeling still with thee in my crush'd feeling's dearth.

Yet must I think less wildly:– I *have* thought
Too long and darkly, till my brain became,
In its own eddy boiling and o'erwrought,
A whirling gulf of phantasy and flame:
And thus, untaught in youth my heart to tame,
My springs of life were poison'd. 'Tis too late!
Yet am I chang'd; though still enough the same
In strength to bear what time can not abate,
And feed on bitter fruits without accusing Fate.

(III.iv–vii)

I have discussed in some detail aspects of the poem which would appear to work against any conventional notion of wholeness; paradoxically Byron achieves a kind of wholeness in spite of everything, and it is this I should now like to examine. The more we look at the poem, the more the images accumulate, until we can begin to talk of a pattern of imagery that gives the poem structure. The notion of seeing, as I have suggested, is central, and the poem can be seen as a set of variations on the concept of sight: the range of reference is wide, and often surprising. Quite often we appear to be settling in for a long stretch of rather mundane, competent verse, when there is a sudden flash of genius, a reaching-out beyond the confines of self-imposed form and narrative structure to something verging on the symbolic. Another way of putting that is to say that the literal becomes metaphorical: what begins as an actual journey into exile turns into a metaphysical exploration of the psyche (these are Byron's terms). Something as basic to the poem as the sea, in its alternating turbulence and placidity (again echoing 'The Ancient Mariner'), comes to act as a comment on the poem's central concerns; just as the waves at the beginning of canto III bear the poet along, so they serve as a metaphorical vehicle, and it is not long before we connect such references with those to water generally, especially the glassy waters, for example, of Lake Leman, or the canals of Venice. A poem about reflection draws strength from the imagery of mirror and reflection provided by such obvious natural phenomena. And it is not surprising that Byron does all he can to make the link between the sea, and what we see; between the eye and 'I'.

Such a nexus of images serves the basic purpose of the poem, which is to do with the relationship between that solitary figure, that exiled wanderer, and the world he moves through. There is no doubt at all that *Childe Harold* explores self-consciousness, in terms of individual isolation; much of what I have said so far has been to do with the facet of the poem. But against the self, both setting it off in further isolation and at the same time defining it, is the vast sweep of history. I have already spoken of definitions, and shall have more to say in conclusion; there is obviously a connection with the bounds of the horizon. Our sight is inevitably circumscribed by the horizon, and yet we want to see beyond it. The Grand Tour across Europe is a stern reminder that we cannot, in fact, get beyond that horizon; it always recedes. Time and history, those enormous abstractions that stalk these pages, offer little comfort to someone already lost.

The vanity of man's claims on the world is transparent very early on in canto I, where Byron tackles the Convention of Cintra. Characteristically he is announcing his intentions from the outset – present personal despair is being placed in a context of present political crisis, which in turn reflects the remorseless processes of history. The inescapable quotation makes reference to the imagery of sea:

> Fresh lessons to the thinking bosom, how
> Vain are the pleasaunces on earth supplied,
> Swept into wrecks anon by Time's ungentle tide!
>
> (I.xxiii)

Time renders most things futile; we inhabit a word of folly, in which even the established abstractions are overturned, as Cintra has so clearly demonstrated.

> Woe to the conqu'ring, not the conquer'd host,
> Since baffled Triumph droops on Lusitania's coast!
> (I.xxv)

The bafflement of the poet, of his hero, complements the bafflement of what we might have supposed were certainties: and by a sudden shift into the past, Byron makes his grim point ring true. 'Time's ungentle tide', in a virtuoso reversal of the process I was describing, becomes a literal torrent which is to flow through this canto with gory predictability and profusion. It is not simply that all things fade: quite often the end comes suddenly and bloodily. This stanza is additionally salutary in that it reminds us of the terms of power: Childe Harold has after all come to grips with the problem of control, with the bounds he can set to his own feelings. How much more necessary to find some reserves of power and control, in the face of this ungentle tide:

> But ere the mingling bounds have far been pass'd
> Dark Guadiana rolls his power along
> In sullen billows, murmuring and vast,
> So noted ancient roundelays among.
> Whilome upon his banks did legions throng
> Of Moor and knight, in mailed splendour drest;
> Here ceas'd the swift their race, here sunk the strong;
> The Paynim turban and the Christian crest
> Mix'd on the bleeding stream, by floating hosts oppress'd.
> (I.xxxiv)

This emphasis on the need for power even whilst power is shown to be useless asserts itself powerfully at the beginning of canto II, in which Byron is to address himself to 'Fair Greece! sad relic of departed worth! / Immortal, though no more; though fallen, great!' (II.lxxiii). Those apparent contradictions which offer hope in the face of defeat are not, initially, embraced with quite such sanguine equanimity. The start of this canto hinges on the link between the past and the dream: but, whereas Wordsworth in the 'Immortality' Ode had mourned the loss of the glory and the dream in terms of the fading of his own inspiration – what Coleridge was to call, almost simultaneously in his own farewell to genius, the 'shaping spirit of Imagination' – Byron is talking in more cosmic terms:

> Ancient of days! august Athena! where,
> Where are thy men of might? thy grand in soul?
> Gone – glimmering through the dream of things
> 　　that were:
> First in the race that led to Glory's goal,
> They won, and pass'd away – is this the whole?
> A school-boy's tale, the wonder of an hour!
> The warrior's weapon and the sophist's stole
> Are sought in vain, and o'er each mouldering tower,
> Dim with the mist of years, grey flits the shade of power.
> 　　　　　　　　　　　　　　　　　　　(II.ii)

We might remember here how Harold had looked truth in the face, and his eyes had grown dim (see p. 93); the reference is one of many we are bound to make, backwards as well as forwards. In the context of power, we pick up the reference to I.xlii, where tyrants are shown to be building their worlds on nothing more substantial than a dream. The 'dream of things that were' is itself a central phrase – the poem concerns itself with dreams that are retrospective but also prospective, as he says a little later in this canto:

> Well – I will dream that we may meet again,
> And woo the vision to my vacant breast . . . .
> 　　　　　　　　　　　　　　　　　　　(II.ix)

Stanza ii suffices to suggest Byron's increasing command, his deepening awareness of the precise nature of this poem. After all, Harold has been watching and wondering (as, by implication, have the poet and his audience) as he traversed the famous European landmarks: but wonder now is undermined, and we are left looking at a blank. Not surprising that it is after this passage of question, doubt and disappearance that Byron should be asking where Harold has got to. Man's futility seems to know no bounds, even though, as Byron reminds us, our bounds are firmly set.

Bound to the earth, he lifts his eye to heaven —
Is't not enough, unhappy thing! to know
Thou art? Is this a boon so kindly given,
That being, thou wouldst be again, and go,
Thou know'st not, reck'st not to what region, so
On earth no more, but mingled with the skies?
Still wilt thou dream on future joy and woe?
Regard and weigh yon dust before it flies:
That little urn saith more than thousand homilies.

(II.iv)

The question, 'is the whole?' is awesome, and of course it reflects on the way the poem works — is this what it is all about? He had asked, in I.liv, 'Is it for this?' (another curiously impossible anticipation of Wordsworth), and the persistence of the questioning does nothing to give us confidence in an answer. If we have had trust in hope, in the future, in dreams, in buildings that would last, in seeing things that would make sense, in constructing wholes, then all we need do is pick up a cracked skull from out of the ground. We have only to grasp the whole by peering into the abyss, the hole — and Byron makes the pun for us.

Remove yon skull from out the scatter'd heaps:
Is that a temple where a God may dwell?
Why ev'n the worm at last disdains her shatter'd cell!

Look on its broken arch, its ruin'd wall,
Its chambers desolate, and portals foul:
Yes, this was once Ambition's airy hall,
The dome of Thought, the palace of the Soul:
Behold through each lack-lusture, eyeless hole,
The gay recess of Wisdom and of Wit
And Passion's host, that never brook'd control:
Can all, saint, sage, or sophist ever writ,
People this lonely tower, this tenement refit?

(II.v–vi)

This is Byron doing more than flexing his muscles: he is exercising himself at something very like full stretch, reworking with aplomb and dexterity what is in essence a common trope, and actually deriving from the Spenserian stanza the authority he had aimed at. Within the confines of the stanza form Byron captures the absurdity of man's hopes, but manages to do it with a dignity and control which lend the verse a precision precisely at the point where everything is being denied. And the next stanza confirms the point, 'All that we know is, nothing can be known.' The poem keeps circling around this alarming truth: but it is a truth the poet, in acknowledging, has to deny, at least by implication. This brings us back to the uselessness of poetry: or rather, Byron brings us back, later in the canto, to the point of nothingness and forgetfulness.

> Oh! where, Dodona! is thine aged grove,
> Prophetic fount, and oracle divine?
> What valley echo'd the response of Jove?
> What trace remaineth of the thunderer's shrine?
> All, all forgotten – and shall man repine
> That his frail bonds to fleeting life are broke?
> Cease, fool! the fate of gods may well be thine:
> Wouldst thou survive the marble or the oak?
> When nations, tongues, and worlds must sink beneath the
>   stroke!
>
> (II.liii)

The vast bulk of the poem is given over to a series of variations on this theme. A particularly classic case occurs in canto III, on the field of Waterloo: it is an extraordinary passage both for the intrusion of the poet into Harold's meditations, and for the way it leads back into an account of battle, culminating in an image of brutal merging, with 'Rider and horse, – friend, foe, – in one red burial blent' (xxviii). The rivers of blood that gush through the poem find their termination here; the stanza I quote contains a shocking variant. If we thought in canto II that Byron was evincing greater control over his material, this demonstrates the advantages of those intervening years. The incongruity of the world's ways calls forth an irony that is increasingly the poem's tone:

> Stop! – for thy tread is on an Empire's dust!
> An Earthquake's spoil is sepulchred below!

Is the spot mark'd with no colossal bust?
Nor column trophied for triumphal show?
None; but the moral's truth tells simpler so,
As the ground was before, thus let it be; —
How that red rain hath made the harvest grow!
And is this all the world has gained by thee,
Thou first and last of fields! king-making Victory?
                                         (III.xvii)

The poem's intimate complexity is well illustrated by this stanza. Again, it is a matter of harking back to a central passage in canto I, where Byron first demonstrates his potential versatility in describing in quick succession the ravages of Spain, of time, the absurdities of society life whether in London or Cadiz. He has constant resort to the imagery of blood and destruction, with even the disturbing implication that the eye itself can be destructive (as later he talks of how Caesar came and saw and conquered, as though the conquest were in the eye):

Death rides upon the sulphury Siroc,
Red Battle stamps his foot, and nations feel the shock.

Lo! where the Giant on the mountain stands,
His blood-red tresses deep'ning in the sun,
With death-shot glowing in his fiery hands,
And eye that scorcheth all it glares upon;
Restless it rolls, now fix'd, and now anon
Flashing afar, — and at his iron feet
Destruction cowers to mark what deeds are done;
For on this morn three potent nations meet,
To shed before his shrine the blood he deems most sweet.
                                         (I.xxxviii–xxxix)

From here we move through the poised satirical account of Spanish society — the more poised in its use of the eye imagery, but also in the contrast made between their warmth and Harold's coldness.

Here dons, grandees, but chiefly dames abound,
Skill'd in the ogle of a roguish eye,

> Yet ever well inclin'd to heal the wound;
> None through their cold disdain are doom'd to die,
> As moon-struck bards complain, by Love's sad archery.
>
> (I.lxxii)

(and we note how the satirical tone is immediately mellowed and softened by that sudden twist in the final line, so that bards are vindicated even as they are scorned – the parenthesis does them a service the dames do not intend). We move through this to the bullfight itself, the snorting animal dependent, like destruction and war, on the power of his eye ('red rolls his eye's dilated glow' reminding us of the insistent 'female eye' of six stanzas previously, which is determined not to shrink).

The significance and reverberation of any one passage in *Childe Harold* depends on the echoes and anticipations of other parts of the poem. It might be objected that the poem's compositional history should make us chary of such leaps backwards and forwards. The only answer to that is the bald one that the poem is, now, what is on the page. And Byron, in the opening poem to Ianthe, explicitly sees *Childe Harold* in these terms, and paradoxically appeals to Ianthe's (and the reader's) eye. Just as the world is prey to the eye (and *vice versa*), so his page will come alive as it is gazed upon.

> Oh! let that eye, which, wild as the Gazelle's,
> Now brightly bold or beautifully shy,
> Wins as it wanders, dazzles where it dwells,
> Glance o'er this page . . . .

Byron in his restlessness may be pressing on breathlessly; but, just as his hero is defining himself as he goes, discovering the meaning of exile in terms of what is left behind as well as what is there, somewhere, to be discovered, so the poet's journey makes sense in retrospect. Byron would have liked that marvellously absurd invention of Flann O'Brien's, the train that lays down and picks up its own track as it goes along.

It is in the final canto that Byron brings together the threads he has been spinning. What he has to do is justify, finally, his choice of the Spenserian stanza, and the reasoning behind that; at the same time, the uncertainties and oscillations have to find some resolution at least, if the poem isn't going to seem hopelessly open-ended. This is where his concern with his medium becomes paramount, so that the self-reflexive nature of the poem comes to the surface as the predominant characteristic (it is now, quite clearly, a poem about itself); it is also where the imagery of turbulence and calm finds its own resolution, in Rome and Venice. Where the ravages of time would seem to be most pressing Byron finds, surprisingly, at least a modicum of succour. Having looked rather desperately forward for most of the poem, he can now look back; and, with some equanimity at last, look forward again.

Towards the end of canto III Byron had expressed a rather hopeless wish to roll all his feelings up into the ball of one word: as he is writing in a storm, the appropriate, Lear-like word would be 'Lightning'. But he knows it to be an impossibility, and he is driven back in upon himself:

> But as it is, I live and die unheard,
> With a most voiceless thought, sheathing it as a sword.
>
> (III.xcvii)

Against this, though, is the optimism expressed later on in this canto, that 'there may be / Words which are things, hopes which will not deceive'. He cultivates this optimism in the final canto. Not that it is anything easy, because his sense of reality is now so totally confused, and he wonders quite what his own voice has to say. He has become conscious of a whole tradition of literature from which he is excluded, and yet which matters to him. Being in Rome reminds him of Italian writers with whom he feels a sympathy, a sense of fellow exile. 'I twine', he says, 'My hopes of being remembered in my line / With my land's language' (IV.ix) – a point echoed later with reference to Petrarch, who achieved precisely that, and is to be valued accordingly:

> He arose
> To raise a language, and his land reclaim
> From the dull yoke of her barbaric foes.
>
> (IV.xxx)

It is a hard task, as he says in IV.clxxviii:

> I love not Man the less, but Nature more,
> From these our interviews, in which I steal
> From all I may be, or have been before,
> To mingle with the Universe, and feel
> What I can ne'er express, yet can not all conceal.

'Yet' is, again, the strong word there, only now the tables have been turned; the word rescues him, and us, from the despair into which he, and we, had in the course of the poem been about to sink (and 'sink' is a word of more than coincidental recurrence). The poet has moved from seeing to feeling (the comparison with a similar progression in Wordsworth's 'Immortality' Ode is instructive); more precisely, seeing has had to be redefined, as it has been in this stanza, where Byron very carefully charts the shifts, alluding as he does to the dilated pupils of those ogling Spaniards as well as the roaring bull in canto II:

> Our outward sense
> Is but of gradual grasp – and as it is
> That what we have of feeling most intense
> Outstrips our faint expression; even so this
> Outshining and o'erwhelming edifice
> Fools our fond gaze, and greatest of the great
> Defies at first our Nature's littleness,
> Till, growing with its growth, we thus dilate
> Our spirits to the size of that they contemplate.
>
> (IV.clviii)

By seeing inwardly, rather than with the outward, picturesque eye, we act in conjunction with the objects of our seeing, we become involved in a creative process, as Byron had realised and explained, rather confusedly, at the start of canto III. So that, in the end, the restless urge to see and gaze and wonder pays off. By 'prying into the abyss' (IV.clxvi) we do in fact see further than if we for ever gaze at the horizon. This is not to say that the revelation is necessarily comforting: the poem is major because it resolutely refuses that kind of resolution, and it is on this paradox that we might appropriately end.

On the one hand, there is the stern moral of the poem, best suggested by direct quotation of III.cxi:

> Thus far have I proceeded in a theme
> Renewed with no kind auspices:– to feel
> We are not what we have been, and to deem
> We are not what we should be, – and to steel
> The heart against itself; and to conceal,
> With a proud caution, love, or hate, or aught, –
> Passion or feeling, purpose, grief or zeal, –
> Which is the tyrant spirit of our thought,
> Is a stern task of soul:– No matter, – it is taught.

And then we might pass without comment to that moment in canto IV (cviii) where Byron seems to be saying that there is no point in poetry anyway: 'Away with words', he cries, un-equivocally. True eloquence is to be found in silence, in con-templation of what Rome has to tell us. This stanza (IV.xlix) sums up the honest confusions on which the poem is based; it helps to explain the constant ebb and flow of the poem, the attempt to capture, in spite of words' inadequacy, that range of experience which makes man the paradox he is. And the paradox from our point of view as readers, and Byron's as a poet, is that whilst throwing words to the wind, he goes on clutching at them, like a juggler throwing his clubs in the air, saying he can do without them. He is in the process of realising precisely the fulfilment of the claims for the Spenserian stanza, made initially by Beattie, but more importantly the claims he makes to be remembered in the line of his land's language. Byron has moved away from the outward trappings of pseudo-Spenserianism, and has ended up with something that can claim the Spenserian sanction even as it asserts its own peculiar authority.

> Admire, exult – despise – laugh, weep, – for here
> There is such matter for all feeling:– Man!
> Thou pendulum betwixt a smile and tear,
> Ages and realms are crowded in this span,
> This mountain, whose obliterated plan

> The pyramid of empires pinnacled,
> Of Glory's gewgaws shining in the van
> Till the sun's rays with added flame were fill'd!
> Where are its golden roofs? where those who dared to
>   build?

> (IV.cix)

On the other hand, there is the final return to the imagery of sea and water. The sea, the ever-rolling ocean, is important because it is outside man's domain: 'Man marks the earth with ruin – his control / Stops with the shore' (IV.clxxix). Similarly the sea is outside time; it is constant. And this is the ultimate paradox within a paradox, that the turbulent ocean, on which both poet and hero have hurled themselves with such reckless, restless abandon, becomes an image of peace and calm. The sea is a mirror, gathering up into itself all those other references to mirrors and glass, and images themselves, so that it is an image of an image (see, for example, the 'broken mirror, which the glass / In every fragment multiplies' – III.xxxiii; or, more complexly, Harold's ruminations on slaughter in III.li: 'Thy tide wash'd down the blood of yesterday, / And all was stainless, and on thy clear stream / Glass'd, with its dancing light, the sunny ray; / But o'er the blacken'd memory's blighting dream / Thy waves would vainly roll, all sweeping as they seem'). It combines the placidity of Lake Leman with the 'matchless cataract' (IV.lxx), so that we get another unexpected reminder of Wordsworth, the beauty and the fear of nature. Control has finally been won: it is the poem's moment of triumph.

> Thou glorious mirror, where the Almighty's form
> Glasses itself in tempests; in all time,
> Calm or convuls'd, – in breeze, or gale, or storm,
> Icing the pole, or in the torrid clime
> Dark-heaving; – boundless, endless, and sublime,
> The image of Eternity – the throne
> Of the Invisible; even from out thy slime
> The monsters of the deep are made; each zone
> Obeys thee; thou goest forth, dread, fathomless, alone.

And I have loved thee, Ocean! and my joy
Of youthful sports was on thy breast to be
Borne, like thy bubbles, onward: from a boy
I wantoned with thy breakers – they to me
Were a delight; and if the freshening sea
Made them a terror – 'twas a pleasing fear,
For I was as it were a child of thee,
And trusted to thy billows far and near,
And laid my hand upon thy mane – as I do here.
                              (IV.clxxxiii–clxxxiv)

4 'The Fitting Medium of Desire': *Childe Harold* (ii)

Childe Harold yields its riches rather reluctantly. Some of the processes whereby Byron confronts his own confusions have been explored in the previous chapter; but there is more to be said on the role of passion in the overall design of the poem. As I have already suggested, the poem turns on Harold's restlessness, on his desire for escape, which in turn mirrors the poet's anxieties. Such yearning for self-abnegation has thematic and stylistic implications, rather similar to those encountered in the narrative poems: *Childe Harold* involves poet and reader in an exploration of the dangers and delights of feeling, an exploration of how such things can be captured in art. Amongst all its other ambitions, this poem wants to pronounce on the vexatious connections between art and life. It would indeed be some relief if we had begun to hear the last of discussions of *Childe Harold* in terms, simply, of 'romantic travelogue'.

Although Harold is presented initially as a cold creature, from whom the poet is anxious to distance himself, there is, early on, an ambiguity about his emotions: we are warned, 'deem not thence his breast of steel'; partings are painful, even for a 'shameless wight'; although he does not allow himself to complain when the boat leaves his native land, the hint is that he is displaying a manly stoicism. But, when he gives vent to his feelings, it is in the form of an eloquent song 'pour'd' forth to the accompaniment of his own harp. Such ambiguity runs through the whole poem.

It is typical, for example, that the account of Spain which immediately follows a bald statement of Harold's confused restlessness (I.xxvii–xxviii), should move from talk of 'romantic hills', and 'sweetness in the mountain air', to this:

More bleak to view the hills at length recede,
And, less luxuriant, smoother vales extend:
Immense horizon-bounded plains succeed!
Far as the eye discerns, withouten end,
Spain's realms appear whereon her shepherds tend
Flocks whose rich fleece right well the trader knows
Now must the pastor's arms his lambs defend:
For Spain is compass'd by unyielding foes,
And all must shield their all, or share Subjection's woes.
                                                    (I.xxxi)

There is an odd combination here of openness and enclosure: although 'less luxuriant', the vales are 'smoother'; the plains are 'immense', but bounded by the horizon, so that it becomes small comfort to be able to see so far. There is, in fact, an implicit threat in such apparent freedom, which is where the literal pastoral image serves its cunning purpose, in that it allows Byron to make the link between affectionate protection and the necessary military extension of that. The verse moves from the 'pastor's arm', through the verb 'shield', to the implied 'arms' of opposing factions. Byron has gone from a fairly conventional loco-descriptive mode to an implicit exploration of historical freedoms and constraints, which have their counterpart in the basic emotions that go with the urge to protect.

The next stanza can ask questions that appear to revel in their own paradoxical rhetoric:

Where Lusitania and her sister meet,
Deem ye what bounds the rival realms divide?
Or ere the jealous queens of nations greet,
Doth Tayo interpose his mighty tide?
Or dark Sierras rise in craggy pride?
Or fence of art, like China's vasty wall? –
Ne barrier wall, ne river deep and wide,
Ne horrid crags, nor mountains dark and tall,
Rise like the rocks that part Hispania's land from Gaul . . . .
                                                    (I.xxxii)

This, however, is undercut by what follows, where the pastoral image returns in its literal application:

> But these between a silver streamlet glides,
> And scarce a name distinguisheth the brook,
> Though rival kingdoms press its verdant sides.
> Here leans the idle shepherd on his crook,
> And vacant on the rippling waves doth look,
> That peaceful still 'twixt bitterest foeman flow;
> For proud each peasant as the noblest duke:
> Well doth the Spanish hind the difference know
> 'Twixt him and Lusian slave, the lowest of the low.
>
> (I.xxxiii)

Such a sequence lends force and complexity to the next stanza, which is precisely about the logical culmination of such contradictions (see above, p. 103); the Guadiana's 'power' is of a remorseless, yet reluctant, kind: those 'sullen billows, murmuring and vast' are not without their own complications, which reflect both on the style and the theme of the poem. There are powerful emotions at play – whether we are talking here about Harold, the poet, or Spain – but they find no easy outlet. In the early stanzas of *Childe Harold* we frequently get disturbing variations in tone and temper as Byron approaches places that are associated with outwardly violent manifestations of passion. However coarse the verse might be, he is anxious to cling on to the possibilities of tenderness. 'How sweet is the Shepherd's sweet lot', sings Blake. Nothing for Byron is ever that simple, but a faint echo of that sentiment can be heard here. It will assume more importance later on in the poem, as images of nature's protectiveness accumulate.

A later passage in canto I addresses itself more directly to the emotional contradictions implied in the landscape: Spain's downfall at the hands of the French is both inevitable and unnatural; power and despotism triumph, and the famous story of the Maid of Saragoza merely serves to highlight the perversion of the natural order ('all unsex'd, the Anlace hath espous'd . . .'). We are urged to 'marvel' at her exploits, but they are no more than those of a wasted 'Glory', a series of denials. The tales have demonstrated the futility of vengeance. Byron steps in to provide the necessary qualifications: the conflicting claims require some kind of reconciliation:

Yet are Spain's maids no race of Amazons,
But form'd for all the witching arts of love:
Though thus in arms they emulate her sons,
And in the horrid phalanx dare to move,
'Tis but the tender fierceness of the dove
Pecking the hand that hovers o'er her mate:
In softness as in firmness far above
Remoter females, fam'd for sickening prate;
Her mind is nobler sure, her charms perchance as great.

The seal Love's dimpling finger hath impress'd
Denotes how soft that chin which bears his touch:
Her lips, whose kisses pout to leave their nest,
Bid man be valiant ere he merit such:
Her glance how wildly beautiful! how much
Hath Phoebus woo'd in vain to spoil her cheek,
Which glows yet smoother from his amorous clutch!
Who round the North for paler dames would seek?
How poor their forms appear! how languid, wan, and
    weak!

(I.lvii–lviii)

The relationship between ferocity and tenderness has been tentatively put, the oxymorons have done their work, and the apparently conventional reference to Phoebus outgrows its conventionality. If the rhyme dictates 'clutch', so much the better for the rhyme.

One of the more virtuoso sections in canto I focuses on the bullfight in Cadiz: it enables Byron to bring together a number of his central themes, in particular the conjunction of love and violence. The bullfight becomes an ironic comment on the ridiculous waste of war; but it is set in an arena which serves also as the playground of all those 'Skill'd in the ogle of a roguish eye'. Those who are watching are really unaware of what it is they are watching, unaware that the bull is a rebuke not only to the absurdity of war, but also to their own cupidinous glances. For all his suffering, it is the bull who keeps his furious dignity, even as he falls on the sand:

Where his vast neck just mingles with the spine,
Sheath'd in his form the deadly weapon lies.

> He stops – he starts – disdaining to decline:
> Slowly he falls, amidst triumphant cries,
> Without a groan, without a struggle dies.
> The decorated car appears – on high
> The corse is pil'd – sweet sight for vulgar eyes –
> Four steeds that spurn the rein, as swift as shy,
> Hurl the dark bulk along, scarce seen in dashing by.
>
> (I.lxxix)

There is no doubt where vulgarity lies. The 'mad crowd' (I.lxviii) aspires to a nobility it ill deserves. This 'ungentle sport that oft invites / The Spanish maid, and cheers the Spanish swain' (I.lxxx) does credit to no one. Byron's point is not that love is futile – but that the game of love, as played in the 'throng'd arena', is pernicious, a travesty of true feeling. The verse operates by implication.

One of the implications – love's apparent fickleness – is explored almost immediately, in terms of Harold's own development. It becomes increasingly important, as the poem develops, for Harold to display feelings that are not all cold and inert: the long sequence of the bullfight is an appropriate prelude to Byron's first broaching of this subject. There is some confusion here. Byron wants to emphasise two contradictory things – the force of love, and its insubstantiality. His immaturity gets the better of him at this point, and he is lured into bluster, hiding behind his own too-easy rhetoric.

> Oh! many a time, and oft, had Harold lov'd,
> Or dream'd he lov'd, since Rapture is a dream;
> But now his wayward bosom was unmov'd,
> For not yet had he drunk of Lethe's stream;
> And lately had he learn'd with truth to deem
> Love has no gift so grateful as his wings:
> How fair, how young, how soft soe'er he seem,
> Full from the fount of Joy's delicious springs
> Some bitter o'er the flowers its bubbling venom flings.

> Yet to the beauteous form he was not blind,
> Though now it mov'd him as it moves the wise;
> Not that Philosophy on such a mind
> E'er deign'd to bend her chastely-awful eyes:

But Passion raves herself to rest, or flies;
And Vice, that digs her own voluptuous tomb,
Had buried long his hopes, no more to rise:
Pleasure's pall'd victim! life-abhorring gloom
Wrote on his faded brow curst Cain's unresting doom.
(I.lxxxii—lxxxiii)

Several important ingredients are there, but they do not add up to more than a series of gestures. Byron is not yet able to stamp coherence on such contradictory emotions. It is therefore the more remarkable that he should introduce a personal element into the penultimate stanzas of this canto, where he mourns the death of his friend John Wingfield, in lines that recall, ironically, the death of the bull. Tenderness reasserts itself when it is most needed:

What hadst thou done to sink so peacefully to rest?

Oh, known the earliest, and esteem'd the most!
Dear to a heart where nought was left so dear!
Though to my hopeless days for ever lost,
In dreams deny me not to see thee here!
And Morn in secret shall renew the tear
Of Consciousness awaking to her woes,
And Fancy hover o'er thy bloodless bier,
Till my frail frame return to whence it rose,
And mourn'd and mourner lie united in repose.
(I.xci—xcii)

We could well argue (as McGann has implied, with his emphasis on the phrase 'Consciousness awaking to her woes'[1]), that this is one of the most important stanzas in the entire poem: the coldness of Harold is replaced by the genuine, puzzled loss of a dear friend. Emotion is full, but held in check; the image of 'Fancy' hovering 'O'er thy bloodless bier' inevitably recalls the comparable, but more fully evoked, image in *The Giaour* (see pp. 51–2), as though Byron finds in that poised moment of bereavement a release and a relief from conflict. He is able, in the last two lines, to look ahead to a union in death: significantly this 'repose' is not 'vile', it is a sign of conclusion and appropriateness. We could at this juncture say that the rest of *Childe Harold* involves an attempt to achieve such repose, in life as well as death, and that in turn requires a due recognition of the tumult and passion that lie behind it.

Repose and self-containment of a fairly obvious and practical kind surface early on in canto II, after the opening colloquy with Athena. Harold has been depicted as the 'cold stranger', unmoved by the ravages wrought on Greece, not only by time, but by such as Lord Elgin. He sails away, leaving 'without a sigh the land of war and crimes'. Byron is at some pains to emphasise the smooth harmony of life on board ship, the sense of everyone working together; but there is some contradictoriness in his appeals, on the one hand to nature, and, on the other, to war. 'The convoy' is 'spread like wild swans in their flight'; but he exclaims three lines later, 'And oh, the little warlike world within!' He seems to want to assimilate the two worlds, rather than point to any differences. The smoothness of the deck reflects what he is to refer to often in this poem, the smooth placid waters of the sea; but here it is associated with the ship's officers, in particular the captain, who keeps his own placidity, in order to preserve the almost synonymous control he has over his men. It is a curious passage, in view of what has a few stanzas earlier been urged against the 'weight of Despot's chains' (II.xii), as represented by Britain's seizure of the marbles from the Acropolis. The oddness, the quaint, sub-Thomsonian comicality of the tone, underlines the awkwardness, as though Byron were half aware that this depiction of a ship at sea is too neat for its own good; perhaps his awareness comes to the fore, when in the next stanza he calls on the winds to keep the ship going. His dread of repose is exposed ('Ah! grievance sore, and listless dull delay, / To waste on sluggish hulks the sweetest breeze!' – II.xx). But that is only after this:

> White is the glassy deck, without a stain,
> Where on the watch the staid Lieutenant walks:
> Look on that part which sacred doth remain
> For the lone chieftain, who majestic stalks,
> Silent and fear'd by all – not oft he talks

> With aught beneath him, if he would preserve
> That strict restraint, which broken, ever balks
> Conquest and Fame: but Britons rarely swerve
> From Law, however stern, which tends their strength
>   to nerve.
>
> (II.xix)

The canto develops at this point, through a sudden burst of energy, to a nightpiece which turns back on itself all that talk of 'strict restraint'; by a nice irony, the 'glassy deck' finds its echo in the moon's reflection in the still waters; the flight of the soul, unlike that of the ship in stanza xx, is not ever onwards, but back into the past. In this moment of meditation and reflection, Byron dwells on the claims of love in an unprecedented fashion. We soon realise that there has been something completely deceptive about the calm, orderly world of the ship; and something just as deceptive about his calls to the 'keel-compelling gale'. In the silence and stillness of 'Meditation', we have some sense of the reality of love, even when it is over, and a more painful sense of the turbulence of such feelings.

> Thus bending o'er the vessel's laving side,
> To gaze on Dian's wave-reflected sphere;
> The soul forgets her schemes of Hope and Pride,
> And flies unconscious o'er each backward year.
> None are so desolate but something dear,
> Dearer than self, possesses or possess'd
> A thought, and claims the homage of a tear;
> A flashing pang! of which the weary breast
> Would still, albeit in vain, the heavy heart divest.
>
> (II.xxiv)

It seems apposite that Byron should move from this exploration of the heart's 'baffled zeal', of the consequent and utter solitude, to an account of Harold's feelings for his own Calypso, 'sweet Florence'. He re-creates with some subtlety, and some amusement, the fluctuations of feeling, as Harold cannot bring himself 'To cast a worthless offering at thy shrine, / Nor ask so dear a breast to feel one pang for mine' (II.xxx). For a brief moment, as their eyes meet, we get an anticipation of what Byron is to perfect in *Don Juan*, the hint of eroticism held at arm's length. Here, he has to resort to the personification of Cupid, which keeps the whole matter in check; it is, though, the second and third lines which announce their own particular Byronic distinctiveness:

> Thus Harold deem'd, as on that lady's eye
> He look'd, and met its beam without a thought,
> Save Admiration glancing harmless by:
> Love kept aloof, albeit not far remote,
> Who knew his votary often lost and caught,
> But knew him as his worshipper no more,
> And ne'er again the boy his bosom sought:
> Since now he vainly urg'd him to adore,
> Well deem'd the little God his ancient sway was o'er.
>
> (II.xxxi)

For her part, Florence is puzzled by Harold's apparent aloofness: she is used to quicker conquests, whether 'real or mimic'. The point is made that Harold is adopting one of his poses, that his 'seeming marble heart . . . was not unskilful in the spoiler's art'; he is, however, not going to continue playing love's games ('Yet never would he join the lover's whining crew' – II.xxxiii). Cynicism takes over, and we are given the traditional rake's view of how to conduct an affair:

> Disguise ev'n tenderness, if thou art wise;
> Brisk Confidence still best with woman copes;
> Pique her and soothe in turn, soon Passion crowns thy
>   hopes.
>
> (II.xxxiv)

This might be what Harold would have Florence believe, and what the poet would have Harold have us believe. But we are clearly being led along by the nose throughout these stanzas, and we do well to recognise the moral for what it is, an echo of the Regency tone cultivated by Byron with heartless delight in many of his lyrics, not because he necessarily believed in it, but because it was a tone he found congenial.

The paltry prize is hardly worth the cost:
Youth wasted, minds degraded, honour lost,
These are thy fruits, successful Passion! these!

(II.xxxv)

Harold and Florence are as much involved in role-playing as the Spanish maids and grandees at the bullfight. One of the several voices in *Childe Harold* is asserting the shallowness of love, but there is no reason to assume it to be the poem's dominant voice, and within two stanzas Byron is careful to allow a more persuasive voice its say.

I have already referred to the deliberate use, in canto I, of the pastoral motif to imply protection. As with Blake, so with Byron, it is a short step from this to the image of nature as mother. There is no need to supply any particularly Freudian reading of *Childe Harold*: Byron quite openly exploits the image of nature's bosom, and this has its special function in his account of the *caritas Romana* in canto IV. But, after the apparently scornful dismissal of true feeling, there is some relief in this appeal to the comforts of nature, even if they are distinctly uneasy comforts:

Dear Nature is the kindest mother still,
Though alway changing, in her aspect mild;
From her bare bosom let me take my fill,
Her never-wean'd, though not her favour'd child.
Oh! she is fairest in her features wild,
Where nothing polish'd dares pollute her path:
To me by day or night she ever smil'd,
Though I have mark'd her when none other hath,
And sought her more and more, and lov'd her best in
    wrath.

(II.xxxvii)

Nature's wildness is part of her comfort, but the paradox is insisted upon: wildness rhymes with mildness. This means that Albania has its own obvious claims, and it is hard not to hear in these lines something of the Wordsworthian bending of the eye in *The Prisoner of Chillon*:

> Land of Albania! let me bend mine eyes
> On thee, thou rugged nurse of savage men!
> (*Childe Harold*, II.xxxviii)

The following stanza brings out the complications of the nursing image: nature's bosom becomes that of the poet Sappho, her 'breast imbued with such immortal fire. . . . Could she not live who life eternal gave?' I have discussed part of this section in connection with Byron's challenge to the validity of poetry; but what is of interest here is that he should be using his basic image of nature's breast in such a variety of ways: in the space of three stanzas it has come to represent, and to question, the nature of poetry itself, in particular the poetry of love. He is recalling here people both real and fictitious who have suffered, even died, for love. Harold's voyage takes him past two absolutely crucial landmarks that have to do with the true feeling that interests Byron, landmarks that reveal those earlier stanzas for the posturing that they are. In such a context, the scenes of war – Actium, Lepanto, Trafalgar – are laughable, even to Harold. Observing a scene of true passion, however, he is moved in a way that is itself moving.

> But when he saw the evening star above
> Leucadia's far-projecting rock of woe,
> And hail'd the last resort of fruitless love,
> He felt, or deem'd he felt, no common glow:
> And as the stately vessel glided slow
> Beneath the shadow of that ancient mount,
> He watch'd the billows' melancholy flow,
> And, sunk albeit in thought as he was wont,
> More placid seem'd his eye, and smooth his pallid front.
> (II.xli)

This is one of those places where Byron's control over his verse form mirrors his understanding of emotion; he rises above the level of Spenserianism that, for much of the first part of the poem, he is happy to settle for. 'The last resort of fruitless love', for example, has its own built-in pun which is almost Miltonic in its density; 'fruitless love' is worlds away from that line in II.xxxv, 'These are thy fruits, successful Passion, these', which I have already mentioned – rather it picks up the 'barren spot' of II.xxxix, without devaluing the love itself. The qualification in the fourth line might seem awkward, perhaps even metrical padding; but it is, I think, an early instance of Byron's increasing tendency to move towards precision in a rather crab-wise fashion. There is a difference, after all, between feeling and thinking one feels, and Byron's scrupulosity dictates that hesitation: he is warning us against giving Harold too much credit. At the same time, though sunk in thought perhaps as much as in feeling (another crucial distinction), Harold has attained – again, apparently ('seem'd') – a greater placidity of eye, so that the earlier Wordsworthian hint might now be more justified; and, if his 'pallid front' is 'smooth', we remember 'that seeming marble heart' of II.xxxiii only to notice the difference between feigned indifference and a more genuine repose.

Childe Harold's meeting with 'Albania's chief, whose dread command / Is lawless law' (II.xlvii) is an occasion for the wildness of nature and of humanity to be set off against each other. Byron has already staked out some of the argumentative possibilities, with his tortuous contemplations on the nature of love and the nature of nature. If it comes as no surprise that he should turn immediately from an initial discussion of power and defiance to a description of 'Monastic Zitza' (II.xlvii), it is equally no surprise to find him resorting to the volcanic image that heralds the violence of a passionate world:

> Dusky and huge, enlarging on the sight,
> Nature's volcanic amphitheatre,
> Chimaera's alps extend from left to right:
> Beneath, a living valley seems to stir;
> Flocks play, trees wave, streams flow, the mountain-fir
> Nodding above: behold black Acheron!
> Once consecrated to the sepulchre.
> Pluto! if this be hell I look upon,
> Close sham'd Elysium's gates, my shade shall seek for
>   none!
>
> (II.li)

The paradoxes are self-evident. It is however worth pointing to the way in which the earlier Thomsonian 'rounding off' of the scene (II.xlii) is disallowed: the setting 'enlarges' on the sight, which in turn has no choice but to absorb it, to register the contradictions, the apparent marriage of heaven and hell. Although the amphitheatre is 'volcanic', the 'living valley seems to stir', like a person waking up. One of Byron's favourite images is here hinted at, before the verse relaxes into something more conventional. But a few stanzas later, where he is using several stock devices of loco-descriptive verse, there is an important sense of lack of complexity, as though tranquillity has momentarily been earned.

> Epirus' bounds recede, and mountains fail;
> Tir'd of up-gazing still, the wearied eye
> Reposes gladly on as smooth a vale
> As ever Spring yclad in grassy dye:
> Ev'n on a plain no humble beauties lie,
> Where some bold river breaks the long expanse,
> And woods along the banks are waving high,
> Whose shadows in the glassy waters dance,
> Or with the moon-beam sleep in midnight's solemn trance.
>
> (II.liv)

The 'Motley scene' (II.lix) of Ali Pasha's court is described at some length, as Byron dwells in his loving fashion on the colourful, outlandish details, on the very aspects that made him return repeatedly to the excitements of the 'Turkish Tales'. In view of the image of nature as mother, which played such a prominent part earlier in this canto, there is no need to do more than point to the role played by woman at court: she is a prisoner in a cage, but a fairly contented one. We might want to question the implications of this image of domestic contentment; but we cannot overemphasise its importance in the overall design. At the centre of a warlike race is the maternal figure, at one with her lot and therefore with nature:

> Here woman's voice is never heard: apart,
> And scarce permitted, guarded, veil'd, to move,
> She yields to one her person and her heart,
> Tam'd to her cage, nor feels a wish to rove:

For, not unhappy in her master's love,
And joyful in a mother's gentlest cares,
Blest cares! all other feelings far above!
Herself more sweetly rears the babe she bears,
Who never quits the breast, no meaner passion shares.
(II.lxi)

Ali himself is more complex, a 'man of war and woes': his 'voluptuous . . . . repose' is deceptive, so much so that the poet has to make the point for us.

Yet in his lineaments ye cannot trace,
While Gentleness her milder radiance throws
Along that aged venerable face,
The deeds that lurk beneath, and stain him with disgrace.
(II.lxii)

For all the pomp and splendour, the ravages of violence cannot be denied – Ali is 'marked . . . with a tyger's tooth':

Blood follows blood, and, through their mortal span,
In bloodier acts conclude those who with blood began.
(II.lxiii)

This, in its crudest, most reductive form, is the moral of many of the verse tales; what is interesting about it here is that Byron speaks out so directly, but can do so only after the extremely elaborate preparation of the previous twenty stanzas.

A rather similar process of accumulation works in his favour in his concluding address, first of all to 'Fair Greece! sad relic of departed worth!' (II.lxxiii), and subsequently to the dead youth Edleston, 'Thou lov'd and lovely one!' (II.xcv). The transition is in itself a daring one. Much of this canto has been about places, beginning and ending with Greece, and all its implications for freedom and wisdom: 'All that we know is, nothing can be known', Socrates's dictum of II.vii, colours the whole of the second canto. On a metaphysical plane it is sufficiently daunting; on the level of historical understanding it could lead to universal despair; but on the level of personal feeling, personal loss, it could result in that sense of futility that has been such a hallmark of Harold. As we have seen, towards the beginning of this canto Byron examined a moment when Harold was on the brink of true feeling, but he edged away; in the course of the canto Byron has explored other moments of feeling less easy to deny. One of the results of his visit to Ali Pasha's court is a fuller understanding of the plight of Greece: that in turn allows him to confront his own sense of loss. The first canto concluded with a sad salute to John Wingfield, as though partly to remind us that true feeling was still a possibility; the second canto, with its greater overall complexity, is to conclude with the cry of affection that Harold himself would not allow. Greece's lost freedom is the vital link. After the 'Tambourgi' war song, with its attempt to win nature's sanction for war ('Ye mountains, that see us descend to the shore / Shall view us as victors, or view us no more!'), the address to Greece is moving in its sensitivity, in its harsh qualifications:

> Fair Greece! sad relic of departed worth!
> Immortal, though no more! though fallen, great!
> Who now shall lead thy scatter'd children forth,
> And long accustom'd bondage uncreate?
>
> (II.lxxiii)

The second line epitomises the contradictions, with its chiastic inversion: immortality, strictly speaking, cannot cease to be, and, if you are fallen, can you still be great? In order to create freedom, bondage has to be uncreated: positives, as so often in *Childe Harold*, require their negatives. Even the appeal to the past seems to be one to defeat, rather than victory:

> Not such thy sons who whilome did await,
> The hopeless warriors of a willing doom,
> In bleak Thermopylae's sepulchral strait –
> Oh! who that gallant spirit shall resume,
> Leap from Eurotas' banks, and call thee from the tomb?
>
> (II.lxxiii)

The carnival in Stamboul, embraced in the succeeding stanzas with a rather puzzled enthusiasm, becomes a chance to meditate on what is real, what feigned. The moon's reflection in the water (as before in this canto) is both a cue for thoughts of love and itself a reflection on love's appropriateness. Byron is fascinated by the reciprocal nature of love. He approaches it here, and we do well to remember not only that glance between Harold and Florence, but – just as important – the lingering glances of *The Giaour*.

> Loud was the lightsome tumult of the shore,
> Oft Music chang'd, but never ceas'd her tone,
> And timely echo'd back the measur'd oar,
> And rippling waters made a pleasant moan:
> The Queen of tides on high consenting shone,
> And when a transient breeze swept o'er the wave,
> 'Twas, as if darting from her heavenly throne,
> A brighter glance her form reflected gave,
> Till sparkling billows seem'd to light the banks they lave.
>
> Glanc'd many a light caique along the foam,
> Danc'd on the shore the daughters of the land,
> Ne thought had man or maid of rest or home,
> While many a languid eye and thrilling hand
> Exchang'd the look few bosoms may withstand,
> Or gently prest, return'd the pressure still:
> Oh Love! young Love! bound in thy rosy band,
> Let sage or cynic prattle as he will,
> These hours, and only these, redeem Life's years of ill!
> (*Childe Harold*, II.lxxx–lxxxi)

It might at this point be tempting to take the poet at his own word, to see him casting himself, as he appeared earlier, in the role of a 'sage Apollonius'. But the sad history of Greece will not allow such a reading, nor such a carefree response as these stanzas apparently celebrate. There is too much false jollity here, too much of the unthinking flirtation that Byron lambasted in the bullfight passage of canto I. The next stanza reminds us of our responsibilities: the sea's 'pleasant moan' becomes something else, and the moon's bright reflection is shown up for what it is.

> But, midst the throng in merry masquerade,
> Lurk there no hearts that throb with secret pain,
> Even through the closest searment half betrayed?

> To such the gentle murmurs of the main
> Seem to re-echo all they mourn in vain;
> To such the gladness of the gamesome crowd
> Is source of wayward thought and stern disdain:
> How do they loathe the laughter idly loud,
> And long to change the robe of revel for the shroud!
>
> (II.lxxxii)

Some consolation is to be found in nature; but Byron can find little to console him when he turns to the loss of his beloved Edleston. The grand, historical gesture shrivels rather before such private pain, such repeated realisations of isolation. *Childe Harold* reaches a genuine crisis at this point. The hero appears to be fading from the scene, unworthy of it rather in the way that the Greeks are unworthy of their past: and if he is unworthy in his 'too protracted song', his 'inglorius lays' (II.xciv), then by extension the poet is equally unworthy; the crisis is magnified by the sudden lurch into the deeply personal grief of the poet himself; after the loss of Greece, the impending loss of the hero – inadequate to his task – comes the loss of the person on whom he depended for his existence. The pain at this stage is too great to be assimilated into the verse: it is an isolated cry of anguish –'What is my being? thou hast ceas'd to be' (II.xcv). If Harold is on the verge of disappearing, the poet is determined to take on some of his characteristics. His answer to loss is not to dwell on it, but to 'plunge again into the crowd'; he will dissemble, as did Harold, as did the Greeks in captivity. But two lines from these concluding stanzas stand out, in their claims for redemption: 'Thou too art gone, thou lov'd and lovely one!' (II.xcv); 'Oh! ever loving, lovely, and belov'd' (II.xcvi). No amount of dissembling can overturn the strength of feeling contained in such reciprocal love.

There is, as I have suggested, a marked difference in tone and quality between the first two cantos of *Childe Harold* and canto III: the biographical and bibliographical facts do not need to be rehearsed here. Some of the effects, though, deserve further exploration. Harold's 'guarded coldness' gives way to a 'nobler aim'; his proud independence is presented as a virtue. For the first time in the poem, the relationship between nature, feeling and passion is stated with a clarity and a reference to Harold that has before merely been hinted at:

> Where rose the mountains, there to him were friends;
> Where roll'd the ocean, thereon was his home;
> Where a blue sky, and glowing clime, extends,
> He had the passion and the power to roam;
> The desert, forest, cavern, breaker's foam,
> Were unto him companionship; they spake
> A mutual language, clearer than the tome
> Of his land's tongue, which he would oft forsake
> For Nature's pages glass'd by sunbeams on the lake.
>
> (III.xiii)

'Passion' and 'power' are the important words here: they are allowed their place, unquestioned by any authorial ambiguity; the mutuality of man and nature is comparable to that between lover and beloved; there is no suggestion that the reflections in the lake are illusions, or delusive. However, the next stanza demonstrates the problem which increasingly haunts Byron – and, indeed, most of the Romantics. Their aspirations to immortality are thwarted. As much of the poem is about bounds and horizons, so we realise here the taunting nature of the relationship between heaven and earth. The imaginative spark remains a spark, immortality (like that of Greece) is denied. This stanza is a reflection not just of the Childe's perplexities, but of Byron's own realisation of the contradictions:

> Like the Chaldean, he could watch the stars,
> Till he had peopled them with beings bright
> As their own beams; and earth, and earth-born jars,
> And human frailties, were forgotton quite:
> Could he have kept his spirit to that flight
> He had been happy; but this clay will sink
> Its spark immortal, envying it the light
> To which it mounts, as if to break the link
> That keeps us from yon heaven which woos us to its brink.
>
> (III.xiv)

The language of love is used to describe the aspirations of mortals; but, subtly, it is heaven which does the wooing, and all we can do is respond. We become like caged birds, beating ourselves against the bars, drawing blood, denied the 'boundless air' which is our true home. This is the dreadful contradiction at the base of canto III.

As usual, war is the strongest challenge to any notion of human aspiration, and Byron gives full weight to the lessons of Waterloo. Where his poetic maturity most fully shows itself is in the reflections that arise out of such scenes: he conjures up a marvellous sequence of grim paradoxes, which stand in their own right, but which also serve as comments on the poem, and how it works. The syntax is pushed across the line breaks, the resisting rhymes are left stranded, barely keeping all these 'fragments' together. There has been a lot of talk in the poem of coldness, of hearts constrained and constricted: much of it, in the first two cantos, has seemed artificial or grandiloquent. Here, however, the thrust of the verse is towards an understanding of what coldness might imply: the heart's triumph here is that it sticks to its task, even though that involves its own inevitable breaking.

Again, at this point, we should remember the stanza 'Fair Greece! sad relic of departed worth!'; the difference is the greater compression of these two stanzas in canto III:

> They mourn, but smile at length; and, smiling, mourn:
> The tree will wither long before it fall;
> The hull drives on, though mast and sail be torn;
> The roof-tree sinks, but moulders on the hall
> In massy hoariness; the ruined wall
> Stands when its wind-torn battlements are gone;
> The bars survive the captive they enthral;
> The day drags through though storms keep out the sun;
> And thus the heart will break, yet brokenly live on:
>
> Even as a broken mirror, which the glass
> In every fragment multiplies; and makes
> A thousand images of one that was,
> The same, and still the more, the more it breaks;
> And thus the heart will do which not forsakes,
> Living in shattered guise, and still, and cold,

> And bloodless, with its sleepless sorrow aches,
> Yet withers on till all without is old,
> Shewing no visible sign, for such things are untold.
> (III.xxxii–xxxiii)

This is a long way from the glassy reflections of the moon in the sea, even from the 'glassy deck' of II.xix. That image of placidity has been well and truly shattered, and it will be difficult to piece it together again; it is one of the many achievements of the poem that Byron can effect such a piecing-together. But at this point in the poem all the heart can do is to contemplate its own fragmented shards, and live on 'in shattered guise'. Byron evinces a kind of desperate stoicism here, which lends a particular colour to the declaration, 'There is a very life in our despair' (III.xxxiv). That is no hollow cry of a jejune Gothicism, but rather the recognition that such despair has its 'vitality' – 'a quick root / Which feeds these branches' (III.lxxxiv).

It is in the context of these insights that Byron's ensuing discussion of Napoleon needs to be seen. On one level, Napoleon recalls, in his aspirations, the vain yearnings of Harold earlier in this canto, yearnings which are supported by Byron's own approach to a tragic vision. On another level, he recalls other Byronic heroes, and by extension Byron himself, 'antithetically mixt', 'Extreme in all things' (III.xxxvi). But Byron is careful to draw the necessary distinctions. Napoleon is both 'Conqueror and captive of the earth' (III.xxxvii), perhaps captive because conqueror; he could crush an empire, but he could not govern his own passions – to that extent, for all his greater potentialities, he is no better than Ali Pasha. Many of the Romantics held Napoleon in peculiar and ambiguous awe: few were able to emulate Hazlitt's sustained admiration. Byron uses his portrait of Napoleon to qualify that earlier passage on human aspiration, and to qualify further the crucial difference between action and repose. III.xlii is a central statement of doctrine which helps to explain much of *Childe Harold*, and much of Byron's other poetry (the 'fever at the core', for instance, is precisely the cause of the Giaour's suffering, and of the Corsair's, and Lara's; the inability to 'dwell in its own being' foreshadows Bonnivard's plight in the *The Prisoner of Chillon*):

> But quiet to quick bosoms is a hell,
> And *there* hath been thy bane; there is a fire
> And motion of the soul which will not dwell
> In its own narrow being, but aspire
> Beyond the fitting medium of desire;
> And, but once kindled, quenchless evermore,
> Preys upon high adventure, nor can tire
> Of aught but rest; a fever at the core,
> Fatal to him who bears, to all who ever bore.

'The fitting medium of desire' is an appropriately decorous phrase in a poem so often denied any decorum at all: Byron's concern for stylistic and ethical decorum becomes increasingly apparent. He is talking here about how to find the *via media*, a matter of perception, behaviour, and expression. Napoleon has not seen things in fragments; he has not allowed his heart to break. But his inability to rest, to know what passions are appropriate, is the downfall of all great men who glory in their power. The verse recoils upon itself in savage mockery, just as the fever spreads its contagion:

> This makes the madmen who have made men mad
> By their contagion; Conquerors and Kings,
> Founders of sects and systems, to whom add
> Sophists, Bards, Statesmen, all unquiet things
> Which stir too strongly the soul's secret springs,
> And are themselves the fools to those they fool;
> Envied, yet how unenviable! what stings
> Are theirs! One breast laid open were a school
> Which would unteach mankind the lust to shine or rule:

> Their breath is agitation, and their life
> A storm whereon they ride, to sink at last,
> And yet so nurs'd and bigotted to strife,
> That should their days, surviving perils past,
> Melt to calm twilight, they feel overcast
> With sorrow and supineness, and so die;
> Even as a flame unfed, which runs to waste
> With its own flickering, or a sword laid by
> Which eats into itself, and rusts ingloriously.
>
> (III.xliii–xliv)

But the fineness of the line separating such extremes from 'the fitting medium of desire' emerges in the imagery Byron deploys here: only ten stanzas earlier, he has said, 'There is a very life in our despair / Vitality of poison'; the fire of the soul has just been scorned because it refuses its own confines, refuses, in fact, to remain 'unfed', to remain, as Byron puts it earlier, the 'immortal spark'; at the same time, the rusted sword recalls the phrase applied to Bonnivard, 'rusted with a vile repose', and the reminiscence – strictly speaking, of course, the anticipation – confronts us with an ambivalence, in that Bonnivard is a figure of sympathy; it is also hard not to recall those lines in II.xxxviii where the suckling-image is dwelt on precisely because it is one of wildness and savagery ('thou rugged nurse of savage men!'). This is not to charge Byron with inconsistency. *Childe Harold* circles around particcular problems, recurring images that are like so many bits of splintered glass. That is why Byron can discuss the nature of Napoleonic power when and where he does, so soon after his reflections on battle and its aftermath, so soon after he has redefined his own position with regard to feeling and suffering. And he can then revert to the imagery of sea and mountain with which this section began (III.xii), and we realise the fragility of Harold's hold on the world: the language of nature is all very well, but here its metaphysical implications are spelled out:

> He who ascends to mountain-tops, shall find
> The loftiest peaks most wrapt in clouds and snow;
> He who surpasses or subdues mankind,
> Must look down on the hate of those below.
> Though high *above* the sun of glory glow,
> And far *beneath* the earth and ocean spread,
> *Round* him are icy rocks, and loudly blow
> Contending tempests on his naked head,
> And thus reward the toils which to those summits led.
>
> (III.xlv)

The italicised prepositions indicate Byron's rather desperate need for emphasis; his irritation in the next stanza – 'Away with these!' – is understandable. His problem is that he has not himself learnt how to dwell in his 'own narrow being';

aspiration has its urgent attractions, which make it even harder to discover 'the fitting medium of desire'.

There is some significance in the fact that Harold should turn at this point to nature, in particular to the hope offered by the Rhine. It is a muted form of hope, in that man's presence is itself a blight. But Harold can recognise that the Rhine has managed to obliterate the traces of slaughter on its banks:

> Thy tide wash'd down the blood of yesterday,
> And all was stainless, and on thy clear stream
> Glass'd with its dancing light the sunny ray . . . .
>
> (III.li)

As he watches, he allows himself a glimmer of joy, which in turn gives way to an expression of love. This is left as something of a mystery, a fact we have to accept:

> and though in solitude
> Small power the nipp'd affections have to grow,
> In him this glowed when all beside had ceased to glow.
>
> (III.liv)

Again, the verbal reminiscences announce themselves: this small flame recalls that of conquerors unable to rest, in turn recalling the immortal spark of Harold himself. Love and power and aspiration become inseparable in this particular nexus of imagery. It is in a way Harold's apotheosis that he should sing his song, 'The castled crag of Drachenfels', and then, to all intents and purposes, disappear from the poem. He has 'learned to love', perhaps the most important and most difficult lesson of all.

The poet discovers that he can aspire in ways that Harold would have found inconceivable: the contraries are increasingly stressed as he contemplates nature in her grandest, most awesome forms. At one moment the gulf still seems to be there:

> All which expands the spirit, yet appals,
> Gather around these summits, as to show
> How Earth may pierce to Heaven, yet leave vain man
> below.
>
> (III.lxii)

But it is possible to circumvent this impasse, by becoming a spiritual being; immortality is not, after all, a spark that cannot become a fire, it can assert itself like the sun, 'like yonder Alpine snow, / Imperishably pure beyond all things below' (III.lxvii). The reflections in Lake Leman are indications of a spirituality which will pave the way for solitude, escape from mankind and the 'contentious world'.

> Lake Leman woos me with its crystal face,
> The mirror where the stars and mountains view
> The stillness of their aspect in each trace
> Its clear depth yields of their far height and hue . . . .
>
> (III.lxviii)

The fragmented mirror has been restored, and in the stillness there is a perfect congruence between those apparent oppositions: earth and heaven are at one in a rare moment of reciprocal repose.

There follows shortly after this a celebrated passage which was mocked at the time by those who thought Byron was simply aping Wordsworth (and the 'Lakists' generally). More recent critics have scoffed at a Byron they regard as out of his depth, reaching towards a nature mysticism which is alien to him.[2] There is no doubt about the awkwardness of this passage: Byron is risking everything here, in an affirmation that is extremely difficult for him to make, but towards which the whole poem has been haltingly moving. There is much of importance in these stanzas, but the two concepts that lend the passage coherence are those which frame it, feeling and passion.

> I live not in myself, but I become
> Portion of that around me; and to me,
> High mountains are a feeling, but the hum
> Of human cities torture: I can see
> Nothing to loathe in nature, save to be
> A link reluctant in a fleshly chain,
> Class'd among creatures, when the soul can flee,
> And with the sky, the peak, the heaving plain
> Of ocean, or the stars, mingle, and not in vain.

And thus I am absorb'd, and this is life:
I look upon the peopled desart past,
As on a place of agony and strife,
Where, for some sin, to Sorrow I was cast,
To act and suffer, but remount at last
With a fresh pinion; which I feel to spring,
Though young, yet waxing vigorous, as the blast
Which it would cope with, on delighted wing,
Spurning the clay-cold bonds which round our being cling.

And when, at length, the mind shall be all free
From what it hates in this degraded form,
Reft of its carnal life, save what shall be
Existent happier in the fly and worm, –
When elements to elements conform,
And dust is as it should be, shall I not
Feel all I see, less dazzling, but more warm?
The bodiless thought? the Spirit of each spot?
Of which, even now, I share at times the immortal lot?

Are not the mountains, waves, and skies, a part
Of me and of my soul, as I of them?
Is not the love of these deep in my heart
With a pure passion? should I not condemn
All objects, if compared with these? and stem
A tide of suffering, rather than forego
Such feelings for the hard and worldly phlegm
Of those whose eyes are only turn'd below,
Gazing upon the ground, with thoughts which dare not
    glow?

(III.lxxii–lxxv)

These are mighty questions, as far-reaching as any we are
likely to find in this poem or elsewhere. In the very posing of
such questions, Byron seems to be answering by implication
the questions that centred around the likes of Napoleon. It is
in fact possible to overcome the confines of the body, to do
more than beat one's wings in helplessness against the bars of
the cage, to escape by denying our 'clay-cold bonds'. Whereas
John Clare, in his nightmare version of *Childe Harold*, was to
cry out, echoing both Hamlet and Byron, 'Now stagnant

grows my too refined clay / I envye birds their wings to flye away',[3] Byron himself effects that escape. His passions and his feelings have been so refined that they have no need of the body.

Byron, though, is enough of a realist to declare that 'this is not my theme' (III.lxxvi), and that the example of Rousseau calls into question much of what he has just claimed. Rousseau is 'the apostle of affliction, he who threw / Enchantment over passion, and from woe / Wrung overwhelming eloquence': Byron's wariness of words, of the flood of eloquence that can so easily attend on passion, is one of his major themes, and it lies at the centre of the paradoxical nature of *Childe Harold*, in that a long poem cannot constantly be questioning its premisses without calling into question its very existence. In the same way, Rousseau's claims for passion can be seen as a challenge to Byron's own claims:

> His love was passion's essence – as a tree
> On fire by lightning; with ethereal flame
> Kindled he was, and blasted; for to be
> Thus, and enamoured, were in him the same.
>
> (III.lxxviii)

Mention of essence recalls Byron's 'essentialist' view of passionate feeling, just as the idealised nature of Rousseau's love makes it apparently similar to Byron's. There is more than a hint of admiration (it is also to be found in Byron's note to the poem at this point) of Rousseau's friendship with the Comtesse d'Houdetot. But admiration can only go so far, in that Rousseau's 'phrenzy' led indirectly to the tumult of the French Revolution. Such a 'fearful monument' is an awesome one to be associated with feelings of love and passion, and this central contradiction in Rousseau's heritage is deeply disturbing to Byron, as it reflects his own anxieties, his own inherent contradictions. He affirms that

> in his lair
> Fix'd Passion holds his breath, until the hour
> Which shall atone for years; none need despair:
> It came, it cometh, and will come.
>
> (III.lxxxiv)

For passion thus to lurk should cause unease. But, whereas earlier despair seemed a necessary, if grim, part of the scenario, here it is eschewed, as the poet turns, almost in exhaustion, once again to the clear waters of the Leman, picking up the earlier address of III.xlviii. This time, however, the placidity is that of someone who has confronted an extreme passion, and found it wanting.

> Clear, placid Leman! thy contrasted lake,
> With the wild world I dwelt in, is a thing
> Which warns me, with its stillness, to forsake
> Earth's troubled waters for a purer spring.
> This quiet sail is as a noiseless wing
> To waft me from distraction; once I loved
> Torn ocean's roar, but thy soft murmuring
> Sounds sweet as if a sister's voice reproved,
> That I with stern delights should e'er have been so moved.
>
> (III.lxxxv)

The poignancy of this derives partly from the fact that the poet has taken on his shoulders the burden of his hero's lessons.

The night scene that follows has about it a richness and fullness that will not ignore night's dangers. In addition to the verse's determination to be distinct, there is a reminder of that backward look that marked an earlier moment of reflection, II.xxiv, where the soul flew 'unconscious o'er each backward year' – here the reference to childhood is as fresh as it is surprising, until we learn that it is echoed by the grasshopper 'who makes / His life an infancy' (III.lxxxviii). This is poetry about itself, about creativity, about a moment when life is conscious of its bounds and purposes.

> It is the hush of night, and all between
> Thy margin and the mountains, dusk, yet clear,
> Mellowed and mingling, yet distinctly seen,
> Save darken'd Jura, whose capt heights appear
> Precipitously steep; and drawing near,
> There breathes a living fragrance from the shore,
> Of flowers yet fresh with childhood; on the ear
> Drops the light drip of the suspended oar,
> Or chirps the grasshopper one good-night carol more;

He is an evening reveller, who makes
His life an infancy, and sings his fill;
At intervals, some bird from out the brakes,
Starts into voice a moment, then is still.
There seems a floating whisper on the hill,
But that is fancy, for the starlight dews
All silently their tears of love instil,
Weeping themselves away, till they infuse
Deep into Nature's breast the spirit of her hues.
(III.lxxxvi–lxxxvii)

The nature that has been the focus of attention for so much of this canto finds its fulfilment here, in an intensity of feeling that requires the concept of love.

But if we might think, when 'All heaven and earth are still' (III.lxxxix), that love and nature have found their final rest, what Byron calls 'Eternal harmony' (III.xc), then we are in for another shock. In a passage added at a fairly late stage in the composition of canto III, Byron suddenly introduces the opposite of the peace and calm he has just celebrated so majestically. Initially, it does not seem as if the terror of thunder and lightning is his concern, but rather the sense of nature in the process of rejoicing in its own creativity. Earlier talk of nature as feeling and passion is here effectively dramatised:

The sky is changed! – and such a change! Oh night,
And storm, and darkness, ye are wondrous strong,
Yet lovely in your strength, as is the light
Of a dark eye in woman! Far along,
From peak to peak, the rattling crags among
Leaps the live thunder! Not from one lone cloud,
But every mountain now hath found a tongue,
And Jura answers, through her misty shroud,
Back to the joyous Alps, who call to her aloud!

And this is in the night:– Most glorious night!
Thou wert not sent for slumber! let me be
A sharer in thy fierce and far delight, –
A portion of the tempest and of thee!
How the lit lake shines, a phosphoric sea,
And the big rain comes dancing to the earth!

And now again 'tis black, – and now, the glee
Of the loud hills shakes with its mountain-mirth,
As if they did rejoice o'er a young earthquake's birth.
                                        (III.xcii–xciii)

Such rapture, however, does not last. The more he writes
about it, the more he introduces elements of disturbance, so
that the scene is likened to one where lovers part in hate; love
has expired, 'but leaving them an age / Of years all winters, –
war within themselves to wage' (III.xciv). A note of desperate
questioning enters in, as he contemplates the tempest's roar:

But where of ye, oh tempests! is the goal?
Are ye like those within the human breast?
Or do ye find, at length, like eagles, some high nest?
                                        (III.xcvi)

The plunge into despair undermines the core of the poem, as
Byron acknowledges the inadequacy of his attempt to make
one word ('Lightning') embrace all that he had ever thought
or felt; what had seemed like a triumph of altered perception
becomes, quite suddenly, the resignation of 'So we'll go no
more aroving': 'I live and die unheard, / With a most voiceless
thought, sheathing it as a sword' (III.xcvii). What had appar-
ently been successful in terms of poetic response and creation,
becomes, the more it is pondered upon, uncertain and deso-
late. This desolation is both aesthetic and emotional; impor-
tantly, Byron effects this shift by using the image of the Rhone
valley as parted lovers, and in doing so he finds himself more
persuaded by the parting than by the love. Passion and feeling
remain abstractions that he can contemplate in some kind of
semi-Platonic absorption in nature; but the reality, involving
real people, is still rather more disturbing than he might wish.
    However, the return of day allows us to 'resume / The
march of our existence' (III.xcviii). The poet addresses
Clarens, and tries to work out the associations with Rousseau
in a way that will clarify the emerging confusions.

Clarens! sweet Clarens, birth-place of deep Love!
Thine air is the young breath of passionate thought;
Thy trees take root in Love; the snows above

The very Glaciers have his colours caught,
And sun-set into rose-hues sees them wrought
By rays which sleep there lovingly: the rocks,
The permanent crags, tell here of Love, who sought
In them a refuge from the worldly shocks,
Which stir and sting the soul with hope that woos, then
    mocks.

Clarens! by heavenly feet thy paths are trod, –
Undying Love's, who here ascends a throne
To which the steps are mountains; where the god
Is a pervading life and light, – so shown
Not on those summits solely, nor alone
In the still cave and forest: o'er the flower
His eye is sparkling, and his breath hath blown,
His soft and summer breath, whose tender power
Passes the strength of storms in their most desolate hour.

(III.xcix–c)

The desolation is admitted, but overcome by 'tender power'.
This second stanza of the sequence demonstrates Byron's
ability to qualify, to arrange his verse around what he calls in
the previous stanza 'passionate thought': he wants to spell out,
with his own form of 'tender power', what it is that is being
concluded. His prose note reinforces the point:

> the feeling with which all around Clarens, and the oppo-
> site rocks of Meillerie, is invested, is of a still higher and
> more comprehensive order than the mere sympathy with
> individual passion: it is a sense of the existence of love in
> its most extended and sublime capacity, and of our own
> participation of its good and of its glory: it is the great
> principle of the universe, which is there more condensed,
> but not less manifested; and of which, though knowing
> ourselves a part, we lose our individuality, and mingle in
> the beauty of the whole.

As the canto finishes, we realise that there is a deeply perso-
nal reason for the long and complex exploration of love and
feeling; the canto is in fact framed by addresses to Byron's
daughter. He draws attention to this framing-device, and in

doing so forces on us, as readers, the realisation that, for all the literary and historical resonances of *Childe Harold*, this is an intimately personal poem; no amount of talk about voices, personae, or a cold hero will alter the basic fact that this becomes a poem about Byron. The third canto has largely been given over to the varieties of feeling amidst natural scenery; but such explorations have had, it becomes clear, as their prime function the essential one of nurturing a bond between father and daughter, a bond the more painful because it has to survive at such a distance. Some of Byron's letters at the time of the separation express his dreadful anguish, his sense of loss; and behind this canto lie his attempts to come to terms with such personal suffering. Passion as strength of feeling, and as suffering, come together again. The imagery of childhood, of growth, of hope, that has accumulated in this canto, focuses itself on his unseen daughter:

> To aid thy mind's development, – to watch
> Thy dawn of little joys, – to sit and see
> Almost thy very growth, – to view thee catch
> Knowledge of objects, – wonders yet to thee!
> To hold thee lightly on a gentle knee,
> And print on thy soft cheek a parent's kiss, –
> This, it should seem, was not reserv'd for me;
> Yet this was in my nature:– as it is,
> I know not what is there, yet something like to this.
>
> . . .
>
> The child of love, – though born in bitterness,
> And nurtured in convulsion, – of thy sire
> These were the elements, – and thine no less.
> As yet such are around thee, – but thy fire
> Shall be more tempered, and thy hope far higher.
> Sweet be thy cradled slumbers! O'er the sea,
> And from the mountains where I now respire,
> Fain would I waft such blessing upon thee,
> As, with a sigh, I deem thou might'st have been to me!
>
> (III.cxvi,cxviii)

The tender sureness of this is deeply moving, as Byron once again puts his faith in a reciprocity that he knows he has, through force of circumstance, lost. This might have seemed an apposite conclusion. Already the poem has become stretched over a vast canvas, its proportions and pretensions verging on the epic; here, we could argue, with his final address to his daughter, he has come to understand what love is. To some extent that is true. There is certainly a comprehension in canto III that we do not get in the earlier cantos, and along with it goes verse of a much greater, more concentrated, force. Some major and difficult distinctions have been made, between for example Ali Pasha and Napoleon, and then again between Napoleon and Rousseau: the 'fever at the core' has been given its due weight, but shown to be suspect; the part that nature might play in an understanding of feeling has been fully canvassed. But there is the blunt fact that Byron's own journey still has some way to go: Rome and Venice in particular demand the Muse. And aesthetically, the poem requires its own continuation. 'Time's ungentle tide' is a cruel historical phenomenon, and the history of Italy has its tales to divulge; but, just as importantly, that tide is one that laps at the feet of any notion of passion, as feeling and as suffering. Byron has still, in other words, to work his way even further towards a grasp of, an apprehension of, 'the fitting medium of desire'.

Canto IV opens abruptly in Venice. It is one of the boldest strokes in an already bold poem: for a work that has confronted so many varieties of fragmentation, any attempt at establishing a coherent vision is going to be severely tempered by the ambiguities of Venice. The Bridge of Sighs, on which the poet stands, seems the entirely appropriate image for an emotion that is celebratory both of the wonder and magic of the place, and of the terrible loss. The past can seem a long time ago. Even in the first stanza, it is a 'dying Glory' that 'smiles / O'er the far times': that smile has reason to be wan.

> She looks a sea Cybele, fresh from ocean,
> Rising with her tiara of proud towers
> At airy distance, with majestic motion,
> A ruler of the waters and their powers:

> And such she was; – her daughters had their dowers
> From spoils of nations, and the exhaustless East
> Pour'd in her lap all gems in sparkling showers.
> In purple was she robed, and of her feast
> Monarchs partook, and deem'd their dignity increas'd.
>
> (IV.ii)

The loss of glory is, significantly, put in terms of the loss of poetry, one of the obsessions, as we have seen, of this poem. But something, it seems, can be salvaged, if only from the natural world. If art fails us, nature will not.

> In Venice Tasso's echoes are no more,
> And silent rows the songless gondolier;
> Her palaces are crumbling to the shore,
> And music meets not always now the ear:
> Those days are gone – but Beauty still is here.
> States fall, arts fade – but Nature doth not die,
> Nor yet forget how Venice once was dear,
> The pleasant place of all festivity,
> The revel of the earth, the masque of Italy!
>
> (IV.iii)

We should not expect things to be that simple. The very fragmentation that Byron seems to be countering begins to take over the poem, as one mood cancels out another. It is as though *Childe Harold* had become a cacophonous sequence of discordant voices, and there is little indication as to which one should be trusted. For example, the following stanza would appear to be an answer to the negativity of III.iii, where he had spoken of the 'sterile track . . . O'er which all heavily the journeying years / Plod the last sands of life, – where not a flower appears'; it also appears to pick up some of the essentialist ideas of canto III, challenging the notion of imprisoned selfhood and bodily confinement:

> The beings of the mind are not of clay;
> Essentially immortal, they create
> And multiply in us a brighter ray
> And more beloved existence: that which Fate
> Prohibits to dull life, in this our state

> Of mortal bondage, by these spirits supplied
> First exiles, then replaces what we hate;
> Watering the heart whose early flowers have died,
> And with a fresher growth replenishing the void.
>
> (IV.v)

But fast on the heels of this comes an apparent refutation of these claims, a refutation with its own contradiction in the last four lines. This is a classic example of Byron thinking aloud from line to line.

> Such is the refuge of our youth and age,
> The first from Hope, the last from Vacancy;
> And this worn feeling peoples many a page,
> And, may be, that which grows beneath mine eye:
> Yet there are things whose strong reality
> Outshines our fairy-land; in shape and hues
> More beautiful than our fantastic sky,
> And the strange constellations which the Muse
> O'er her wild universe is skilful to diffuse . . . .
>
> (IV.vi)

Dissatisfied with this, the poet then makes it quite clear how confused he is, how anything (and therefore nothing) is possible. One of Byron's favourite phrases is 'let it go': it usually indicates a recognition of the full value of what is being allowed out of sight (I am thinking, for example, of the end of Julia's letter in *Don Juan*, I.cxcv).[4] Here there are two variants of the phrase within one stanza. Letting go so deliberately makes us wonder just how anxious he is to do the opposite.

> I saw or dreamed of such, — but let them go —
> They came like truth, and disappeared like dreams;
> And whatsoe'er they were — are now but so:
> I could replace them if I would, still teems
> My mind with many a form which aptly seems
> Such as I sought for, and at moments found;
> Let these too go — for waking Reason deems
> Such over-weening phantasies unsound,
> And other voices speak, and other sights surround.
>
> (IV.vii)

Within the space of seven stanzas, a process of almost complete disorientation has set in. In a climate where it is hard to take anything on trust, any claims to importance have to assert themselves strongly.

Byron keeps returning to the obvious attractions of Venice, even in its desolation; he clings onto what the past has to offer, as though from that perspective the shattered image can be restored. But it is a tenuous hold.

> Statues of glass – all shiver'd – the long file
> Of her dead Doges are declin'd to dust;
> But where they dwelt, the vast and sumptuous pile
> Bespeaks the pageant of their splendid trust;
> Their spectre broken, and their sword in rust,
> Have yielded to the stranger: empty halls,
> Thin streets, and foreign aspects, such as must
> Too oft remind her who and what enthrals,
> Have flung a desolate cloud o'er Venice' lovely walls.
>
> (IV.xv)

The stubbornness of nature suggests a source of hope, even if hope has in the first few stanzas been scoffed at; the imagery of creativity picks up some of the vitality Byron had found in canto III.

> But from their nature will the tannen grow
> Loftiest on loftiest and least shelter'd rocks,
> Rooted in barrenness, where nought below
> Of soil supports them 'gainst the Alpine shocks
> Of eddying storms; yet springs the trunk, and mocks
> The howling tempest, till its height and frame
> Are worthy of the mountains from whose blocks
> Of bleak, grey, granite, into life it came,
> And grew a giant tree; – the mind may grow the same.
>
> (IV.xx)

As the poet stands, contemplating himself – 'A ruin amidst ruins' (IV.xxv) – he gradually elaborates on the hint, contained in that stanza, of the conjunction of art and nature; and the implication is that, if this ruin of Venice has its beauties and glory, then he too might acquire something of the same. What he rather quaintly calls her 'immaculate charm' (IV.xxvi) is permanent, ineradicable; once again, the resort to natural imagery serves his purposes:

> The Moon is up, and yet it is not night –
> Sunset divides the sky with her – a sea
> Of glory streams along the Alpine height
> Of blue Friuli's mountains; Heaven is free
> From clouds, but of all colours seems to be
> Melted to one vast Iris of the West,
> Where the Day joins the past Eternity;
> While, on the other hand, meek Dian's crest
> Floats through the azure air – an island of the blest!
>
> A single star is at her side, and reigns
> With her o'er half the lovely heaven; but still
> Yon sunny sea heaves brightly, and remains
> Roll'd o'er the peak of the far Rhaetian hill,
> As Day and Night contending were, until
> Nature reclaim'd her order . . . .
>
> (IV.xxvii–xxviii)

Nature and art appear to be in a state of suspended harmony: those 'contentious worlds' to which he has so frequently addressed himself have been subdued, controlled. It is Tasso's lasting glory that he, in his own way, has effected a similar kind of control over warring elements; although imprisoned, he attained a freedom of the spirit which shames his captors. Art, it would seem, can, in its repose, give a sense of life and vitality.

The stanzas on sculpture anticipate what Byron is to say in *Don Juan*, rather more paradoxically. The rich potentialities of art are celebrated in several stanzas, but this one in particular deserves comment:

> Glowing, and circumfused in speechless love,
> Their full divinity inadequate
> That feeling to express, or to improve,
> The gods become as mortals, and man's fate
> Has moments like their brightest; but the weight
> Of earth recoils upon us; – let it go!

> We can recal such visions, and create,
>   From what has been, or might be, things which grow
> Into thy statue's form, and look like gods below.
>   (*Childe Harold*, IV.lii)

As I shall suggest later, much of Byron's concern in *Don Juan* is with the weight of human suffering and the need to lighten it; although he nearly catches himself out here, he wants to emphasise the possibility of the 'burden of the mystery' being lifted, through the combination of art and feeling. He goes on to make the same point towards the end of the canto, at the moment when he has established his bearings in Rome. He has moved from what he calls the 'sating gaze of wonder' to a depth of contemplation that can only be hinted at. The reader is urged to visit the Vatican, to see the Laocoön statue, or the 'Lord of the unerring bow'. Art, in the form of sculpture, makes sense of the suffering of mortals, makes the connection with immortality, and in so doing provides the justification for Prometheus. The figure of passionate revolt has become the artist.

> Or, turning to the Vatican, go see
> Laocoon's torture dignifying pain –
> A father's love and mortal's agony
> With an immortal's patience blending: – Vain
> The struggle; vain, against the coiling strain
> And gripe, and deepening of the dragon's grasp,
> The old man's clench; the long envenomed chain
> Rivets the living links, – the enormous asp
> Enforces pang on pang, and stifles gasp on gasp.

> Or view the Lord of the unerring bow,
> The God of life, and poesy, and light –
> The Sun in human limbs arrayed, and brow
> All radiant from his triumph in the fight;
> The shaft hath just been shot – the arrow bright
> With an immortal's vengeance; in his eye
> And nostril beautiful disdain, and might,
> And majesty, flash their full lightnings by,
> Developing in that one glance the Deity.

> But in his delicate form – a dream of Love,
> Shaped by some solitary nymph, whose breast
> Long'd for a deathless lover from above,
> And madden'd in that vision – are exprest
> All that ideal beauty ever bless'd
> The mind with in its most unearthly mood,
> When each conception was a heavenly guest –
> A ray of immortality – and stood,
> Starlike, around, until they gathered to a god!
>
> And if it be Prometheus stole from Heaven
> The fire which we endure, it was repaid
> By him to whom the energy was given
> Which this poetic marble hath array'd
> With an eternal glory – which, if made
> By human hands, is not of human thought;
> And Time himself hath hallowed it, nor laid
> One ringlet in the dust – nor hath it caught
> A tinge of years, but breathes the flame with which 'twas
> wrought.
>
> (IV.clx–clxiii)

In the context of *Childe Harold*, this seems to be the perfect statement of art's supremacy, its ability to embrace the contradictions of life, in particular those contradictions that arise from agony and passionate feeling. Mortal passion, in fact, as that first stanza suggests, becomes immortal patience.

Byron arrives at this conjunction by a pained and tortuous route: contradictions are rife on every page; the very landscape in its violent upheavals is a mirror of human pain. There is a very remarkable passage (famously commented on by Hazlitt[5]), devoted to the river Velino hurling itself through the gorge, a 'matchless cataract, / Horribly beautiful': 'on the verge' sits an iris, 'Like Hope upon a death-bed . . . Resembling, 'mid the torture of the scene, / Love watching Madness with unalterable mien' (IV.lxxii). Hope, that elusive phantom, has been reinstated; but, more importantly, love is actually looking at its own distortion; so often has love turned to passion and then to madness. The irony and complexity of this passage cannot be lost on us: love and madness are inextricably linked, even if, here, it is the 'unalterable mien' of love

that is allowed the final word. The very symbol of Rome itself
is a reminder of the basic ambiguity.

> And thou, the thunder-stricken nurse of Rome!
> She-wolf! whose brazen-imaged dugs impart
> The milk of conquest yet within the dome
> Where, as a monument of antique art,
> Thou standest: — Mother of the mighty heart,
> Which the great founder suck'd from thy wild teat,
> Scorch'd by the Roman Jove's etherial dart,
> And thy limbs black with lightning — dost thou yet
> Guard thine immortal cubs, nor thy fond charge forget?
>
> (IV.lxxxviii)

Byron is back with his dominant image of the nursing breast,
one that inevitably offers hope, but paradoxically in this con-
text can soon take it away again.

There are perhaps two further moments in canto IV that
could be regarded as crucial. The first is the address to Egeria,
where natural and human gentleness come together. Typical-
ly, Byron goes on to challenge his own premisses, but then
retracts the challenge: the force of the initial passage is too
powerful to be dismissed.

> Egeria! sweet creation of some heart
> Which found no mortal resting-place so fair
> As thine ideal breast; whate'er thou art
> Or wert, — a young Aurora of the air,
> The nympholepsy of some fond despair;
> Or, it might be, a beauty of the earth,
> Who found a more than common votary there
> Too much adoring; whatsoe'er thy birth,
> Thou wert a beautiful thought, and softly bodied forth.

> The mosses of thy fountain still are sprinkled
> With thine Elysian water-drops; the face
> Of thy cave-guarded spring, with years unwrinkled,
> Reflects the meek-eyed genius of the place,
> Whose green, wild margin now no more erase
> Art's works; nor must the delicate waters sleep,

Prisoned in marble, bubbling from the base
  Of the cleft statue, with a gentle leap
The rill runs o'er, and round, fern, flowers, and ivy, creep,

  Fantastically tangled; the green hills
  Are clothed with early blossoms, through the grass
  The quick-eyed lizard rustles, and the bills
  Of summer-birds sing welcome as ye pass;
  Flowers fresh in hue, and many in their class,
  Implore the pausing step, and with their dyes
  Dance in the soft breeze in a fairy mass;
  The sweetness of the violet's deep blue eyes,
Kiss'd by the breath of heaven, seems coloured by its skies.

  Here didst thou dwell, in this enchanted cover,
  Egeria! thy all heavenly bosom beating
  For the far footsteps of thy mortal lover;
  The purple Midnight veil'd that mystic meeting
  With her most starry canopy, and seating
  Thyself by thine adorer, what befel?
  This cave was surely shaped out for the greeting
  Of an enamour'd Goddess, and the cell
Haunted by holy Love — the earliest oracle!

  And didst thou not, thy breast to his replying,
  Blend a celestial with a human heart;
  And Love, which dies as it was born, in sighing,
  Share with immortal transports? could thine art
  Make them indeed immortal, and impart
  The purity of heaven to earthly joys,
  Expel the venom and not blunt the dart —
  The dull satiety which all destroys —
And root from out the soul the deadly weed which cloys?

                                        (IV.cxv−cxix)

The second crucial moment is supplied by the *caritas Romana*
passage, where the suckling-image receives its most gently
surprising fulfilment, in the portrait of the daughter feeding
her father at her breast, as they languish in prison. The hint —
almost *Don Juan*esque — of paradise lost does not detract from
the moment's significance. If there is to be such a thing as 'the

fitting medium of desire', then it is perhaps here that Byron attains it.

> Full swells the deep pure fountain of young life,
> Where *on* the heart and *from* the heart we took
> Our first and sweetest nurture, when the wife,
> Blest into mother, in the innocent look,
> Or even the piping cry of lips that brook
> No pain and small suspense, a joy perceives
> Man knows not, when from out its cradled nook
> She sees her little bud put forth its leaves –
> What may the fruit be yet? – I know not – Cain was Eve's.
>
> But here youth offers to old age the food,
> The milk of his own gift:– it is her sire
> To whom she renders back the debt of blood
> Born with her birth. No; he shall not expire
> While in those warm and lovely veins the fire
> Of health and holy feeling can provide
> Great Nature's Nile, whose deep stream rises higher
> Than Egypt's river; – from that gentle side
> Drink, drink and live, old man! Heaven's realm holds no
> such tide.
>
> The starry fable of the milky way
> Has not thy story's purity; it is
> A constellation of a sweeter ray,
> And sacred Nature triumphs more in this
> Reverse of her decree, than in the abyss
> Where sparkle distant worlds:– Oh, holiest nurse!
> No drop of that clear stream its way shall miss
> To thy sire's heart, replenishing its source
> With life, as our freed souls rejoin the universe.
>
> (IV.cxlix–cli)

Although, as I argued in the previous chapter, control in the end is won, in the image of the ocean, it is not a consistent thing. The central truth is perhaps contained in the stanza in which Byron admits, once again, to the fragmentary nature of our vision.

Thou seest not all; but piecemeal thou must break,
To separate contemplation, the great whole;
And as the ocean many bays will make,
That ask the eye – so here condense thy soul
To more immediate objects, and control
Thy thoughts until thy mind hath got by heart
Its eloquent proportions, and unroll
In mighty graduations, part by part,
The glory which at once upon thee did not dart . . . .

(IV.clvii)

We could say that *Childe Harold* is very largely concerned with the assault on some great vastness, which will always defeat us; the final appeal to the ocean offers hope and comfort, but even that cannot be wholly convincing. There has been too much fragmentation, too many shattered images. To look at 'more immediate objects', to 'control' our 'thoughts', and understand the significance of 'eloquent proportions': Byron finds that to do all of this he must turn wholeheartedly to the *ottava rima* he had found so congenial when confronting his own shattered self, in the 'Epistle to Augusta'. The rest of this study devotes itself to Byron's attention to feeling in his major satire, *Don Juan*.

5   'Due Bounds' and 'Due Precision': *Don Juan* (i)

One of Byron's most sustained flights occurs in canto VI of *Don Juan*, where he pursues the ramifications of his hero's plight, disguised as a woman in a harem: on the one hand there is the innocent Dudù, with her less-than-innocent dreams as she shares a bed with Juan; on the other is the lustful Gulbeyaz, with her own thoughts about this new arrival. Byron plays off the one relationship against the other, and the canto as a whole depends for its effect on this juxtaposition and eventual intermingling of feelings, and ideas about feelings. Towards the end of the canto, when Dudù has finally been settled after her 'fond hallucination', Byron turns his attention towards Gulbeyaz:

> With the first ray or rather grey of morn,
>   Gulbeyaz rose from restlessness, and pale
> As Passion rises with its bosom worn,
>   Arrayed herself with mantle, gem, and veil.
> The nightingale that sings with the deep thorn,
>   Which fable places in her breast of wail,
> Is lighter far of heart and voice than those
> Whose headlong passions form their proper woes.
>
> And that's the moral of this composition,
>   If people would but see its real drift.
> But *that* they will not do without suspicion,
>   Because all gentle readers have the gift
> Of closing 'gainst the light their orbs of vision,
>   While gentle writers also love to lift
> Their voices 'gainst each other, which is natural;
> The numbers are too great for them to flatter all.
>
> (VI.lxxxvii–lxxxviii)

Although many writers have refused to take Byron's word for it (and his word is not lightly taken), I am inclined to agree with Ridenour here, that *Don Juan* is, indeed, about the passions and their consequences, even if we might want to question the notion of the poem's having any one particular 'moral'.[1] In a poem that, as we have seen, depends for much of its force and strength on notions of seeing, and on the paradox, canvassed in the Dedication, of the blind Milton's divine insight, there is considerable point in Byron's talk of his 'gentle readers' (elsewhere more harshly wooed) having 'the gift / Of closing 'gainst the light their orbs of vision' – that brilliant line has the effect of evoking simultaneously the blind eyes of the unseeing and the open, understanding gaze of the blind. As he says repeatedly in this poem, people will do all they can to shun the truth: only two stanzas earlier he has declared, 'All that I know is that the facts I state / Are true as truth hath ever been of late', which allows him both to appeal to the concept and to have, as so often, the last laugh. The truth of these two stanzas, the truth of Gulbeyaz's passion, is set off against the literary nightingale. It is typical of Byron to gauge his – and our – reactions in this way, to remind us constantly of a literary tradition to which he stands in a particular relation, and which in turn stands in a particular relation to the truth. Moral and aesthetic values are often synonymous, which is why at this point there is some propriety in his reference to 'proper woes'. That deeply moving, deeply honest poem, the 'Epistle to Augusta' had declared,

> I have been cunning in mine overthrow,
> The careful pilot of my proper woe.

Our 'proper woe' is what we deserve; it is ours in particular; it is commensurate with what has caused it; it is appropriate in the sense of being somehow 'within bounds', not beyond what we would expect from 'propriety', from 'proper' behaviour. That final line of stanza lxxxvii, 'Whose headlong passions form their proper woes', sums up, not just the 'moral' of *Don Juan* but the delicate balance between cause and effect, between the 'headlong passions' and how they are experienced and given utterance. The antithesis of 'headlong' and 'proper' is the antithesis of the poem as a whole.

Which is why, amongst other things, Byron is so particular at this moment, in his determination to do more than point a moral: the qualifications assist the 'proper woes'. The previous stanza had put it rather jokily, as it could afford to do, after the painful tensions of the Dudù scene: 'And so good night to them, or if you will, / Good morrow, for the cock had crown' (VI.lxxxvi). But there is nothing joky about the first four lines of stanza lxxxvii, which are in fact an extended pun: 'ray' becomes 'grey'; Gulbeyaz 'rose from restlessness' – almost as though 'restlessness' brought forth the etymological possibility of 'rose'; the descriptive clause allows the present tense 'rises', which, of course, is what passion does, though less often 'pale' and therefore the more striking – pale passion's rising here implies a sinking too; the fourth line continues the pun with 'Arrayed herself' – in other words she has to provide the ray that has been denied by the first line's qualification 'first ray or rather grey'. The pun reaches out beyond this stanza: two stanzas previously, Juan and Dudù have embraced –

> Her neck alone was seen, but that was found
> The colour of a budding rose's crest.
>
> (VI.lxxxv)

Byron's description of the morning in stanza lxxxvii hints at the standard epic simile 'rosy fingered dawn', but does no more than hint, helped along by the 'ray' – 'rose' – 'rises' – 'Arrayed' sequence, and then by the 'deep thorn' of line 6; helped along, too, by stanza lxxxix, where verb and noun enclose the lines –

> Rose the Sultana from a bed of splendour,
> Softer than the soft Sybarite's, who cried
> Aloud because his feelings were too tender
> To brook a ruffled rose leaf by his side . . . .

The pun continues with the rising, afterwards, of 'her great lord': 'Also arose about the self-same time, / Perhaps a little later'; 'And now he rose, and after due ablutions / Exacted by the customs of the East' (VI.xc, xcii). Once more, the sense of propriety, which sends us back to those 'proper woes', and to the fuller realisation of what they entail and imply. Gulbeyaz might not be an attractive person in any moral scale, but there is a very clear distinction between her and her husband, a distinction which works aesthetically in her favour.

Byron is determined to give passion its full weight, whatever the woes that follow. He is to speak out, in his own voice, later in the poem,

> I would not be a tortoise in his screen
>   Of stubborn shell, which waves and weather wear not.
> 'Tis better on the whole to have felt and seen
>   That which humanity may bear or bear not.
> 'Twill teach discernment to the sensitive
> And not to pour their ocean in a sieve.
>
>   (XIV.xlix)

This might seem to anticipate Tennyson's self-consoling cry of *In Memoriam*: ''Tis better to have loved and lost / Than never to have loved at all'; but Byron's observation does not run the risk of becoming an apparently trite aphorism of comfort. This is partly because of the sequence of rhymes, which, though 'feminine', are emphatically negative: the effect is for us to dwell on what we cannot bear, so that we cannot hide behind any easy stoicism. 'On the whole' is sufficient qualification to remove the possibility of sententiousness (upbraiding the 'maxim' of line 1 of this stanza: 'But this is not my maxim'); and the importance of 'discernment' is that it is not something cold or abstract, but learnt from feeling and seeing.

Hence, when Johnson expounds his philosophy to Juan, when they are both awaiting purchase in the slave market, he can be apparently dispassionate ('"You take things coolly sir", said Juan'), because he knows what passion is: 'All, when life is new, / Commence with feelings warm and prospects high' (V.xxi). Johnson, thrice married, is not the phlegmatic character he seems to the wide-eyed Juan. He has learnt 'not to pour' his 'ocean in a sieve', which is a different matter from being a stoic.

> 'But after all what *is* our present state?
>   'Tis bad and may be better – all men's lot.
> Most men are slaves, none more so than the great,
>   To their own whims and passions and what not.

> Society itself, which should create
>   Kindness, destroys what little we had got.
> To feel for none is the true social art
> Of the world's stoics – men without a heart.'
>   (V.xxv)

As if to emphasise the point, Johnson and Juan are bought by 'a black old neutral personage / Of the third sex', who examines them 'as to discover / If they were fitted for the purposed cage' (VI.xxvi). Baba's sexlessness is a short step away from heartlessness.

Just as it was appropriate to make the connection between Gulbeyaz and the 'Epistle to Augusta', so we can see something of Byron in Johnson. Byron stands behind his creation because he himself understands the need for feeling: it is necessary for life; it is necessary, too, for poetry. This emerges in canto III, where the court poet, introduced with many a qualification but clearly to some degree a mocking self-portrait, sings the famous 'The isles of Greece, the isles of Greece!' It is a song about the loss of liberty, which entails the loss of poetry:

> On thy voiceless shore
> The heroic lay is tuneless now,
>   The heroic bosom beats no more!

The poet has little to offer, beyond his 'burning teardrop' and the 'mutual murmurs' shared with the waves. It is a song of despair, but with its own inherent ambiguities, made starker by the enclosing framework. What Byron says afterwards deserves some attention, for, whilst he does not want to make too many claims for it, he recognises the song's symbolic and functional importance:

> Thus sung or would or could or should have sung
>   The modern Greek in tolerable verse.
> If not like Orpheus quite, when Greece was young,
>   Yet in these times he might have done much worse.
> His strain displayed some feeling, right or wrong,
>   And feeling in a poet is the source

Of others' feeling; but they are such liars
And take all colours – like the hands of dyers.
                     (III.lxxxvii)

For all the implied criticisms and contradictions, the display of emotion is clearly what matters. Those alternatives in the first line reinforce the point, demonstrating that we are indeed in a world of make-believe, that poets lie even whilst they affirm the truth. Byron is adverting to a much more complex and paradoxical process than Sidney's proposition that the poet 'nothing affirms, and therefore never lieth', and his determination to confront this process head-on is stamped on every canto of *Don Juan*. For the moment, though, I want to concentrate on Byron's concentration on feeling. It is a word and a concept that has become too much abused: for the Romantics generally it held a particularly important place, leading as it so often did to a form of knowledge.[2] The poet has to cultivate his feelings so that he can in turn help his readers to cultivate theirs; but if the poet is a liar, or at best a Keatsian chameleon, the question arises as to what feelings can be taken to be true, right or wrong. The only way to approach an answer to that is to be open about the limits of knowledge ('All that we know is nothing can be known'), but open, too, to the need for precision. Byron is very clear about the relationship between precision and propriety, even as he affirms the fictionality of his work:

What Juan saw and underwent shall be
    My topic with of course the due restriction
Which is required by proper courtesy.
    And recollect the work is only fiction . . . .
                   (XI.lxxxviii)

Some of the ironic implications of this idea of a decorous satire are spelled out in the extraordinarily compressed and savage Dedication to the Poet Laureate, Robert Southey, taken as an exemplum, 'a common case'.[3] Southey is mocked for his epic pretensions, for that attempt at sublimity evident in a later passage already discussed, the morning rise of Gulbeyaz's lord and master; and in that connection we get reinforced what it is perhaps wrong to think of as merely a sexual undertone — Southey's failure is because his aspirations are too great, but they are too great for him only, because of his impotence. At least Coleridge, in his flight, is 'like a hawk'.

> You, Bob, are rather insolent, you know,
>   At being disappointed in your wish
> To supersede all warblers here below,
>   And be the only blackbird in the dish.
> And then you overstrain yourself, or so,
>   And tumble downward like the flying fish
> Gasping on deck, because you soar too high, Bob,
> And fall for lack of moisture quite a dry Bob.
>
> (Dedication, iii)

Thus early in the poem is the notion of sexuality alluded to, in particular a sexuality that is misplaced because inappropriate; to telescope one of the poetic arguments, Southey is another version of the eunuch Baba. Moisture of any kind, from tears to the rich oozings Byron occasionally hints at, is preferable to the arid heartlessness of a Baba, a Southey, or any of the other poets of the day, secluded in their safe complacency. Milton becomes the standard by which the others are to be judged. Byron recognises in *Paradise Lost* the values of true epic, true sublimity, true feeling: we are not allowed, for long, to forget that behind *Don Juan* lies the image of Eden, and what that meant in terms of human drama, the love of Adam and Eve:

> Would he [Milton] adore a sultan? He obey
> The intellectual eunuch Castlereagh?
>
> (Dedication, xi)

It has been suggested that the attack on Castlereagh is itself a breach of decorum, an instance of Byron's not knowing where to stop. But the political dimension is essential to the structure of the poem. Castlereagh is 'The vulgarest tool that tyranny could want' (another pun that Byron relishes), a Urizenic figure of constriction, the dangerous political extension of the 'narrowness' of the Lakers, with an equally insidious 'trash of phrase':

> A bungler even in its disgusting trade,
>   And botching, patching, leaving still behind
> Something of which its masters are afraid,
>   States to be curbed and thoughts to be confined,
> Conspiracy or congress to be made,
>   Cobbling at manacles for all mankind,
> A tinkering slave-maker, who mends old chains,
> With God and man's abhorrence for its gains.
>
> If we may judge of matter by the mind,
>   Emasculated to the marrow, it
> Hath but two objects, how to serve and bind,
>   Deeming the chain it wears even men may fit,
> Eutropius of its many masters, blind
>   To worth as freedom, wisdom as to wit,
> Fearless, because no feeling dwells in ice;
> Its very courage stagnates to a vice.
>
> (Dedication, xiv—xv)

Eutropius continues the line of eunuchs that runs through the poem; to be 'unmanned' is one thing (several of the narratives explore the state), to be 'emasculated' another. Eutropius's distinction had been, like Castlereagh's, to 'serve and bind', and of course what 'may fit' becomes that which befits, or is fitting. Byron is signalling that other major theme of his poem, the erosion of freedom, and, as with poetic decorum, so here, he chooses to attack on the grounds of the enemy: he will challenge intellectual and emotional emasculation, he will attack accustomed and received ideas of what is fit. Similarly, to fear is at least to feel: to be fearless is to be feelingless. In the courage that 'stagnates to a vice' we hear an echo of *The Prisoner of Chillon*, rusted in his vile repose. Feeling, Byron is saying, is a matter of openness, of changing 'lakes for ocean', of refusing the 'mind forg'd manacles' (there is a terrible appositeness in 'manacles for all mankind'). Byron is able to refuse: 'Where shall I turn me not to view its bonds, / For I will never feel them' (*Don Juan*, Dedication, xvi). The play on 'feel' makes the verse double back on itself, to reinforce the strength of the earlier appearance of the word. To feel properly demands a denial of bonds, a refusal to 'feel' them in the literal sense. What is required is the 'honest simple verse' that is to be *Don Juan*, the 'skill' the other poets 'need' (and lack). For a brief moment we might be reminded of a line near the opening of Sidney's *Astrophel and Stella*: 'While with a feeling skill I paint my hell'.

As we saw in our discussion of *Childe Harold*, Byron is fascinated by boundaries, by how far we can see beyond the horizon. In *Don Juan* he sets himself a task more demanding than any he had previously faced: he wants to explore human feelings, especially human passion; he refuses to acknowledge the bonds (or bounds) placed on feeling and its expression by his contemporaries (whether poets or politicians); and yet bounds of some sort have to be set, if only because he is so aware of the dangers of an unbridled passion. He needs to be in a position where decorum itself can be both undermined and elevated to the greatest virtue. His mastery of the *ottava rima* is obviously one of the most important elements in this process, in that the final couplet is always there as a forceful conclusion or an equally forceful rebuff; his own attitude towards himself and his role as a poet setting the world to rights is in itself a precarious balancing-act; but it is his dependence on the myth of a lost Eden which deserves some fuller exploration at this point, as it is this which lies behind everything else he says on the subject of feeling and passion.

I have already pointed to the significance of Milton's presence, not only in the Dedication, but in the poem as a whole. Against the obvious *gravitas* of that initial mention we might set the first appearance of Adam and Eve in the poem proper. Byron is describing Juan's parents, in particular the too-perfect Donna Inez:

> Perfect she was, but as perfection is
>   Insipid in this naughty world of ours,
> Where our first parents never learned to kiss
>   Till they were exiled from their earlier bowers,
> Where all was peace and innocence and bliss
>   (I wonder how they got through the twelve hours).
> Don Jóse, like a lineal son of Eve,
> Went plucking various fruit without her leave.
>
> (I.xviii)

At this early stage in the poem, the tone is light; Byron is not anxious to conjure up much sympathy for someone very like his wife. This 'naughty world of ours' is not so terrible, and certainly preferable to the chaste innocence of Eden; if Donna Inez seems to belong, in her perfection, to a prelapsarian world, then thank God for the fall.

But when Byron is trying to describe the nature of love, later on in the first canto, the reference to Eden assumes a darker colour. The passage in which this occurs is complicated, because it is part of a long rhetorical device which appeals to the very rules it is anxious to break; furthermore, the reference to chastity acquires, in retrospect, an irony we might not, at first reading, give it credit for:

> Here my chaste Muse a liberty must take.
>   Start not, still chaster reader, she'll be nice hence-
> Forward, and there is no great cause to quake.
>   This liberty is a poetic licence,
> Which some irregularity may make
>   In the design, and as I have a high sense
> Of Aristotle and the rules, 'tis fit
> To beg his pardon when I err a bit.
>
> (I.cxx)

The poet then launches into a series of repetitive clauses — ''Tis sweet to see . . . 'tis sweet to listen . . . 'tis sweet view', and so on, covering a whole range of experiences commonly celebrated in verse. The list extends over five stanzas, and, the longer it continues, the more the reader expects some kind of rebuff. Eventually it comes:

> But sweeter still than this, than these, than all
>   Is first and passionate love. It stands alone,
> Like Adam's recollection of his fall.
>   The tree of knowledge has been plucked; all's known,
> And life yields nothing further to recall
>   Worthy of this ambrosial sin, so shown
> No doubt in fable as the unforgiven
> Fire which Prometheus filched for us from heaven.
>
> (I.cxxvii)

This is far removed from that earlier jauntiness with which Byron treated Don Jóse's peccadilloes. Whatever the ambivalence of the images, there is no equivocation in the utterance:

the poet is speaking out, in the way he does, announcing a truth it is important for us to grasp. We are not in a position to question the value that is being placed on 'first and passionate love'. But what is intriguing is the immediate emphasis on loss; whereas in stanza xviii, quoted above, Eden seemed well lost, here passionate love is a literally singular occurrence likened not just to the fall, but to 'Adam's recollection' of it. The previous stanza had concluded, 'and dear the schoolboy spot / We ne'er forget, though there we are forgot' (I.cxxvi). That potentially sentimental view of the past is here transformed: we move from the adult remembering a sweet childhood, to our first father's remembering of the event; recollection is part of the experience, and once it has occurred, there is 'nothing further to recall / Worthy of this ambrosial sin'. For all the implied claims of the phrase 'ambrosial sin', we cannot evade sin's consequences. Once the 'tree of knowledge has been plucked', there is nothing left to know. Adam's finest moment is also his saddest; and yet there is no recollection to match that one. The full weight of 'alone', at the end of the second line, becomes apparent: there is a desperate sense of isolation, precisely the experience of Adam and Eve. Whereas before the fall they were harmonious and intertwined, mutually dependent, after the fall they became two separate people, going their sad and solitary way. All of this is contained in Byron's economical stanza. He does not, however, leave it at that. He likens the 'ambrosial sin' to the 'unforgiven / Fire which Prometheus filched for us from heaven'. The myth of Prometheus was a potent one for most of the Romantics, but Byron cannot here aspire to Shelley's optimism. What he does is to inject into the myth the unforgiving Calvinism which so easily attaches itself to the fall. Although there is an attempt to shrug off the comparison ('so shown /No doubt in fable . . .'), we cannot readily evade the implications. The effect is that by the end of the stanza 'first and passionate love' has become a much more complicated blessing than that first sentence would have led us to suppose.

The stanzas that follow demonstrate how seriously Byron takes those complications. It is not possible to talk of love and passion, in his terms, without talking about knowledge. The myths of Adam and Eve, and of Prometheus, raise the question of the nature of humanity and creativity, of the relationship between knowledge and feeling. Byron opens out into a series of stanzas in which he marvels, particularly, at the wonders of the present day:

> Man's a strange animal and makes strange use
> Of his own nature and the various arts,
> And likes particularly to produce
> Some new experiment to show his parts.
> This is the age of oddities let loose . . . .

> What opposite discoveries we have seen,
> Signs of true genius and of empty pockets!
> One makes new noses, one a guillotine,
> One breaks your bones, one sets them in their sockets.
> But vaccination certainly has been
> A kind of antithesis to Congreve's rockets,
> With which the Doctor paid off an old pox,
> By borrowing a new one from an ox.

> Bread has been made (indifferent) from potatoes;
> And galvanism has set some corpses grinning,
> But has not answered like the apparatus
> Of the Humane Society's beginning,
> By which men are unsuffocated gratis.
> What wondrous new machines have late been spinning!
> I said the smallpox has gone out of late;
> Perhaps it may be followed by the great.

> . . .

> Man's a phenomenon, one knows not what,
> And wonderful beyond all wondrous measure.
> 'Tis pity though in this sublime world that
> Pleasure's a sin and sometimes sin's a pleasure.
> Few mortals know what end they would be at,
> But whether glory, power or love or treasure,
> The path is through perplexing ways, and when
> The goal is gained, we die you know – and then?
>
> (I.cxxviii–cxxx, cxxxiii)

The references to syphilis were removed from the first edition, to spare offence; but we can see how crucial those stanzas are to the tone of the whole, which is offered as a digression ('What then? I do not know, no more do you, / And so good night. Return we to our story'), but which is a logical progression from the mention of Adam and Prometheus. Byron confronts the possible consequences of that first 'ambrosial sin', makes the connection between Adam's recollected nakedness and modern man's inclination 'to show his parts', the connection between sexual passion and its extreme results. Since the fall, there is no clear certainty about anything: smallpox could be replaced by something worse, sin and pleasure can become interchangeable; we do not know where we are going or why. The expulsion from Eden entails a world and a lifetime of wandering, with no knowledge of what awaits us. The question 'and then?' is asked frequently in *Don Juan*; Byron always reserves the right to withhold an answer – this is as true of his narrative technique as it is of his moral universe. The irony in this particular instance is that, after that image of Adam looking at his fall, after the facetious extension of Promethean defiance to new discoveries such as Congreve's rockets and the Davy lamp (just to limit the instances to those picking up the image of fire) – after that, Byron proceeds to the continuation of the affair between Juan and Julia, where, again, the question 'and then?' has considerable importance. But he does not let the Eden reference slip quietly away.

There is a remarkable mingling of tones within one stanza at the point where the wronged husband Alphonso has entered the bedroom with his suspicions, but his searches have revealed nothing; he has apologised ('He would not justify what he had done; / To say the best, it was extreme ill-breeding'), and he is on the verge of departure. This is a perfect example of Byron's ability to keep the verse poised, before the narrative turn of the final line, which leads to the pragmatic question of the next stanza.

> Alphonso closed his speech and begged her pardon,
> Which Julia half withheld and then half granted
> And laid conditions, he thought, very hard on,
> Denying several little things he wanted.
> He stood like Adam lingering near his garden,

> With useless penitence perplexed and haunted,
> Beseeching she no further would refuse,
> When lo! he stumbled o'er a pair of shoes.
>
> A pair of shoes. What then?
>
> (I.clxxx–clxxxi)

In the first part of the stanza, Julia is entirely in control: her reluctance to give ground is caught in 'half withheld and then half granted', which do not cancel each other out, because it is a temporal sequence of events: half-granted pardon is often worse than pardon fully withheld. The reference to Adam, though, lends Alphonso a certain literary dignity, at least for a brief moment. The Miltonic echo requires the reader's recollection:

> Whereat
> In either hand the hastening angel caught
> Our lingering parents, and to the eastern gate
> Led them direct.
>
> (*Paradise Lost*, XII.636–9)

The final lines of *Paradise Lost* are almost unbearably poignant, with their quiet containment of loss and possible hope. There is no doubt that these lines moved often through Byron's mind: for him, as for Wordsworth, that conclusion, that expulsion from Eden, was a challenge to which he returned repeatedly. If the earth lay all before him, behind lay Paradise. That Byron should allude to the passage at this point of high farce (with Juan hiding in the closet and Julia denying his very presence) is an indication of how seriously he is taking the episode. The only appropriate comparison (and I am aware of the dangers) would be with the Mozart of *Figaro*. Mozart can make his music do what words by themselves never could: he can render absurdity into sublimity and give due weight to both. Byron's use of the *ottava rima* comes close to a similar kind of effect. The farcical episode is there, throughout the stanza; but the Miltonic reference is like a beautiful aria that we do not expect here, an echo of another, higher world, where questions such as 'What then?' have little relevance.

It is instructive to notice Byron's first thoughts here:

> He stood like Adam lingering near his garden,
> His Eve with all the innocence she vaunted . . . .[4]

The temptation to introduce Eve in the same breath as Adam is understandable; but it makes Julia into Eve, in terms of the simile, and undermines the Miltonic reference – by the end of the last book of *Paradise Lost* Adam and Eve are beyond the stage of mutual reproach, and they leave the garden 'hand in hand'. Milton emphasises the contrast between 'the hastening angel' with a job to do, and 'Our lingering parents', reluctant to leave their Paradise. Byron's second thought takes a different tack.

> He stood like Adam lingering near his garden,
> With base suspicion now no longer haunted . . . .

Although the reference to Eve has gone, the alteration is in no other respect an improvement: in Milton, base suspicion is neither here nor there, and to have the other single line doing all the work of the literary allusion is to ask too much of it. The third version, we can now see, has a particular quality which Byron knew he wanted to keep:

> He stood like Adam lingering near his garden,
> With useless penitence perplexed and haunted . . . .

Both these lines refer to Alfonso; but they also refer to Adam, in a way that the earlier versions could not. In this moment of pause, this backward look – so typical of Byron early and late – Alfonso and Adam merge. Adam too was uselessly penitent and perplexed; and we remember the 'unforgiven / Fire which Prometheus filch'd for us from heaven': penitence is useless when there is no forgiveness. This is a far remove, it would seem, within the space of nine lines, from Alfonso's 'begged her pardon', and Julia's coy response: social graces give way to theological perplexities of some magnitude. And those perplexities have already reared their heads: 'The path is through perplexing ways . . . and then?' Byron expects us to catch this echo, to be haunted by it as are his protagonists. As

Alfonso stands there in perplexity, he recollects, like Adam of stanza cxxvii, the fall and its implications, he remembers what he is about to lose, he remembers the paradise of 'first and passionate love'. It is a remarkable and moving moment of empathy with Don Alfonso, who is otherwise not allowed much psychological leeway; but it is, equally, a pointer to the imagery of a lost Eden that colours encounters ranging from the apparently ridiculous to the idyllic.

The most idyllic relationship in the poem is that between Juan and Haidée, and it is not surprising that Byron should resort to the paradisal reference; it is, perhaps, more surprising that the reference is so sparse. It seems to be important for Byron that early in his description of Haidée he should hint at her destructive force; she is, it transpires, a Lamia-like figure, immensely attractive and colourful, but with a hint of corruption about her. All the work, though, is done by the phrase describing the colour of her eyes, those dark eyes that Byron himself always found so appealing.

> Her hair, I said, was auburn, but her eyes
>   Were black as death, their lashes the same hue,
> Of downcast length, in whose silk shadow lies
>   Deepest attraction, for when to the view
> Forth from its raven fringe the full glance flies,
>   Ne'er with such force the swiftest arrow flew.
> 'Tis as the snake late coiled, who pours his length
> And hurls at once his venom and his strength.
>
>   (II.cxvii)

Out of context, much of this could seem very similar to Byron's descriptions of eyes in his narrative poems; and even the snake of the final couplet might be taken in our stride, were it not for the startling way this whole passage is isolated, as an authorial comment. It is curiously insidious, in that Haidée is being presented to us as something of a goddess; but she becomes for us – not for Juan, not for herself – a serpent, and we are tempted to think of Satan, disguised as a serpent in the Garden of Eden. So Byron has first of all introduced the serpent and its connotations; he then proceeds to construct Eden around it, or more properly around the two central characters who are unaware of the serpent.

The account of that relationship is one of the best things Byron ever did, and it is only when he has established its uniqueness and importance that he mentions Eden by name. This is at the famous beginning of canto IV, after he has announced,

> And the sad truth which hovers o'er my desk
> Turns what was once romantic to burlesque.
>
> (IV.iii)

Don Juan as a whole demonstrates that the reversal is by no means so simple or clear-cut as this would imply. There is no sense of burlesque about this account of the two lovers:

> They were alone once more; for them to be
>   Thus was another Eden. They were never
> Weary, unless when separate. The tree
>   Cut from its forest root of years, the river
> Dammed from its fountain, the child from the knee
>   And breast maternal weaned at once forever
> Would wither less than these two torn apart.
> Alas, there is no instinct like the heart —
>
> The heart — which may be broken. Happy they,
>   Thrice fortunate who of that fragile mould,
> The precious porcelain of human clay,
>   Break with the first fall. They can ne'er behold
> The long year linked with heavy day on day
>   And all which must be borne and never told,
> While life's strange principle will often lie
> Deepest in those who long the most to die.
>
> (IV.x–xi)

This soltitude is not that of Adam and Eve expelled from the Garden, but of Adam and Eve in harmony, working together in perfect interdependence. Byron appeals to some of his most frequent naturalistic images in order to stress the perfection of this couple. But, as with Adam and Eve, it is a perfection that depends on their staying together – Byron will have none of Eve's pragmatic independence. And so he puts the state of their Eden in terms of what it would be like if they were not together. The word 'apart' provides him with the obvious rhyme – 'heart' – which enables him to explore the intense fragility of 'human clay'. Eden has already disappeared, for we are now talking about mortals, not immortals, and the imagery of broken pottery does not by any means eliminate the full significance of that 'first fall'. The notion of the *felix culpa* is perverted: 'Happy they / Thrice fortunate who . . . Break with the first fall.' The torture of the myth is that we are granted life after the fall. For Byron, Eden would ideally be a place of youth, not eternal, but happy so long as it lasted:

> And yet they could not be
> Meant to grow old, but die in happy spring,
> Before one charm or hope had taken wing.
>
> (IV.viii)

In the ninth stanza Byron first wrote:

> Lightning might assail
> And shiver them to ashes, but to trail
> A long and withering life of slow decay
> Was not for them – they had too little clay . . . .

That penultimate line became, 'A long and snake-like life of dull decay', and in that change Byron rounded the circle of the image he had hinted at two cantos previously in his description of Haidée's eyes.

The ambiguities of Eden emerge very starkly in Byron's description of Haidée later in the same canto, after the confrontation between Juan and her father. Once again, it is Byron's final thought that counts. He originally wrote,

> Her mother was a moorish maid from Fez,
> Born of the Sun as Afric's climate is . . . .

The weakness of this is sufficiently evident; the blotting of this line produced a much more disturbing final couplet:

> Her mother was a Moorish maid from Fez,
> Where all is Eden, or a wilderness.
>
> (IV.liv)

The alternative is a startling one, for the implication is that Eden contains within itself its opposite. Once again, the description of Fez is, in essence, a description of Eden:

> There the large olive rains its amber store
> In marble fonts; there grain and flower and fruit
> Gush from the earth until the land runs o'er;
> But there too many a poison-tree has root,
> And midnight listens to the lion's roar,
> And long, long deserts scorch the camel's foot
> Or heaving whelm the helpless caravan.
> And as the soil is, so the heart of man.
>
> (IV.lv)

The universalising final sentence takes us beyond Fez, to humanity in general: we all carry within us the poison-tree of Eden. The next stanza, more specific, is also dependent on the earlier use of the Prometheus myth, and on the notion of 'human decay'. That 'unforgiven fire' and the 'first fall' are part of the same process.

> Afric is all the sun's, and as her earth
> Her human clay is kindled. Full of power
> For good or evil, burning from its birth,
> The Moorish blood partakes the planet's hour,
> And like the soil beneath it will bring forth.
> Beauty and love were Haidée's mother's dower,
> But her large dark eye showed deep passion's force,
> Though sleeping like a lion near a source.
>
> (IV.lvi)

The comforts of Eden become increasingly bleak as the poem moves into its savage attack on war in cantos VII and VIII. Byron resorts to the idea of Eden to demonstrate how well and truly lost it is.

> 'Let there be light', said God, and there was light!
> 'Let there be blood', says man, and there's a sea!
> The fiat of this spoiled child of the night
> (For day ne'er saw his merits) could decree
> More evil in an hour than thirty bright

Summers could renovate, though they should be
Lovely as those which ripened Eden's fruit,
For war cuts up not only branch, but root.

(VII.xli)

The appeal to Eden, even in a simile, is useless. The image of loveliness turns on the summers that 'ripened Eden's fruit', and of course there is one fruit in particular that had better not been ripened. The surprised decorum of the third line is overwhelmed by the tide of blood.

Byron has one other allusion to the 'fruit of that forbidden tree' in his war cantos, and it is a *tour de force* of utter ghastliness. He extends Milton's own play with ideas of taste/distaste/disgust beyond Milton's wildest nightmares.[5]

A Russian officer in martial tread
  Over a heap of bodies felt his heel
Seized fast, as if 'twere by the serpent's head,
  Whose fangs Eve taught her human seed to feel.
In vain he kicked and swore and writhed and bled
  And howled for help as wolves do for a meal.
The teeth still kept their gratifying hold,
As do the subtle snakes described of old.

A dying Moslem, who had felt the foot
  Of a foe o'er him, snatched at it and bit
The very tendon which is most acute
  (That which some ancient Muse or modern wit
Named after thee, Achilles), and quite through't
  He made the teeth meet, nor relinquished it
Even with his life, for (but they lie) 'tis said
To the live leg still clung the severed head.

(VIII.lxxxiii–lxxxiv)

Love and glory, addressed at the beginning of canto VII, here find their grim apotheosis. Byron drives the point home by using the very verb – 'feel' – he has earlier celebrated as necessary to humanity.

It is perhaps that very opening of canto VII which best sums up the tenor of the poem as a whole. In terms of the narrative, Byron jumps very suddenly from the lengthy account of

Juan's stay in the harem and his encounter with the voracious Gulbeyaz to an equally lengthy account of war. He offers it, in fact, as a 'digression' (VI.cxx), but it is of course no such thing. How Juan gets out of the harem and into the lines of battle is unimportant; what matters is that we see the thematic and causal connections. Love and warfare are not only not so very different; the one can easily lead to the other.

> Oh Love! Oh Glory! what are ye who fly
>   Around us ever, rarely to alight?
> There's not a meteor in the polar sky
>   Of such transcendent and more fleeting flight.
> Chill and chained to cold earth, we lift on high
>   Our eyes in search of either lovely light.
> A thousand and a thousand colours they
> Assume, then leave us on our freezing way.
>
> And such as they are, such my present tale is,
>   A nondescript and ever varying rhyme,
> A versified aurora borealis,
>   Which flashes o'er a waste and icy clime.
> When we know what all are, we must bewail us,
>   But ne'ertheless I hope it is no crime
> To laugh at all things, for I wish to know
> What after all are all things – but a show?
>
> (VII.i–ii)

It is all too easy for us to refer to Byron's 'versified aurora borealis', as though he were involved in some magnificent firework display. The pyrotechnics are there, certainly, and they provide some of the richest rewards for Byron's readers – as he himself suggests at the end of that second stanza, everything might just be 'a show' anyway, in which case we might as well join in the fun, 'showing our parts' as best we can. But there is more to it than that. Byron is saying here that his own performance matches that of love and glory, those tantalising abstractions which do nothing so much as remind us of our own mortality. He reverts to one of his frequent and favourite images of confinement to express the conflicting tugs, as we recognise a freedom and a light that is to be denied us: the transcendental is linked to – and cancelled out by – its fleetingness. We can marvel briefly at the glorious display, high above us, but then we are left 'on our freezing way', perplexed as ever ('The path is through perplexing ways' – I.cxxxiii). All Byron as poet can do is to match those 'thousand and a thousand colours', producing a performance 'Which flashes o'er a waste and icy clime'. He is dismissing his 'nondescript and ever varying rhyme', but at the same time it is equivalent to love and glory, equivalent to the brightest meteors in the sky. Like them, his verse is transcendent and fleeting, both a blessing and a curse, providing at least a brief and glorious splash of colour, even whilst reminding us of the 'waste and icy clime' we inhabit. He can, in his verse, make the transcendent leap, escaping the cold chains, but to do so is to be reminded of the meteor's teasing, 'fleeting flight'. This all takes us back to the talk of aspirations in the Dedication, where he spoke of chains, of the lack of fear 'because no feeling dwells in ice'. He had spoken of his determination not to acknowledge those chains, that frozen world of non-feeling. But here we seem to have a conjunction that cannot be denied,

> A versified aurora borealis,
> Which flashes o'er a waste and icy clime.

The two coexist, but there is no doubt about which is the more permanent. Furthermore, glory itself is not just an attractive chimera.

The invocation to canto VIII is unequivocal:

> Oh blood and thunder! And oh blood and wounds!
>   These are but vulgar oaths as you may deem,
> Too gentle reader, and most shocking sounds.
>   And so they are; yet thus is glory's dream
> Unriddled, and as my true Muse expounds
>   At present such things, since they are her theme,
> So be they her inspirers. Call them Mars,
> Bellona, what you will – they mean but wars.

> . . .

> History can only take things in the gross;
>   But could we know them in detail, perchance

> In balancing the profit and the loss,
>   War's merit it by no means might enhance,
> To waste so much gold for a little dross,
>   As hath been done, mere conquest to advance.
> The drying up a single tear has more
> Of honest fame than shedding seas of gore.
>
> (VIII.i, iii)

Glory's dream, then, has been unriddled, and so, by extension and implication, has love's. Love and glory were, a canto earlier, two 'lovely lights', the meteors Byron's verse would emulate. Now, however, they are shown in their true colours, and this is no time to be decorous. We have to be honest, and learn, as he says elsewhere, 'to call things by their right name'. It is Byron's insistence on things as they are that makes him such a devastating critic of war. He turns to the details, for only then can we learn the truth – which means attending to this 'waste and icy clime', in part denying the dreams of poetry, as well as those of love and glory. Particularity and precision bring him back to human feeling, to recognition of others' suffering.

The paradox is that human feeling itself, in the form of passionate love, can lead to war. Byron addresses this paradox in a characteristically paradoxical fashion when he contemplates Catherine the Great of Russia. This deserves some discussion before we explore further his desire to approach love with 'due decorum' and 'due precision'.

> Oh thou *teterrima causa* of all *belli* –
>   Thou gate of life and death – thou nondescript!
> Whence is our exit and our entrance. Well I
>   May pause in pondering how all souls are dipt
> In thy perennial fountain. How man fell, I
>   Know not, since knowledge saw her branches stript
> Of her first fruit; but how he falls and rises
> Since, thou hast settled beyond all surmises.
>
> Some call thee 'the worst cause of war', but I
>   Maintain thou art the best, for after all
> From thee we come, to thee we go, and why
>   To get at thee not batter down a wall

Or waste a world, since no one can deny
    Thou dost replenish worlds both great and small?
With or without thee all things at a stand
Are or would be, thou sea of life's dry land!
                                        (IX.lv—lvi)

Byron's Horatian quotation is, as his editors point out, 'prudent', in that he omits the crucial word *cunnus*, whereby Horace reduces all of womankind to one common organ.[6] But the omission, whilst 'prudent', is pointless unless we supply the Latin word: any translation such as 'wench' or 'woman' is totally inadequate, for everything that is said about the 'worst cause of war' has reference to female sexuality. All the Shakespearean talk of exits and entrances will not conceal what it is that is being entered; similarly the gate of life and death, whatever its other possible references, is the place of sexual consummation, of the life that can be the consequence thereof, a life that in Byron's terms leads only to death, but also the death that goes with such consummation (not to mention the impotence of a Southey or a Castlereagh). That 'perrenial fountain' provides a curious moisture, whereby we are in some odd way baptised; at least we have moved from 'quite a dry Bob'. It is as though Byron had himself made that transition of thought, for the rest of the stanza is devoted to a *double entendre* which plays on impotence but also on the fall in the Garden of Eden. Byron claims not to know how man fell, since the tree of knowledge was in the process 'stript / Of her first fruit'; but he is in no doubt about the subsequent 'falls and rises', and we are in no doubt that the discussion has moved from the female to the male organ (when, in XI.xxv, he describes the Mansion House as 'a stiff yet grand erection', the humour is more blatantly coarse, but even there the architectural dismissal is balanced by the sexual admiration). At this juncture in the poem, Byron is prepared to challenge the Horatian dictum; far from being the 'worst cause of war', the female and her organ is the best, and, again, the *double entendre* of the final couplet makes his point for him. It is, all in all, an extremely witty, if cynical, passage, and ironically, in that it is so cynical, a reversal of the deeply gloomy view of love that had emerged in the course of the war cantos. The brief moment of sexual fulfilment is worth a war, since it is the potential source of such fecundity – even the 'waste and icy clime' might be reclaimed. To make us remember that chilled phrase from the beginning of canto VII, Byron calls this *teterrima causa*, this *cunnus*, what he had called his own verse – 'thou nondescript!' The ever-varying rhyme, the aurora borealis, love, war, death, sex – they are all focused in these two stanzas, and those final two lines make the ironic point that, depending on the level of innuendo, 'all things' are 'at a stand' anyway. The next stanza spells it out:

> Catherine, who was the grand epitome
>   Of that great cause of war or peace or what
> You please (it causes all the things which be,
>   So you may take your choice of this or that) . . . .
>
> (IX.lvii)

Just in case we think this is an isolated instance of Byron's doing rather more than making the best of things, the 'exordium' to canto X picks up the same image of sexual potency, and links it to Adam's fall and to the acquisition of knowledge. Perhaps the arguments of the serpent – and Eve – were not all that far-fetched: perhaps that knowledge was necessary.

> When Newton saw an apple fall, he found
>   In that slight startle from his contemplation –
> 'Tis said (for I'll not answer above ground
>   For any sage's creed or calculation) –
> A mode of proving that the earth turned round
>   In a most natural whirl called gravitation;
> And this is the sole mortal who could grapple,
> Since Adam, with a fall or with an apple.
>
> Man fell with apples and with apples rose,
>   If this be true; for we must deem the mode
> In which Sir Isaac Newton could disclose
>   Through the then unpaved stars the turnpike road
> A thing to counterbalance human woes.
>   For ever since immortal man hath glowed
> With all kinds of mechanics, and full soon
> Steam-engines will conduct him to the moon.
>
> (X.i–ii)

This is another instance of Byron's brilliance when it comes to making connections. The innocent noun and verb of the first line become, by the ninth line, two separate nouns, and yet in that separation they are linked more significantly, just as Newton and Adam become on a par. But, whereas before, particularly in canto I, Adam was a potentially tragic figure, aware of loss and pain, here he is someone who can cope with the problem, who can take fall and apple in his stride. The first fall was perhaps fortunate after all, in that sexuality led to knowledge, an understanding that made sense of those 'perplexing ways'. These stanzas seem to be an answer to that long section in canto I where the implications of the fall, and of the filching of the fire from heaven, were explored in ways that offered little comfort: the 'patent age of new inventions' (I.cxxxii) was beyond comprehension. But here there is the glow of excitement that comes with scientific discovery, and it is matched by the 'glorius glow' within the poet's bosom, the glow of hope and aspiration. The rhyme 'rose'/'woes' is an echo of the 'proper woes' of Gulbeyaz in canto VI, with which I began this chapter. It is a complicating echo, for Byron is here suggesting that what he can do as a poet is comparable to what the scientists can offer: it is possible to 'counterbalance human woes', and to do so with a combination of daring, knowledge and spiritual fire. Man, it transpires, is immortal – a far cry from being a 'strange animal'. He is a reconstituted Adam, but also, in his fiery glow, a Prometheus unbound, a Prometheus forgiven.

The personal application of this revelation to Byron's own role as a poet is honest, simple, and strangely touching. The bounds observed by most have to be crossed, whatever the risks:

> In the wind's eye I have sailed and sail, but for
>   The stars, I own my telescope is dim.
> But at the least I have shunned the common shore,
>   And leaving land far out of sight, would skim
> The ocean of eternity. The roar
>   Of breakers has not daunted my slight, trim,
> But still seaworthy skiff, and she may float
> Where ships have foundered, as doth many a boat.
>
> (X.iv)

A similar urge had been there in *Childe Harold*, but there was, by the end, a sense of failure. What Byron is saying here has all the courage earned by someone who has refused to let it 'stagnate to a vice'. He had, we should remember, taken a passionate leave of passion at the end of canto I:

> No more – no more – oh never more on me
>   The freshness of the heart can fall like dew,
> Which out of all the lovely things we see
>   Extracts emotions beautiful and new,
> Hived in our bosoms like the bag o' the bee.
>   Think'st thou the honey with those objects grew?
> Alas, 'twas not in them, but in thy power
> To double even the sweetness of a flower.
>
> No more – no more – oh never more, my heart,
>   Canst thou be my sole world, my universe!
> Once all in all, but now a thing apart,
>   Thou canst not be my blessing or my curse.
> The illusion's gone forever, and thou art
>   Insensible, I trust, but none the worse,
> And in thy stead I've got a deal of judgement,
> Though heaven knows how it ever found a lodgement.
>
>   (I.ccxiv–ccxv)

This is not, though, to disown what he had championed in the Dedication: *Don Juan* is given over to a scrupulous examination of varieties of feeling, the more scrupulous, perhaps, because of that 'deal of judgement' (however it got there). He goes on, in a subsequent stanza,

>   A chymic treasure
> Is that same Time so common yet so precious
> Of which we are lavish first and then rapacious

but, dissatisfied with that, he produces this:

>   A chymic treasure
> Is glittering youth, which I have spent betimes,
> My heart in passion and my head on rhymes.
>   (I.ccxvii)

I would not want to go along with the rather too easy notion that this sums up the Byronic contradiction of 'Romantic' and 'Augustan'.[7] But the opposition within the line deserves attention. If passion and rhymes are antithetical, they are also complementary; if Byron is saying farewell to his 'days of love', he is also acknowledging their beauty and loveliness; and in continuing to rhyme he is continuing to pay his dues to passion. (No poet is more conscious that to be a poet is to rhyme.) This farewell to love is no straightforward matter. The 'illusion' might have gone but the true feeling is still there. What he has gained is 'judgement', which enables the poem to proceed. At a significant moment, much later in the poem, when he is discussing what he is doing in *Don Juan*, Byron makes a point that has a particular bearing on this. However modest the work, however desultory the rhyme, things have to be ordered just so. Once he has examined the details (which history refuses) he has to make of them a general application:

> The difficulty lies in colouring
> (Keeping the due proportions still in sight)
> With Nature manners which are artificial,
> And rendering general that which is especial.
>
> (XV.xxv)

It is those due proportions which are essential.

There are, of course, different kinds of balance, different forms of correctness. The irony in his comments arising out of his account of relations between Gulbeyaz and her husband should put us on our guard:

> A slight blush, a soft tremor, a calm kind
> Of gentle feminine delight and shown
> More in the eyelids than the eyes, resigned
> Rather to hide what pleases most unknown,
> Are the best tokens (to a modest mind)
> Of love, when seated on his loveliest throne,
> A sincere woman's breast, for over warm
> Or over cold annihilates the charm.

> For over warmth, if false, is worse than truth.
>   If true, 'tis no great lease of its own fire,
> For no one, save in very early youth,
>   Would like (I think) to trust all to desire,
> Which is but a precarious bond in sooth
>   And apt to be transferred to the first buyer
> At a sad discount; while your over chilly
> Women, on t'other hand, seem somewhat silly.
>
> That is, we cannot pardon their bad taste,
>   For so it seems to lovers swift or slow,
> Who fain would have a mutual flame confest
>   And see a sentimental passion glow,
> Even were St Francis' paramour their guest
>   In his monastic concubine of snow.
> In short, the maxim for the amorous tribe is
> Horatian: *medio tu tutissimus ibis*.
>
>   (VI.xv–xvii)

Such apparent scorn of passion, however, is not the universal mode of Byron's works, not even in *Don Juan*. There are sufficient indications of his deep respect for true feeling, as I have been suggesting; the problem, though, is how to put some kind of check on passions that, if we are not careful, can be volcanically destructive. His appeal to taste here is typically double-edged: although taste can form part of his essential vocabulary, he is not persuaded by the forms of taste that are, in fact, little more than convenience and convention. That Horace is being abused here seems clear by the turn the next stanza takes, in which he debates the correctness of his own Latinity, and of his own prosody.

Byron's subsequent description of Lady Adeline calls into question the very maxim he seems to be espousing here: her 'perfectly correct' conduct is no guarantee of real control.

> She loved her lord or thought so, but that love
>   Cost her an effort, which is a sad toil,
> The stone of Sisyphus, if once we move
>   Our feelings 'gainst the nature of the soil.
> She had nothing to complain of or reprove,
>   No bickerings, no connubial turmoil;

Their union was a model to behold,
Serene and noble, conjugal, but cold.

There was no great disparity of years,
  Though much in temper, but they never clashed.
They moved like stars united in their spheres,
  Or like the Rhone by Leman's waters washed,
Where mingled and yet separate appears
  The river from the lake, all bluely dashed
Through the serene and placid glassy deep,
Which fain would lull its river child to sleep.
                              (XIV.lxxxvi–lxxxvii)

On the surface, then, everything is fine, the perfect society marriage. It is an interestingly careful account of such a union, in that Byron elicits sympathy, as so often, for an otherwise unsympathetic character. The effort of her love is precisely in its unnaturalness, in its denial of feelings. At the same time, that second stanza has indeed the serenity and nobility mentioned as public virtues in the first. Byron had resorted to the same image of Lake Leman in *Childe Harold*, III.lxxi (see p. 137), where it had been a celebration of passion. The 'stars united in their spheres' might even recall that beautiful evocation of domestic harmony in the prose gloss to 'The Ancient Mariner'; certainly the relationship between river and lake, as spelled out here, could be regarded as a model of marital harmony, where the mingling of waters does not deny their individuality. And the hint of mother and child is strong enough for it to seem a desirable virtue.

None the less, this cluster of stanzas needs to be taken as a whole; as the passage proceeds, it becomes a matter of moral and semantic distinctions. Firmness, for example, can become obstinacy:

And 'twill perplex the casuists in morality
To fix the due bounds of this dangerous quality.

. . . .

  I leave it to your people of sagacity
To draw the line between the false and true . . . .
                              (XIV.lxxxix–xc)

Byron is not shrugging off the problem of definition: rather, he is drawing his readers into that moral area where judgements are apt to be too easy and therefore wrong. There are feelings developing between Adeline and Juan which demand our full attention, because they make such imperious and yet such equivocal claims. The serenity that exists between Adeline and her master has that dangerous coldness about it against which Byron frequently warns. But love presents its complications:

> Love bears within its breast the very germ
>   Of change; and how should this be otherwise?
> That violent things more quickly find a term
>   Is shown through nature's whole analogies.
> And how should the most fierce of all be firm?
>   Would you have endless lightning in the skies?
> Methinks love's very title says enough;
> How should the tender passion e'er be tough?
>
> (XIV.xciv)

In the face of such questions, it suits Byron to leave Juan and 'chaste Adeline', at the end of the canto, 'hovering, as the effect is fine / And keeps the atrocious reader in suspense' (XIV.xcvii). This is not just a matter of narrative or commercial convenience. In terms of emotion, of the extent and depth of feeling and passion, he wants to leave the matter undecided, so that definitions can be worked out, to establish what exactly are the 'due bounds'. The pun on 'term' is significant: in finding their 'ends', things find their bounds and definitions (see p. 80). But Byron is no longer ready to seek solace in Horace.

In the previous canto, Byron had come up against the paradox presented by Adeline and her 'calm patrician polish'. It is an important passage for its very deliberate reworking of a familiar image. It has an obvious bearing on the 'waste and icy clime' of canto VI, but it has a further bearing on the very notion of coldness, and I think helps to explain the later passage I have just been discussing. Definitions and due bounds are that much harder to be precise about if this coldness has a value 'beyond all price': and dramatic irony is lent to Adeline's dismissal of the young Aurora Raby as 'silent' and 'cold' (XV.xlix; see p. 223).

But Adeline was not indifferent, for –
    Now for a commonplace – beneath the snow,
As a volcano holds the lava more
    Within, et cetera. Shall I go on? No.
I hate to hunt down a tired metaphor,
    So let the often used volcano go.
Poor thing. How frequently by me and others
It hath been stirred up till its smoke quite smothers.

I'll have another figure in a trice.
    What say you to a bottle of champagne,
Frozen into a very vinous ice,
    Which leaves few drops of that immortal rain.
Yet in the very centre, past all price,
    About a liquid glassful will remain,
And this is stronger than the strongest grape
Could e'er express in its expanded shape.

'Tis the whole spirit brought to a quintessence,
    And thus the chilliest aspects may concentre
A hidden nectar under a cold presence.
    And such are many, though I only meant her,
From whom I now deduce these moral lessons,
    On which the Muse has always sought to enter.
And your cold people are beyond all price,
When once you have broken their confounded ice.

(XIII.xxxvi–xxxviii)

Byron's point is in no way lessened by the attention he draws
to his role as virtuoso performer. He gets away with his im-
patient gesture at the end because he has established the value
of the other half of the equation, the balancing part of that
final couplet. The repetition of the rhyme suggests the
seriousness of the image he wants to pretend is just fished out
of nowhere. I do not think it fanciful to hear an echo of
Donne's extraordinary resort, in the 'Nocturnall upon St
Lucy's Day', to the image of a quintessence of nothingness in
order to express a terrible fullness of emotion.

Don Jóse and Donna Inez in canto I of *Don Juan* seem to
approach the Horatian middle way in their marital discord;
the tone is lighter, in any case, and the emphasis on being well-

bred has none of the quandaries attaching to Lady Adeline's 'perfect conduct'.

> Don José and Donna Inez led
>   For some time an unhappy sort of life,
> Wishing each other, not divorced, but dead.
>   They lived respectably as man and wife,
> Their conduct was exceedingly well-bred
>   And gave no outward signs of inward strife,
> Until at length the smothered fire broke out
> And put the business past all kind of doubt.
>
> (I.xxvi)

Inez's 'serenity' is of a purely social cast; propriety is for her a matter of form. This emerges in her education of her son, Juan, particularly when it comes to the classical poets. Byron is making a point about books, but more importantly about false notions of taste and decency; in a poem that focuses on the varieties of feeling, love and sexuality, he needs to set out the terms of the argument at the beginning.

> And then what proper person can be partial
> To all those nauseous epigrams of Martial?
>
> Juan was taught from out the best edition,
>   Expurgated by learnèd men, who place
> Judiciously from out the schoolboy's vision
>   The grosser parts, but fearful to deface
> Too much their modest bard by this omission
>   And pitying sore his mutilated case,
> They only add them all in an appendix,
> Which saves in fact the trouble of an index,
>
> For there we have them all at one fell swoop,
>   Instead of being scattered through the pages.
>
> (I.xliii–xlv)

Once again, those who would be most proper are shown to be anything but: unwittingly but not without guilt they elevate false modesty into a virtue, but simultaneously parade offending obscenities like Priapic garden gnomes. Those 'grosser parts' anticipate modern man's inclination, dwelt on later in this canto, 'to show his parts'. It is to be Dudù's nightmare that she confronts in her sleep those 'grosser parts' of which she had not, hitherto, dreamt.

The affair between Julia and Juan is the first in the poem to explore the contradictions of desire. Byron's description of her harks back to the immorality (because dishonesty) of a 'proper' education, and looks forward to the eruption of the volcano. Although he was later to dismiss such an image as 'commonplace', there is nothing commonplace about this.

> Her eye (I'm very fond of handsome eyes)
>   Was large and dark, suppressing half its fire
> Until she spoke; then through its soft disguise
>   Flashed an expression more of pride than ire,
> And love than either. And there would arise
>   A something in them which was not desire,
> But would have been, perhaps, but for the soul
> Which struggled though and chastened down the whole.
>
>   (I.lx)

This struggle is indeed much more like the Sisyphean toil of Adeline. The more she sees of Juan, the more she wants to see; she recognises the temptation, and retreats behind a false notion of Platonic love:

> Love then, but love within its proper limits
>   Was Julia's innocent determination
> In young Juan's favour . . . .
>
>   (I.lxxxi)

That is the crux of the matter: can love be thus confined? Julia's self-deception is such that she feels she is proof against corruption, and 'from that hour dispensed / With any kind of troublesome control' (I.lxxxii). But to do that is to be as out of control as Juan, who hides for as long as he can behind metaphysical speculations, until he is undone by thinking of Julia's eyes. Byron makes the authorial point that has been lurking beneath the surface.

How beautiful she looked! Her conscious heart
　　Glowed in her cheek, and yet she felt no wrong.
Oh Love, how perfect is thy mystic art,
　　Strengthening the weak and trampling on the strong.
How self-deceitful is the sagest part
　　Of mortals whom thy lure hath led along.
The precipice she stood on was immense,
So was her creed in her own innocence.

(I.cvi)

It is like watching a tightrope-walker poised and humbly proud, before the fall.

Thirty stanzas before this we have had the first, slight physical contact between Juan and Julia. It is a beautiful passage, illustrative not just of Julia's timid advance, which is presented almost as a retreat, but also of Byron's own controlled timidity, at the very point where control is beginning to slip from the pair.

Yet Julia's very coldness still was kind,
　　And tremulously gentle her small hand
Withdrew itself from his, but left behind
　　A little pressure, thrilling and so bland
And slight, so very slight that to the mind
　　'Twas but a doubt . . . .

(I.lxxi)

The excitement is reduced, attenuated gradually through those lines, into a doubt. But such potent doubt is the stuff of amorous attachments, certainly as they present themselves in *Don Juan*. This same image is remembered when Julia is next with Juan, and she is sternly reminding herself of Don Alfonso. Byron plays on the unconsciousness that he is later to find so appealing in Dudù.

One hand on Juan's carelessly was thrown,
Quite by mistake – she thought it was her own.

Unconsciously she leaned upon the other,
　　Which played within the tangles of her hair . . . .

The hand which still held Juan's, by degrees
   Gently but palpably confirmed its grasp,
As if it said, 'Detain me, if you please.'
    Yet there's no doubt she only meant to clasp
His fingers with a pure Platonic squeeze.
    She would have shrunk as from a toad or asp,
Had she imagined such a thing could rouse
A feeling dangerous to a prudent spouse.

                            (I.cix−cxi)

The two of them are taken aback, with a delighted, bashful surprise ('Love is so very timid when 'tis new' − I.cxii). The irony at Julia's expense cannot be denied, the irony at the expense of the whole Platonic tradition. But although he is to launch into a full-scale assault on such a creed, Byron captures the honesty of these overtures, the truth of the feeling between the pair, when the 'full soul' is in a position 'To open all itself, without the power / Of calling wholly back its self-control' (I.cxiv). There is a gentleness about this whole sequence which removes it from the realms of cynicism or anti-romanticism. Byron recognises the emotion and the sexuality: he keeps it all on a tight rein, as though he still has the control the protagonists are in the process of losing.

Just how much weight Byron wants to give to the mutual affection and desire is shown at a crucial dramatic moment later in the canto, when Don Alfonso returns at the wrong moment. The Miltonic echo (from 'Lycidas') has even greater force when it is Juan's hand that is in Julia's hair.

He turned his lip to hers and with his hand
   Called back the tangles of her wandering hair.
Even then their love they could not all command
   And half forgot their danger and despair.

                            (I.clxx)

This time, the maid Antonia undercuts this with her own sense of what is right and proper:

Antonia's patience now was at a stand;
   'Come, come, 'tis no time now for feeling there,'

> She whispered in great wrath. 'I must deposit
> This pretty gentleman within the closet.'
>
> (I.clxx)

Such matter-of-factness has its place, especially when the lord and master is at the door. But there is something even more appropriate in the lovers' gesture, in that solicitous calling-back of the straying (and therefore erring) hair; there is in fact an air of control and command in the very act, as there is too in the defiance of danger and despair. This is rather like the aged Khan's 'scorn of life' in Canto VIII (see. p. 221). Matters of fact are all very well, but emotion has its greater claims. The syntactic qualifications, which become such a common feature of Byron's love poetry, as though the immensity of the precipice requires as many toeholds as possible – these qualifications make the hesitations more precise, redefine the sense of what is proper.

Propriety seems less appropriate in the idyllic surroundings of canto II. Haidée's maid, Zoe, is there to remind them of the need for caution: she serves her lady with 'due precision' (II.158). But the love between Juan and Haidée can expand, because they feel no terror, 'they were / All in all to each other' (II.clxxxix). There is a reciprocity which calls forth from Byron some of his most lyrical writing. Their love is based on generosity, and, whilst passion is there, intensely so, it is followed by perfect repose as they sleep. Of the loved one asleep, Byron offers his own perfect version of what Keats had done in 'The Eve of St Agnes':

> For there it lies so tranquil, so beloved;
>   All that it hath of life with us is living,
> So gentle, stirless, helpless, and unmoved,
>   And all unconscious of the joy 'tis giving.
> All it hath felt, inflicted, passed, and proved,
>   Hushed into depths beyond the watcher's diving,
> There lies the thing we love with all its errors
> And all its charms, like death without its terrors.
>
> (Don Juan, II.cxcvii)

This insight lies behind Byron's later sympathy with Aurora Raby, who has a sense of the depths, in their silent immensity.

But in this earlier episode, he demonstrates his understanding of passion's paradox. For all its startling extremes, it gives way to the all-encompassing control of mutuality. Whatever the narrative brings to upset this paradise, paradise is for a time attained and contained.

6 'Emblems of Emotion': *Don Juan* (ii)

One of the central antitheses of *Don Juan* is stated at the beginning of canto XV.

> Ah! What should follow slips from my reflection.
>   Whatever follows ne'ertheless may be
> As apropos of hope or retrospection
>   As though the lurking thought had followed free.
> All present life is but an interjection,
>   An 'oh!' or 'ah!' of joy or misery
> Or a 'ha, ha!' or 'bah!' a yawn or 'pooh!'
> Of which perhaps the latter is most true.
>
> But more or less the whole's a *syncope*
>   Or a *singultus*, emblems of emotion,
> The grand antithesis to great ennui,
>   Wherewith we break our bubbles on the ocean,
> That watery outline of eternity
>   Or miniature at least, as is my notion,
> Which ministers unto the soul's delight
> In seeing matters which are out of sight.
>
> (XV.i–ii)

The worst thing for Byron is that terrible sense of eternal boredom, for which only the French word seems appropriate; it can sometimes appear something of a Romantic affectation, especially as it is dramatised in some of the earlier poems. But against it Byron sets his paradoxically rhetorical terms for swoons and sobs, which in turn become 'emblems of emotion'; what have in the first stanza been no more than barely articulate 'interjections' are transformed into something formal, part of a rhetorical structure. We could say that this is one aspect of Byron's distinctiveness, that he makes out of such simple cries of joy or sorrow something more elaborate and lasting. It seems apposite that the obvious recollection at this point is of *Childe Harold*, IV, and its elaborate image of the ocean – apposite because as we make that connection we can see the wholeness of Byron's *oeuvre*: Harold, after all, is a characterisation of the 'great ennui' in its grand, Romantic manner, and the sea becomes one of those all-embracing emblems. 'The grand antithesis' is there in both poems, but it is in *Don Juan* that Byron draws particular attention to it: his 'emblems of emotion' provide him with a means of confronting and controlling the claims of feeling. In a poem that for the most part is in various ways headlong, Byron finds it appropriate to stop dead in his tracks from time to time. It is these moments of stillness that I should like to explore; they are the logical extension of those 'due bounds' and 'due proportions' I was discussing in the previous chapter.

In canto II, Byron lavishes much of his energy on the shipwreck and the resultant cannibalism. It is one of those places where he takes great risks, embracing deep emotion and worldly cynicism in ways that manage not quite to cancel each other out. After the death of Pedrillo, Byron turns to two fathers and their sons (II.lxxxvii); the stronger son dies first, and is thrown overboard like a piece of bad meat, 'without a tear or groan'. It is the weaker boy of the other father who lasts longer.

> The other father had a weaklier child,
>   Of a soft cheek and aspect delicate,
> But the boy bore up long and with a mild
>   And patient spirit held aloof his fate.
> Little he said and now and then he smiled,
>   As if to win a part from off the weight
> He saw increasing on his father's heart,
> With the deep deadly thought that they must part.
>
> And o'er him bent his sire and never raised
>   His eyes from off his face, but wiped the foam
> From his pale lips, and ever on him gazed,
>   And when the wished-for shower at length was come,
> And the boy's eyes, which the dull film half glazed,

> Brightened and for a moment seemed to roam,
> He squeezed from out a rag some drops of rain
> Into his dying child's mouth — but in vain.
>   (II.lxxxviii—lxxxix)

This strikes me as a peculiarly Byronic image, the father bent over the son, the lover bent over the loved one, the mourner bent over the dead: from those remarkable opening lines of *The Giaour* onward, Byron has resorted to variations on this image, this emblem of emotion. It sums up the inherent contradiction of the very notion: the fullness of emotion, and the dryness, the spareness, of an emblem. Some (including Wordsworth) have argued the claims of epitaphs and inscriptions along similar lines: the pathos derives from that compression of feeling, someone's death (and life) reduced to a few words and to chiselled silence. Byron seems to think rather of a stylised, statuesque pose, reaching out for the kind of response elicited by a piece of sculpture, in which the moment is caught and held. To think thus is of course to think of Keats, and to do that is to realise (not for the first time) the un-Keatsian nature of what it is that Byron is doing. He does not approach the Keatsian richness. But his cooler, more appraising eye results in verse no less poignant. The greater detachment allows for a fullness of emotion every bit as moving as anything in Keats. What is immediately striking about this passage is the reciprocity between father and son: Byron is continually arrested by the mutual interaction of those who love each other. He recognises that the love he most values is that characterised by complete selflessness. After all the revolting details of cannibalism and madness, it is essential for him to establish this moment of repose, whilst at the same time avoiding the obvious dangers of sentimentality. There are many occasions when he uses the witty turn of the final couplet in order to ensure we do not slip into easy emotion. But to rely entirely on that built-in property of the *ottava rima* would be to depend on a formula, and Byron is careful to show that the final couplet does not have to have the snap of an epigram — indeed, he demonstrates how it can be part of a much more organic process, rather like the Miltonic as opposed to the Shakespearean sonnet. In a poem where so much seems to end in cynical despair, Byron repeatedly places these moments of emotional truth. I do not think it an accident that he is here drawn to the actual sea, in anticipation of 'That watery outline of eternity' to which he refers in XV.ii. The *syncope* and the *singultus* need to be set not simply in antithesis to some abstract idea, but in the terrible context of reality. That is why this whole episode of the shipwreck is so important, and why it is important for it to occur this early in the poem. It is impossible to read the whole poem without registering the central point that Don Juan has been flung on this wide sea, and that somehow or other he survives. How we 'break our bubbles on the ocean' is one of the poem's main preoccupations. If he can, in canto XV, reduce it all to a series of 'ohs' and 'ahs', Byron can also (as he implies there) invest those cries with an emotional significance whereby everything else can be judged. Ennui is inverted.

The weak child's patience (and as before Byron gives the word its due and proper weight) fascinates Byron. The boy can actually smile, he does what he can to make the inevitable end easier for his father. Byron combines a diction that is evidently 'poetic' with one that is deliberately casual ('and now and then he smiled'). Even at this poignant juncture he draws strength from his puns. The whole stanza is about the weight of suffering, and in that context 'the boy bore up long' is of special significance: there is a buoyant lightness about his spirit, as he 'held aloof his fate' (anticipating the line in II.cxvi, where Juan 'buoyed his boyish limbs'). As elsewhere, 'heart' has its inevitable rhyme in 'part', but, more than that, it is sandwiched between this and another 'part', which has the strange effect of lending some of the child's own buoyancy to his father, even as they both recognise 'that they must part' (for who can say to whom we should attach that final line, if not to them both equally?). The second stanza gives all of itself – one long sentence – to that reciprocal gaze of love, whereby both are momentarily strengthened, only to be deceived, or rather frustrated (behind 'but in vain' lurks the Latin *frustra*). The sense of weight and balance is carried over into the syntax, in that the final 'but in vain' has its curt echo at the start of the next stanza, 'The boy expired', before another long sentence in which the weight 'increasing on his father's heart' of stanza lxxxviii becomes the heavy weight of the dead body. And still the gaze is prolonged.

> The boy expired. The father held the clay
>   And looked upon it long, and when at last
> Death left no doubt, and the dead burden lay
>   Stiff on his heart, and pulse and hope were past,
> He watched it wistfully, until away
>   'Twas borne by the rude wave wherein 'twas cast.
> Then he himself sunk down all dumb and shivering,
> And gave no sign of life, save his limbs quivering.
>
>   (II.xc)

Within the space of three stanzas Byron has presented us with all that can be said of a dying father and son. It is difficult to imagine anything more tender or more true.

In a poem that works by echoes, by internal allusions, the 'deep deadliness' of this finds its answer before the canto is out. Juan swims to the shore, and collapses.

> And as he gazed, his dizzy brain spun fast
>   And down he sunk, and as he sunk, the sand
> Swam round and round, and all his senses passed.
>   He fell upon his side, and his stretched hand
> Drooped dripping on the oar (their jury mast),
>   And like a withered lily, on the land
> His slender frame and pallid aspect lay,
> As fair a thing as e'er was formed of clay.
>
>   (II.cx)

It is important for Byron to emphasise the almost theatrical posture of this, because in his swooning Juan resembles 'that weaklier child'; he is pale, on the verge of death, he too is 'formed by clay' and we realise that that in itself is far from being a guarantee of survival. Byron points the crucial difference between the dying boy and Juan coming back to life, in terms that are similar to those he is to apply to other statuesque figures. But, if Juan revives, we cannot but be aware how close he has been to death.

> How long in his damp trance young Juan lay
>   He knew not, for the earth was gone for him,
> And time had nothing more of night nor day
>   For his congealing blood and senses dim.

And how this heavy faintness passed away
  He knew not, till each painful pulse and limb
And tingling vein seemed throbbing back to life,
  For Death, though vanquished, still retired with strife.
                                        (II.cxi)

Furthermore, the echo is made the more powerful – and the more ominous – by the sight that greets Juan's eyes (ironically 'swimming', for he is still half asleep, and has imagined himself back in the boat – rarely can the apparently clichéd 'swimming eyes' have had such dramatic connotations): what he sees is a woman's face bending over his, in that posture of the father over the dying son. The extension is clear: Juan is like the frail youth, Haidée is like the father, and they each reflect the other.

  'Twas bending close o'er his, and the small mouth
    Seemed almost prying into his for breath.
  And chafing him, the soft warm hand of youth
    Recalled his answering spirits back from death,
  And bathing his chill temples tried to soothe
    Each pulse to animation, till beneath
  Its gentle touch and trembling care, a sigh
  To these kind efforts made a low reply.
                                        (II.cxiii)

Byron is to refer to Haidée as 'one / Fit for the model of a statuary' (II.cxviii), and although he is to dismiss immediately the breed (at some length), we drink in the image, the one head bent over the other, that moment of stillness. The earlier sculpted monument is reversed, in that she is able to bring him back to life, she provides a pillow for his 'death-like forehead', which is other than the stiff dead burden of the boy on his father's heart. But, as I suggested in the previous chapter, she is unwittingly aligned with death, with the serpent (II.cxvii), so that the reversal is only partial. What is to be the crucial erotic experience of the poem is already shadowed, not just by the serpent, and the 'eyes . . . black as death', but just as importantly by the sad echo of the father–son emblem. Even the incipient eroticism is at this point held in check, both by its apparent quaintness (the kiss of life in all its evident comicality and desperation is caught here quite surprisingly), and by the fact that the father had in his own desperation been obsessed with his child's mouth: 'He squeezed from out a rag some drops of rain / Into his dying child's mouth – but in vain'. There is not much, it would seem, between the kiss of life and the kiss of death.

Byron prolongs this particular emblem of emotion over many more stanzas; although the narrative pushes forward, and Juan is tended and taken to the cave, where he sleeps, the next time the two are together we seem to be witnessing the same image. Once again, she bends over him in silence, with that same mixture of protectiveness, timidity and quietly erotic love. It is beautiful; but, just as the morning air is raw, so there is a chillness about her. We are back with the figure of Death at the start of *The Giaour*.

> And when into the cavern Haidée stepped
>   All timidly, yet rapidly, she saw
> That like an infant Juan sweetly slept.
>   And then she stopped and stood as if in awe
> (For sleep is awful) and on tiptoe crept
>   And wrapt him closer, lest the air, too raw,
> Should reach his blood, then o'er him still as death
> Bent, with hushed lips, that drank his scarce drawn breath.
>
> (*Don Juan*, II.cxliii)

If we are beginning to think of Haidée as some kind of angelic figure of mercy, Byron gets in first:

> And thus like to an angel o'er the dying
>   Who die in righteousness she leaned; and there
> All tranquilly the shipwrecked boy was lying,
>   As o'er him lay the calm and stirless air . . . .
>
> (II.cxliv)

Immediately he undercuts this, as though he senses the pose has been held for too long. But in the switch to Zoe, Haidée's maid, who always has a sense of what is appropriate in practical terms, Byron is doing more than merely providing the comic antithesis, the burlesque that is the counterpart to the romantic. He is certainly drawing attention to the fact that

life has to go on, that we can't all lie around all day. But there is
the further point that she is 'less in love', and actually finds the
sea a little chilly – but to make the point is to make a comment
on the sea as metaphor, 'The watery outline of eternity'.
Furthermore, even if she yawns – as Byron is to elsewhere –
she recognises the need for food, the need for the appetite to
be satisfied, and in that recognition the connection is made
between the feelings and sustenance. In spite of the lightness
of tone – welcome after the sustained pathos that has pre-
ceded it – there is little doubt but that Byron is making a point
of some complexity.

> But Zoe the meantime some eggs was frying,
>   Since, after all, no doubt the youthful pair
> Must breakfast; and betimes, lest they should ask it,
> She drew out her provision from the basket.
>
> She knew that the best feelings must have victual,
>   And that a shipwrecked youth would hungry be.
> Besides, being less in love, she yawned a little
>   And felt her veins chilled by the neighbouring sea.
> And so she cooked their breakfast to a tittle;
>   I can't say that she gave them any tea,
> But there were eggs, fruit, coffee, bread, fish, honey,
> With Scio wine, and all for love, not money.
>
> (II.cxliv–cxlv)

The respite is temporary; the breakfast is allowed to go
cold, since Juan is not yet awake. He is still, in fact, only just
this side of death, and the poignancy and fragility of that is the
stronger after the down-to-earth commonsense of Zoe. The
light tone is displaced, and the verse resumes the heaviness
that has been associated throughout this canto with imminent
death.

> For still he lay, and on his thin worn cheek
>   A purple hectic played like daying day
> On the snow-tops of distant hills. The streak
>   Of sufferance yet upon his forehead lay,
> Where the blue veins looked shadowy, shrunk, and weak;
>   And his black curls were dewy with the spray,

Which weighed upon them yet, all damp and salt,
Mixed with the stony vapours of the vault.
(II.cxlvii)

It is hard not to remember the father and son in the boat, and to remember the compression of that scene; by comparison this is drawn-out, part of an emotional and dramatic complexity which allows Byron a variety of tones from stanza to stanza. Against the consistency, for example, of this stanza, in which he has restored the dominant tone of romantic pathos, Byron places the next, in which he combines that pathos with the detachment hinted at by Zoe. But here it is the poet's detachment.

And she bent o'er him, and he lay beneath,
    Hushed as the babe upon its mother's breast,
Drooped as the willow when no winds can breathe,
    Lulled like the depth of ocean when at rest,
Fair as the crowning rose of the whole wreath,
    Soft as the callow cygnet in its nest.
In short he was a very pretty fellow,
Although his woes had turned him rather yellow.
(II.cxlviii)

The final couplet draws attention away from the scene, to the poet; but it does nothing to diminish the potency of what has gone before – rather the reverse, in that we question the poet's readiness to hide from feeling.

Quite what Byron has achieved with his long lingering over this particular emblem of emotion emerges two cantos later. All the mutuality of the gaze of love is to be found as Juan and Haidée watch the sun set, and go to sleep, as Adam and Eve in Paradise. Extraordinarily, Byron repeats the 'swimming looks' with which Juan had first, in his troubled waking, gazed upon the unknown Haidée; and, as with the dying son and his loving father, there is no need for words.

Juan and Haidée gazed upon each other
    With swimming looks of speechless tenderness,
Which mixed all feelings, friend, child, lover, brother,
    All that the best can mingle and express

When two pure hearts are poured in one another
  And love too much and yet cannot love less,
But almost sanctify the sweet excess
By the immortal wish and power to bless.

Mixed in each other's arms and heart in heart,
  Why did they not then die? They had lived too long
Should an hour come to bid them breathe apart . . . .
(IV.xxvi–xxvii)

The irony, like the feeling, is intense. It is precisely the cruel
arrival of death that has made such a scene before in the poem
so tender; Haidée's role in canto II was to rescue Juan from
the death that had taken off all his companions. But now,
mingled in each other's arms, they deserve death rather than
life, in particular a life that involves parting; they experience a
perfection that makes them unfit for the world.

The world was not for them, nor the world's art
  For beings passionate as Sappho's song.
(IV.xxvii)

In *Childe Harold*, II, Byron had attempted to say something
similar about the futility of passion, and the corresponding
futility of art and poetry. Sappho's death leap had itself
seemed to be a denial, even if in another sense it might be seen
– and this is the implication here – as a fulfilment.

The two lovers slumber, with all the apparent innocence of
children. Eroticism is given plenty of room in *Don Juan*, but
there are times when Byron emphasises those aspects of feel-
ing that have little to do with sexuality. Juan is not just a lover,
he is 'friend, child . . . brother'; Haidée is sister and mother.
Earlier, 'her transparent cheek' had 'Pillowed his death-like
forehead' (II.cxiv); now, they are like songbirds:

Now pillowed cheek to cheek in loving sleep,
  Haidée and Juan their siesta took,
A gentle slumber, but it was not deep,
  For ever and anon a something shook
Juan and shuddering o'er his frame would creep;
  And Haidée's sweet lips murmured like a brook

A wordless music, and her face so fair
Stirred with her dream as rose leaves with the air.

Or as the stirring of a deep clear stream
  Within an Alpine hollow when the wind
Walks o'er it, was she shaken by the dream,
  The mystical usurper of the mind,
O'erpowering us to be whate'er may seem
  Good to the soul which we no more can bind.
Strange state of being (for 'tis still to be),
Senseless to feel and with sealed eyes to see!

(IV.xxix–xxx)

Even in this disturbance they reflect each other: the two are shaken by emotions they cannot define. I find it impossible at this point not to think of the end of *The Corsair*, where the hero returns to find Medora dead, and he 'set the anxious frame that lately shook'; I think also of the quivering limbs of the dying father in the boat (*Don Juan*, II.xc); I think of the clear, placid Leman in *Childe Harold*, and all the ambiguities of that glassy image; I think, too, of the end of the first canto of *Lara*, which provides a crucial gloss to this whole section of *Don Juan*:

The crowd are gone, the revellers at rest;
The courteous host, and all-approving guest,
Again to that accustomed couch must creep
Where joy subsides, and sorrow sighs to sleep,
And man o'er-laboured with his being's strife,
Shrinks to that sweet forgetfulness of life:
There lie love's feverish hope, and cunning's guile,
Hate's working brain, and lull'd ambition's wile,
O'er each vain eye oblivion's pinions wave,
And quench'd existence crouches in a grave.
What better name may slumber's bed become?
Night's sepulchre, the universal home,
Where weakness, strength, vice, virtue, sunk supine,
Alike in naked helplessness recline;
Glad for awhile to heave unconscious breath,
Yet wake to wrestle with the dread of death,

And shun, though day but dawn on ills increased,
That sleep, the loveliest, since it dreams the least.
                                        (*Lara*, I.629–45)

Not only is the reference to dreams remarkably similar; much of the language and imagery is the same: 'quench'd existence', for example, anticipates the 'quenched heart' of Juan in Haidée's dream (*Don Juan*, IV.xxxiv). It is salutary to realise, at the moment when Byron is so evidently in control of the *ottava rima* and of the emotions at the centre of *Don Juan*, how able he is, in the earlier narratives, to aspire to a comparable control of a very different medium. It makes me even less ready to concur with those who regard such a poem as *Lara* as a quaint failure.

Haidée dreams of being chained, Prometheus-like, to a rock on the seashore, threatened by waves, but not released by death. The Prometheus reference is not dwelt on, but it is sufficiently striking for us to remember the 'unforgiven fire' of I.cxxvii and all the implications of that. The sea is, in her dream, frighteningly real, and yet clearly symbolic, as it is throughout the poem: she is now in the position that Juan was in earlier, the same position as that of the dying boy, and all the others in the doomed boat. Her dreams shift, but the final image is of Juan, finally dead at her feet.

And wet and cold and lifeless at her feet,
    Pale as the foam that frothed on his dead brow,
Which she essayed in vain to clear (how sweet
    Were once her cares, how idle seemed they now),
Lay Juan, nor could aught renew the beat
    Of his quenched heart. And the sea dirges low
Rang in her sad ears like a mermaid's song,
And that brief dream appeared a life too long.
                                        (IV.xxxiv)

Juan has become that dead child, and all attempts to revive him are 'in vain'. She is, as she was two cantos earlier, bent over the dead. Only this time it is she who is gradually awaking from a dream. The parallel with the passage from *Lara* requires no comment.

> And gazing on the dead, she thought his face
>   Faded, or altered into something new,
> Like to her father's features, till each trace
>   More like and like to Lambro's aspect grew
> With all his keen worn look and Grecian grace.
>   And starting, she awoke, and what to view?
> Oh powers of heaven! What dark eye meets she there?
> 'Tis – 'tis her father's – fixed upon the pair!
>
>   (IV.xxxv)

The ambiguity and complexity of the initial emblem have found their fulfilment in the narrative twist, at the moment when we might (forgivably) have forgotten there was a narrative to worry about. Juan 'grows' (for Byron a mighty word) into Lambro, he comes alive only to be transformed into someone else, the antithesis of what Juan and Haidée together represent; Juan becomes the means to his own end, so far as his love for Haidée is concerned. The images of death have been appropriate, because Lambro's return is to ring out the death knell of his paradisal love. The irony of the contrast is almost too painful to dwell on. Lambro's 'Grecian grace' sends us back to that marvellous stanza in canto II where Haidée and Juan gaze at each other, she sitting on his knee in a pose that has its quiet comedy, but also its statuesque rightness, as art and nature come together:

> They look upon each other, and their eyes
>   Gleam in the moonlight, and her white arm clasps
> Round Juan's head, and his around hers lies
>   Half buried in the tresses which it grasps.
> She sits upon his knee and drinks his sighs,
>   He hers, until they end in broken gasps;
> And thus they form a group that's quite antique,
> Half naked, loving, natural, and Greek.
>
>   (II.cxciv)[1]

As father and daughter confront each other, Haidée in her pale sternness is both statue and sensual lover: 'Pale, statue-like, and stern, she wooed the blow' (IV.xliii). Once again, the emblematic movement of the poem and the moral narrative are conjoined. Haidée is now the waking child, but also the protective lover; she is also not only like her father, but in some essential sense she *is* her father, as the penultimate line of this next stanza shows:

> He gazed on her, and she on him. 'Twas strange
>   How like they looked. The expression was the same,
> Serenely savage, with a little change
>   In the large dark eye's mutual-darted flame,
> For she too was as one who could avenge,
>   If cause should be – a lioness, though tame.
> Her father's blood before her father's face
> Boiled up and proved her truly of his race.
>
> I said they were alike, their features and
>   Their stature differing but in sex and years;
> Even to the delicacy of their hand
>   There was resemblance, such as true blood wears.
> And now to see them, thus divided, stand
>   In fixed ferocity, when joyous tears
> And sweet sensations should have welcomed both,
> Show what the passions are in their full growth.
>
> (IV.xliv–xlv)

For the time being, the emblem of one figure leaning over another seems to have worked itself out, and the final paradox is stated: an image of death and mourning becomes one of living passion, the volcano that in its eruption proves itself true. And at that point of confrontation, of division even whilst they stand in front of each other, 'in fixed ferocity', both of them like statues, cold and implacable, they are simultaneously warm, and, like the passions, at the point of 'their full growth'.

At this point in the narrative, Juan fights Lambro, and is wounded. For Haidée it is the end. Her slow death is yet another in this long sequence, balancing that of the boy in the boat. Haidée was doomed from her first entry into the poem; that doom is now to find its fitting expression, in a way that is dramatically much more potent than the less savage doom meted out to Julia in canto I. Passion works itself out:

Her daughter, tempered with a milder ray —
　　Like summer clouds all silvery, smooth, and fair,
Till slowly charged with thunder they display
　　Terror to earth and tempest to the air —
Had held till now her soft and milky way,
　　But overwrought with passion and despair,
The fire burst forth from her Numidian veins,
Even as the simoom sweeps the blasted plains.

. . .

A vein had burst, and her sweet lips' pure dyes
　　Were dabbled with the deep blood which ran o'er;
And her head drooped as when the lily lies
　　O'ercharged with rain. Her summoned handmaids
　　　bore
Their lady to her couch with gushing eyes.
　　Of herbs and cordials they produced their store,
But she defied all means they could employ,
Like one life could not hold, nor death destroy.

　　　　　　　　　　　　　　　　　　(IV.lvii, lix)

Haidée is once again, but this time more cruelly, like Juan,
between life and death. He had been described 'like a with-
ered lily' when he collapsed on the shore; she is now the lily,
ironically weighted down like those characters in the boat,
burdened by the rain they lacked. She is in that state of
'neither life nor death', 'between two worlds' (XV.xcix); the
process that we saw with Juan is being reversed; the decline is
into death, even though there is at this moment a poised
stillness about it. The image of the statue is the natural one to
resort to — it has, after all, offered hope before, and is to do so
again. The contradictions of Haidée's condition are those
most readily associated with the paradoxes of statues.

Days lay she in that state unchanged; though chill
　　With nothing livid, still her lips were red.
She had no pulse, but death seemed absent still.
　　No hideous sign proclaimed her surely dead;
Corruption came not in each mind to kill
　　All hope. To look upon her sweet face bred

New thoughts of life, for it seemed full of soul;
She had so much, earth could not claim the whole.

The ruling passion, such as marble shows
   When exquisitely chiselled, still lay there,
But fixed as marble's unchanged aspect throws
   O'er the fair Venus, but forever fair,
O'er the Laocoon's all eternal throes,
   And ever-dying Gladiator's air.
Their energy like life forms all their fame,
Yet looks not life, for they are still the same.

(IV.lx—lxi)

Byron had made a similar reference in *Childe Harold*, IV, but less poignantly (see p.150). There is a terrible paradox about a passion that is 'fixed' and 'chiselled' in this way, especially when only four stanzas previously it had been likened to a fire, to the simoom sweeping across the plains; there is no movement here, no force. The dreadful anguish of the Laocoön group is in itself a contradiction in terms: such figures are like life, but unlike it, for precisely similar reasons. Gotthold Lessing, of course, had said it all before;[2] but he lacked all of Byron's saddened eloquence.

Byron teases us at this point, actually bringing Haidée back to life, again perversely, in that she awakes as the dead do, 'for life seemed something new, / A strange sensation which she must partake perforce'. She still has with her that dead weight that has been pressing on the spirits of all the characters in this canto, and yet, with this 'heavy ache', she has a momentary respite, rather as though she were back in that dream she had had earlier. Her plight, though, is one of total loss of memory, perhaps the most terrible fate of all, other than death, for the sane. 'Gentle, but without memory she lay' (*Don Juan*, IV.lxiv). In its simplicity of utterance, this is on a par with the famous Arnoldian touchstone from Wordsworth's 'Michael': 'And never lifted up a single stone'. There is no need, however, to hide behind any of Arnold's vagueness as to what effect is being achieved here. In psychological terms, Byron has identified the crucial aspect of character, the ability to remember, to have a past. To have no past is to have no present; it is to have no feeling; it is to be, to all intents and purposes, dead:

'she gave / No sign, save breath, of having left the grave'
(IV.lxiii). Her gentleness remains, but it is that of a corpse, and
therefore all but denied. But, when she hears a song of love,
she comes briefly to life. To feel, however tenuously, is to be.

> Anon her thin wan fingers beat the wall
>   In time to his old tune. He changed the theme
> And sung of love. The fierce name struck through all
>   Her recollection; on her flashed the dream
> Of what she was and is, if ye could call
>   To be so being. In a gushing stream
> The tears rushed forth from her o'erclouded brain,
> Like mountain mists at length dissolved in rain.
>   (IV.lxvi)

The subtlety of what is happening here can be clarified by a
reference back to the end of canto II:

> The heart is like the sky, a part of heaven,
>   But changes night and day too, like the sky.
> Now o'er it clouds and thunder must be driven,
>   And darkness and destruction as on high,
> But when it hath been scorched and pierced and riven,
>   Its storms expire in water drops. The eye
> Pours forth at last the heart's blood turned to tears,
> Which make the English climate of our years.
>   (II.ccxiv)

That echo seems to underline the qualifications Byron is
making: there is relief, certainly, but it is of a muted kind. The
potential ambiguities of Larkin's 'Whitsun Weddings' might
quite fruitfully present themselves to us here; but the conclu-
sion to that earlier stanza (II.ccxiv) is rather more daunting:
the aphorism, whilst witty, has nothing joky about it.

Haidée's death provides an echo of other spiritual deaths –
particularly of Bonnivard in *The Prisoner of Chillon*; she moves
through that half-world, where everything fragments. And,
crucially, she will not now look at her father: that is one gaze
she will not indulge.

Yet she betrayed at times a gleam of sense.
   Nothing could make her meet her father's face,
Though on all other things with looks intense
   She gazed, but none she ever could retrace.
Food she refused and raiment; no pretence
   Availed for either. Neither change of place
Nor time nor skill nor remedy could give her
Senses to sleep – the power seemed gone forever.
(IV.lxviii)

Her death, when it comes, is almost impossible to discern.
There is, though, one distinctive sign which takes us full circle,
back to the initial description of Haidée and her eyes in
canto II.

Twelve days and nights she withered thus. At last
   Without a groan or sigh or glance to show
A parting pang, the spirit from her past.
   And they who watched her nearest could not know
The very instant, till the change that cast
   Her sweet face into shadow, dull and slow,
Glazed o'er her eyes, the beautiful, the black.
Oh to possess such lustre – and then lack!
(IV.lxix)

The long, painful lingering over this statue-like figure, neith-
er dead nor alive, is eventually terminated with a precision
that only the poet himself is fully aware of. We should not be
surprised to note that Byron worked on that final line, his first
thought ('Oh what a soul was that which now they lack') rightly
giving way to the more powerful antithesis, which in turn
allows the Shakespearean echo from *As You Like It* ('looking on
it with lacklustre eye'). The compression is stunning: for a
brief moment 'lack' offers itself as a noun, the thing now
ironically possessed, as though one could in death possess a
lack (which is one way of defining death); the noun then
(picking up the penultimate word of the line – 'then') trans-
forms itself into a verb, and we are left with the play on
'lacklustre'. Furthermore, it is not just Haidée's possession we
are talking about: those who knew her, who gazed upon her

on her deathbed, possessed in their watching the lustre of her eyes. If love is reciprocal, so too is loss.

However, the loss is not entire. Haidée is vindicated by the poet, and by her memorial in others' songs. For all the desolation of the island, for all the lack of any form of gravestone, Haidée lies where she lived, and where she died. She has ceased to be a statue that might transform itself into something living; she has ceased, in fact, to embrace the contradictions of her state. Her death is proper, an indication of her warm heart, of her passion. She has lost Juan, she has lost the child that is in her womb, she has lost her own life. Without sentimentalising her death, though, Byron makes it appear a resolution, an outcome both inevitable and desirable. Dead, she becomes a figure asleep on the seashore, an image of possibility, an emblem, even in death, of emotion:

> Thus lived, thus died she. Never more on her
>   Shall sorrow light or shame. She was not made
> Through years or moons the inner weight to bear,
>   Which colder hearts endure till they are laid
> By age in earth. Her days and pleasures were
>   Brief, but delightful, such as had not stayed
> Long with her destiny. But she sleeps well
> By the seashore, whereon she loved to dwell.
>
> (IV.lxxi)

A very different set of circumstances is explored in canto VI, where Juan finds himself in the harem, disguised as 'Juanna' on the instigation of the eunuch Baba. This episode provides Byron with a wonderful opportunity for more than mere sexual innuendo: he describes the girls in terms that are extremely gentle and sympathetic, without being either prurient or sentimental. He recognises the attractions of this harem, both for the disguised male, and for the women themselves. As so often the effect depends upon poise. Byron gives us a glimpse of the three girls who befriend Juan: it is Dudù who is especial.

Lolah was dusk as India and as warm;
   Katinka was a Georgian, white and red,
With great blue eyes, a lovely hand and arm
   And feet so small they scarce seemed made to tread,
But rather skim the earth; while Dudù's form
   Looked more adapted to be put to bed,
Being somewhat large and languishing and lazy,
Yet of a beauty that would drive you crazy.

A kind of sleepy Venus seemed Dudù,
   Yet very fit to 'murder sleep' in those
Who gazed upon her cheek's transcendent hue,
   Her Attic forehead and her Phidian nose.
Few angles were there in her form 'tis true;
   Thinner she might have been and yet scarce lose,
Yet after all 'twould puzzle to say where
It would not spoil some separate charm to pare.

She was not violently lively, but
   Stole on your spirit like a May day breaking.
Her eyes were not too sparkling, yet half-shut,
   They put beholders in a tender taking.
She looked (this simile's quite new) just cut
   From marble, like Pygmalion's statue waking,
The mortal and the marble still at strife,
And timidly expanding into life.

(VI.xli–xliii)

Dudù is no sylph, no figure of perfection; her companions are more conventionally attractive, and can be accounted for accordingly, in swift descriptive phrases. In some respects she seems a rather Rubens-like woman, plumper than might be good for her, and yet, the more you consider her, appropriately plump. Byron avoids such an obviously condemnatory word in his desire to be precise about her particular kind of size and shape. The alliteration in the penultimate line of stanza xli has its attractions, obviously, but there are more important reasons for Byron's having altered 'indolent' to 'languishing'. 'Somewhat large and indolent and lazy' verges not so much on Keats as on Jane Austen's description of Lady Bertram, lolling around Mansfield Park like a fat and lazy seal. In Dudù's case, the laziness needs to be minimised, to be transmogrified into something almost voluptuous: 'languishing' performs this radical qualification, assisted of course by the next line, which takes us carefully away from any suggestion of a Lady Bertram. The following stanza continues to make her a Greek statue of a particularly fleshy kind, a goddess reluctant to acknowledge her own divinity – that seems to be the force of 'A kind of sleepy Venus' (although there is the hint of the erotic here, harking back to the suggestion that she is 'more adapted to be put to bed'); she is also, momentarily, out of *Macbeth*. The next stanza pursues the image of the statue, making the reference to Pygmalion explicit; she is both marble and yet not, she is growing even as she retains her quality of a newly cut statue. Expansiveness and enlargement are associated by Byron with love (see II.clxxiii), and it is as though, in expanding as she does, with all the timidity of first love (see p. 191), she is acting out her role as Venus.

Byron pushes the narrative on. There is a debate as to who should share a bed with 'Juanna'; but he keeps returning to Dudù, resting his entirely non-prurient gaze upon her. He does not want to claim for her the kind of sublime passion to which Haidée was doomed; she has not the commandeering attitude of her mistress Gulbeyaz; she is quiet and natural, and entirely unself-conscious. It is this that makes her so delightful and so beguiling.

> But she was a soft landscape of mild earth,
>   Where all was harmony and calm and quiet,
> Luxuriant, budding, cheerful without mirth,
>   Which if not happiness is much more nigh it
> Than are your mighty passions and so forth,
>   Which some call 'the sublime'. I wish they'd try it;
> I've seen your stormy seas and stormy women
> And pity lovers rather more than seamen.

> But she was pensive more than melancholy,
>   And serious more than pensive, and serene
> It may be more than either. Not unholy
>   Her thoughts, at least till now, appear to have been.
> The strangest thing was, beauteous, she was wholly

> Unconscious, albeit turned of quick seventeen,
> That she was fair or dark or short or tall;
> She never thought about herself at all.
>
> (VI.liii–liv)

So unaware is she of herself that she is taken by surprise by her reflection in the mirror:

> In perfect innocence she then unmade
>   Her toilet, which cost little, for she was
> A child of Nature, carelessly arrayed.
>   If fond of a chance ogle at her glass,
> 'Twas like the fawn which in the lake displayed
>   Beholds her own shy, shadowy image pass
> When first she starts and then returns to peep,
> Admiring this new native of the deep.
>
> (VI.lx)

Those ogles of the Spanish maids and grandees in *Childe Harold* I have little in common with this demure delight. It is relatively rare in Byron for reflections to be so uncomplicated, and that is Dudù's charm and point. Whatever dreams she might have when once in bed with 'Juanna' – and they form one of the most highly charged portions of *Don Juan*, in terms of veiled sexuality – Dudù's innocence does not carry around with it the shadow of Eden lost that we associate with Haidée. 'Perfect innocence' is just that. In the structure of the poem as a whole such a recognition matters enormously; the temptations of cynicism need countering, and this particular emblem of emotion acts as a yardstick whereby to judge other, more complicated forms of innocence.

Before her dream is recounted, Dudù is placed in the context of those who sleep around her. Byron disclaims some of what he is doing here ('My similes are gathered in a heap, / So pick and choose' – VI.lxviii); but it is impossible to pass over these two stanzas, with their emphasis on the natural world, on growth in the simplest sense:

> Many and beautiful lay those around,
>   Like flowers of different hue and clime and root
> In some exotic garden sometimes found,

> With cost and care and warmth induced to shoot.
> One with her auburn tresses lightly bound
>   And fair brows gently drooping, as the fruit
> Nods from the tree, was slumbering with soft breath
> And lips apart, which showed the pearls beneath.
>
> One with her flushed cheek laid on her white arm,
>   And raven ringlets gathered in dark crowd
> Above her brow, lay dreaming soft and warm
>   And smiling through her dream, as through a cloud
> The moon breaks, half unveiled each further charm,
>   As slightly stirring in her snowy shroud,
> Her beauties seized the unconscious hour of night
> All bashfully to struggle into light.
>
>   (VI.lxv–lxvi)

This is imagistically and emotionally on a par with Dudù ('And timidly expanding into life' – VI.xliii): not only is beauty in this setting unconscious of self, so too is the night. It is a wonderful reciprocity between people and the natural world.

As I have suggested, *Don Juan* confronts much in the world that is ugly and disturbing, much that is redolent of loss and death: we have already seen how the apparent paradise of the island becomes a chimera, how Haidée's innocence is undercut. All the more important, then, if the poem is not to sink into nihilism, for Byron to cling onto those moments when feeling and emotion have their unquestioned validity. That is the functional role of the central part of canto VI; but to see it merely as functional would be to wrong it dreadfully. In the midst of a long section of the poem in which Byron is joking with his readers, and joking with his characters' plight, he places before us the beauty of perfect innocence that is still not without its fleshly attractions. Hence the paradox of Dudù, with the 'mortal and the marble still at strife'. In II.cxi Juan lies in a faint, and we get the same rhyme:

> And tingling vein seemed throbbing back to life,
> For Death, though vanquished, still retired with strife.

If 'mortal' means living, we can take it as the replacement for death in the earlier section; but to be reminded of that earlier couplet is to be reminded that mortality is, in reality, far from being a replacement for death: it is a recognition of it. Dudù's fragility is all the more touching, as she expands into life. There is a parallel with Byron's own verse; the sleeping girl in VI.lxvi is an image of how his poetry works. There can be full sympathy of response with her as she emerges like the moon from behind a cloud, because Byron's Muse gives off the same sense of timid expansion into a life that is both natural and the result of art:

> Her beauties seized the unconscious hour of night
> All bashfully to struggle into light.

A grim reminder of this passage is to be found in one of the two cantos on war, where Byron spares no one in the savagery of his attack on savagery. In the midst of the carnage of canto VIII he focuses on the rescue of Leila, another of the female figures who is central to the narrative line but also to the emotional force of the poem (there are indications that Byron might have intended to make more of the relationship between Juan and Leila). It is worth dwelling on the way Byron dwells on this dramatic scene, picking up some of the images and ironies of his earlier set pieces in which complex emotions were examined.

> Upon a taken bastion where there lay
>   Thousands of slaughtered men, a yet warm group
> Of murdered women, who had found their way
>   To this vain refuge, made the good heart droop
> And shudder; while, as beautiful as May,
>   A female child of ten years tried to stoop
> And hide her little palpitating breast
> Amidst the bodies lulled in bloody rest.
>
> (VIII.xci)

What might earlier have seemed at times like a convenient trope – the closeness of sleep to death, of death to life – here takes on all the urgency of Byron's critique of war. The warmth of the murdered women recalls those earlier images of women asleep, just as it recalls the chill of the marble statues to which they were likened; the drooping heart echoes the drooping head of Haidée as she approached death – the crucial difference is that in this case the heart that droops is ours, as participants and observers: we are absorbed into the picture, into the statuesque 'group'. The young girl, in her attempts to bend down and find her own refuge, mirrors the desperation of the dead women, mirrors the inclined bodies of Haidée over Juan, of the father over the dying son, and mirrors our own drooping and shuddering hearts. For the awful truth is that death would be a deliverance; her 'palpitating breast' is the antithesis of the 'bodies lulled in bloody rest': the dead have acquired a calm that seems like sleep.

Leila is pursued by two wild Cossacks, 'with flashing eyes and weapons'. Her death seems inevitable, and is in fact anticipated in the syntax:

> Their sabres glittered o'er her little head,
>   Whence her fair hair rose twining with affright;
> Her hidden face was plunged amidst the dead.
>
> (VIII.xciii)

The difference between this and Keats's wonderful anticipatory description of Lorenzo's death in 'Isabella' is that Byron's line works on the literal level, too.[3] The girl has hidden her face in the pile of 'yet warm' bodies; but to all intents and purposes, he is implying, she has taken that plunge into the next world. Simultaneously, her hair moves in the opposite direction, and perhaps we should remember the lesson of the Dedication, that fear does at least imply feeling: her 'affright' is an indication of her value. It is even more complex than that, though. The basic image is of her hair standing on end; but Byron's use of the commonplace transforms it, in that the verb 'rose', in its other manifestation as a noun, dictates the participial 'twining', and for a moment the tangled, startled hair is not only twisting in fear; it is apparently in a literal sense wrapping itself up and around the abstraction that is, at this instant, such a terrible reality.

Juan comes to the rescue, when he catches 'a glimpse of this sad sight':

> One's hip he slashed and split the other's shoulder
>   And drove them with their brutal yells to seek
> If there might be chirurgeons who could solder
>   The wounds they richly merited, and shriek
> Their baffled rage and pain. While waxing colder
>   As he turned o'er each pale and gory cheek,
> Don Juan raised his little captive from
> The heap a moment more had made her tomb.
>
> (VIII.xciv)

Little needs to be said about this stanza, except that, quite extraordinarily, Byron elicits sympathy for the Cossacks he had two stanzas previously regarded as beyond redemption: their baffled rage and pain is a reminder of their humanity, of their ability to feel (rather like his earlier redeeming of Suwarrow). Byron understands bafflement too well for him to let it pass without understanding. Reciprocity extends to war. That central contradiction is contained in the paradox of the rest of that line, as Juan's passion cools: few poets could lend such weight to that chill oxymoron 'waxing colder'. The next stanza emphasises how close Leila is to death; but also, in her startled reaction, how close she is to Haidée.

> And she was chill as they, and on her face
>   A slender streak of blood announced how near
> Her fate had been to that of all her race.
>   For the same blow which laid her mother here
> Had scarred her brow and left its crimson trace
>   As the last link with all she had held dear.
> But else unhurt, she opened her large eyes
> And gazed on Juan with a wild surprise.
>
> (VIII.xcv)

The turbulence of emotion at this point needs to be dwelt on, and Byron devotes a whole stanza to it (although careful to make it subordinate to the main clause of the next stanza, just in case he should be tempted to allow sentiment too much purchase):

> Just at this instant while their eyes were fixed
>   Upon each other with dilated glance,

> In Juan's look, pain, pleasure, hope, fear, mixed
>   With joy to save and dread of some mischance
> Unto his protégée, while hers, transfixed
>   With infant terrors, glared as from a trance,
> A pure, transparent, pale, yet radiant face,
> Like to a lighted alabaster vase;
>
> Up came John Johnson . . . .
>
>   (VIII.xcvi–xcvii)

This mingling of tenderness and terror is in many ways the emotional climax of the canto, epitomising as it does the absurd contradictions of war. But there is a further, complementary, scene, where death has the last word; I should like to refer briefly to this.

Johnson and Juan confront an aged Tartar khan and his five sons, who will not submit. In a terrible fight to the finish, all five sons are slaughtered. As the last son falls, the old man looks at him with something like rapture. For all the atrociousness of war, there is a recognition of dignity and decorum which brings the pell-mell action to a complete halt.

> But with a heavenly rapture on his face,
>   The good old khan, who long had ceased to see
> Houris or aught except his florid race,
>   Who grew like cedars round him gloriously,
> When he beheld his latest hero grace
>   The earth, which he became like a felled tree,
> Paused for a moment from the fight and cast
> A glance on that slain son, his first and last.
>
>   (VIII.cxvi)

His opponents are stopped in their tracks, and Byron dwells on the old man's unspoken feelings as he registers his loss.

> The soldiers, who beheld him drop his point,
>   Stopped as if once more willing to concede
> Quarter, in case he bade them not 'aroint'
>   As he before had done. He did not heed
> Their pause nor signs. His heart was out of joint
>   And shook (till now unshaken) like a reed

As he looked down upon his children gone
And felt, though done with life, he was alone.
                                    (VIII.cxvii)

The poet himself is to cry, echoing Hamlet, '"The time is out
of joint", and so am I!' (IX.xli). In fact, the ghost of Hamlet
stalks the later cantos, and with it goes an increasing sense of
tragic isolation. Byron shows himself extremely sensitive to
the pathos of solitude. The acknowledgement here is the
more moving because of its brevity. The aged khan embraces
death, hurling himself at the 'Russian steel'.

But 'twas a transient tremor. With a spring
    Upon the Russian steel his breast he flung,
As carelessly as hurls the moth her wing
    Against the light wherein she dies. He clung
Closer, that all the deadlier they might wring,
    Unto the bayonets which had pierced his young,
And throwing back a dim look on his sons,
In one wide wound poured forth his soul at once.
                                    (VIII.cxviii)

In pouring forth his soul, he is like the inspired poet: but of
course he is expiring, the word Byron used of the boy in the
boat (II.xc). In his death he finds his tragic consummation,
linked with his sons in that final backward glance.

There is an appalling generosity about his 'one wide wound'
which stirs even the 'rough, tough soldiers' who have caused
it, who 'Touched by the heroism of him they slew / Were
melted for a moment'. To 'melt' in Byron is rather like to feel.
When he is describing in canto IX the meeting of Juan and
Catherine of Russia he uses the same word, not to describe
their feelings for each other, but the response of the Court:
'The whole court melted into one wide whisper' (IX.lxxviii),
which is echoed four stanzas later: 'But when the three rose,
and all was bustle / In the dissolving circle' (IX.lxxxii). How-
ever, the melting in canto VIII is only momentary:[4]

Though no tear
Flowed from their bloodshot eyes, all red with strife,
They honoured such determined scorn of life.
                                    (VIII.cxix)

The bloodshot eyes hark back to similar dilated eyes of destruction in *Childe Harold*. The rhyme harks back to one that has served Byron well already in *Don Juan*, but the force of it here is very different from that of II.cxi, in that here it is those who remain – the conquerors in fact – who are the ones in strife; the dead man deserves honouring because he has so warmly embraced death. His scorn of life has become a virtue in a battlefield where, otherwise, life is only too readily and easily scorned. The paradox stands because it is at the centre of Byron's vision, and his echoing emblems of emotion have served to strengthen it at the most necessary moment. We are invited to pause and watch, and to be 'Touched by the heroism of him they slew'.

A very different kind of isolation occurs in Byron's description of Aurora Raby in canto XV. She continues the line of female figures in the poem, but has apparently none of the guile of Julia, none of the fallen nature of Haidée, none of the voluptuousness of Dudù: she is 'A lovely being, scarcely formed or moulded' (XV.xliii). For Byron that is probably her most salient and attractive quality: she is the true embodiment of someone who is still to find their true embodiment. She views the world with the silent awe of someone who has seen it all before.

> Early in years and yet more infantine
>   In figure, she had something of sublime
> In eyes which sadly shone, as seraphs' shine.
>   All youth but with an aspect beyond time,
> Radiant and grave, as pitying man's decline,
>   Mournful, but mournful of another's crime,
> She looked as if she sat by Eden's door
> And grieved for those who could return no more.

>   . . .

> She gazed upon a world she scarcely knew,
>   As seeking not to know it. Silent, lone,
> As grows a flower, thus quietly she grew
>   And kept her heart serene within its zone.

There was awe in the homage which she drew;
  Her spirit seemed as seated on a throne
Apart from the surrounding world and strong
In its own strength, most strange in one so young.
                                    (XV.xlv, xlvii)

Aurora has some of those qualities Byron had previously associated with marble statues. Although young, she is curiously timeless, so that 'All youth' comes to suggest that she is representative of 'all youth', not just that she is young through and through. She is like the sad but wise observer of the world's follies, self-contained and removed, untainted by the world and yet fully aware of the expulsion from Eden. But, whereas Haidée had been a fragile innocent, Aurora has an inner strength, a strength that the poet admires even as he is puzzled by it. Aurora cannot be fully explained, however much we are told about her family, her Catholicism; in a poem about growth, she has still to grow. Small wonder that Adeline understands her not at all:

  She marvelled what he saw in such a baby
  As that prim, silent, cold Aurora Raby?
                                    (XV.xlix)

It is this lack of possible comprehension that fascinates Byron: he has found in Aurora the image the whole poem has been looking for, the emblem of something on the verge of fulfilment, something itself on the verge of understanding. In the brittle social world of London, so dextrously demolished in the later cantos, she does indeed stand out like a 'star'.

In canto XVI Byron enters the unexpected realms of Gothic horror: since the poem was left unfinished, we cannot say what he would have done with these props.[5] But in the context of this apparent absurdity, his final passing allusion to Aurora is all the more arresting. After some sharp satire at Adeline's expense, he reintroduces this mysterious figure, whose mystery is so much more important than anything to do with ghosts and apparitions.

  Aurora – since we are touching upon taste,
    Which nowadays is the thermometer

> By whose degrees all characters are classed –
>   Was more Shakespearian, if I do not err.
> The worlds beyond this world's perplexing waste
>   Had more of her existence, for in her
> There was a depth of feeling to embrace
> Thoughts, boundless, deep, but silent too as space.
>   (XVI.xlviii)

'The waste and icy clime' of VII.ii, and the 'perplexing ways' of I.cxxxiii are concentrated in 'this world's perplexing waste'. But Aurora is beyond this world, just as she is beyond time. Those final lines celebrate a kind of deliverance: Aurora embraces thoughts that are boundless; goes, in other words, beyond the bounds that restrict and clog the rest of us. What allows this deliverance, this liberation, for her and for us, is her 'depth of feeling' which matches the depth of her thoughts. There might be an echo here of that apparently autobiographical comment at the end of canto I, where Byron takes his leave of love and feeling ('And in thy stead I've got a deal of judgement' – I.ccxv). The echo, however, works against that earlier authorial posture: Aurora embraces feeling and thought together, and as she does so we are confronted with the fact that these are silent thoughts. But it is a silence with all the immensity of space. Such silent thought, such thoughtful silence, might seem a denial of all the words of this poem. 'Away with words', Byron had cried in *Childe Harold*, IV, appealing there to images of art and to the ruins of time. In *Don Juan* his recourse is to such silent 'emblems of emotion' as we get here. It is by virtue of these that we can at least approach the wisdom of Aurora, and 'minister unto the soul's delight / In seeing matters which are out of sight' (XV.ii).

Notes

Unless otherwise stated, all books listed were published in London.

CHAPTER 1. THE 'EYE OF APPETITE'

1. *The Letters of John Keats*, ed. Hyder Edward Rollins (Cambridge, Mass., 1958) II, 200.

2. *The Letters of William and Dorothy Wordsworth*, 2nd edn, rev. Mary Moorman (Oxford, 1969) II, 268.

3. There is a memorable line about Coleridge in John Mortimer's play *A Voyage round my Father*: 'Green around the gills. And a stranger to the lavatory.'

4. *Byron's Letters and Journals*, ed. Leslie A. Marchand (1973–82) II, 122.

5. Ibid., II, 237.

6. Ibid., III, 199.

7. Ibid., III, 240.

8. Ibid., III, 51.

9. For 'pissabed' and 'f–gg–g', see *Letters and Journals*, VII, 200, 225.

10. *The Letters of John Keats*, II, 43.

11. *Byron's Letters and Journals*, IV, 101.

12. Ibid., III, 91.

13. Ibid., III, 145.

14. See Byron's prose account of this episode, *Letters and Journals*, VII, 247. An illuminating comparison might be made with Clough's *Amours de Voyage*, II. vii.

15. *The Letters of John Keats*, I, 281.

16. See especially Robert F. Gleckner, *Byron and the Ruins of Paradise* (Baltimore, 1967), and Jerome J. McGann, *'Don Juan' in Context* (1976).

17. *Byron's Letters and Journals*, III, 62.

18. Ibid., III, 57.

19. Ibid., III, 101.

20. Ibid., III, 168.

21. What Michel Foucault has to say on this topic is of some interest here: see 'The Eye of Power', in *Power/Knowledge*, ed. Colin Gordon (Brighton, 1980) pp. 146–65.

22. *Byron's Letters and Journals*, III, 45.

23. Ibid., III, 53.

24. Ibid., III, 257.

25. Bernard Blackstone makes some germane points about this in his otherwise rather quirky book *Byron: A Survey* (1975).

26. 'I am', *The Later Poems of John Clare*, ed. Eric Robinson and David Powell (Oxford, 1984) I, 396.

27. *Byron's Letters and Journals*, II, 11, and VI, 118.

28. See '"The Eloquence of Indifference": Byron', in Mark Storey, *Poetry and Humour from Cowper to Clough* (1979) pp. 77–114.

CHAPTER 2. THE 'FEVER AT THE CORE': THE POETRY
OF PASSION

1. See especially Philip W. Martin, *Byron, a Poet before his Public* (Cambridge, 1982); but see also my comments on this in *English*, XXXII (Spring 1983) 75–81.

2. *Byron's Letters and Journals*, III, 100.

3. Both Jerome McGann, in *Fiery Dust: Byron's Poetic Development* (Chicago and London, 1968), and Robert Gleckner, in *Byron and the Ruins of Paradise*, address themselves to the composition of *The Giaour*, much more successfully than William H. Marshall in his *The Structure of Byron's Major Poems* (Philadelphia, 1962).

4. In the Preface to *Lyrical Ballads* (1800).

5. *Coleridge's Shakespeare Criticism*, ed. T. M. Raysor (1930) I, 56.

6. '[Poetry] is the lava of the imagination whose eruption prevents an earthquake' (*Byron's Letters and Journals*, III, 171).

7. Ethel C. Mayne, *Byron* (1924) p. 177; quoted in McGann's commentary, *Byron: The Complete Poetical Works* (Oxford, 1980–) III, 416.

8. John Clare, 'The Flitting', *The Midsummer Cushion*, ed. Anne Tibble and R. K. R. Thornton (Ashington, 1978) p. 216.

9. J. R. Watson comments on the Wordsworthian nature of these lines, but with a different emphasis, in his *Picturesque Landscape and English Romantic Poetry* (1970) p. 175.

10. I am indebted to Jerome McGann's chapter on *Mazeppa* in *Fiery Dust*, pp. 174–85.

CHAPTER 3. 'A WHIRLING GULF OF PHANTASY AND FLAME':
CHILDE HAROLD (i)

1. See *Byron's Letters and Journals*, IV, 77: 'but – but – always a *but* to the end of the chapter'; and IV, 243: 'and yet – and yet – always *yet* and *but*'. See also M. G. Cooke, *The Blind Man Traces the Circle* (Princeton, NJ, 1969) pp. 44–5.

2. *Byron's Letters and Journals*, II, 63.

3. See especially Peter Thorslev, *The Byronic Hero: Types and Prototypes* (Minneapolis, 1962).

4. See Mark Storey, *Poetry and Humour from Cowper to Clough* (1979) pp. 94–7.

CHAPTER 4. 'THE FITTING MEDIUM OF DESIRE': *CHILDE HAROLD* (ii)

1. McGann, *Fiery Dust*, p. 58.
2. See *Byron: The Critical Heritage*, ed. Andrew Rutherford (1970) pp. 81–98; see also Martin, *Byron, a Poet before his Public*, pp. 64–96.
3. *The Later Poems of John Clare*, ed. Eric Robinson and David Powell (Oxford, 1984) I, 46.
4. See *Byron's Letters and Journals*, III, 154: 'no matter – let it go – '.
5. Hazlitt is particularly worth reading on this passage, even if he is wrongheaded: *Complete Works*, ed. P. P. Howe (London and Toronto, 1930–4) X, 258.

CHAPTER 5. 'DUE BOUNDS' AND 'DUE PRECISION': *DON JUAN* (i)

1. George M. Ridenour, *The Style of 'Don Juan'* (New Haven, Conn., 1960) p. 76.
2. See John Jones, *John Keats's Dream of Truth* (1969) pp. 270–95.
3. Ridenour's analysis in *The Style of 'Don Juan'* remains essential reading.
4. I derive these and other variants from the Penguin edition of *Don Juan*, ed. T. G. and E. Steffan and W. W. Pratt (Harmondsworth, 1973, rev. 1977).
5. See Christopher Ricks, *Milton's Grand Style* (Oxford, 1963) pp. 69–72.
6. The Penguin edition of *Don Juan*, p. 682. The full sentence in Horace reads 'Nam fuit ante Helenam cunnus teterrima belli / causa'.
7. W. W. Robson talks rather in these terms in 'Byron and Sincerity', in *English Romantic Poets*, ed. M. H. Abrams (London, Oxford, New York, 1975) pp. 275–302; his essay remains none the less one of the most stimulating discussions of Byron.

CHAPTER 6. 'EMBLEMS OF EMOTION': *DON JUAN* (ii)

1. This stanza receives the careful attentions of Christopher Ricks in *Keats and Embarrassment* (Oxford, 1974) pp. 66–7.
2. Gotthold Lessing, *Laokoon* (Berlin, 1766); see Jean H. Hagstrum, *The Sister Arts* (Chicago, 1958), and Ralph Cohen, *The Art of Discrimination* (1964).
3. 'So the two brothers and their murder'd man / Rode past fair Florence . . .' (Keats, 'Isabella', xxvii).
4. How often Byron seems to anticipate and outwit the commonplaces of latterday advertising, which in turn mirror the cheap sentiments of popular songs.
5. Edward E. Bostetter, in *The Romantic Ventriloquists* (Seattle and London, 1963), is suggestive on the later cantos of *Don Juan*.

Index